Instructor's Manual/Test Bank

interactions access

Second Edition

Prepared by
Patricia K. Werner

With Contributions by
John P. Nelson
Marilyn Spaventa
Pamela Hartmann
James Mentel
Emily A. Thrush
Robert Baldwin
Laurie Blass

McGraw Hill

Boston   Burr Ridge, IL   Dubuque, IA   Madison, WI   New York   San Francisco   St. Louis
Bangkok   Bogotá   Caracas   Lisbon   London   Madrid   Mexico City   Milan   New Delhi
Seoul   Singapore   Sydney   Taipei   Toronto

This is an  book

McGraw-Hill

A Division of The McGraw·Hill Companies

Instructor's Manual/Test Bank to Accompany
INTERACTIONS Access Second Edition

ISBN 0-07-069604-7

3 4 5 6 7 8 9 0 BKMBKM 9 0 9

http://www.mhhe.com

Interactions Access: Table of Contents

Instructor's Manual/Test Bank

interactions access

Second Edition

I n t r o d u c t i o n

Introduction to the *Interactions Access, Interactions* **and** *Mosaic* **Programs**

Flexibility and coordination are key aspects of any effective program for English language instruction. The *Interactions Access, Interactions* and *Mosaic* texts were created to address these key needs. The texts offer both flexibility for programming and built-in coordination across skill areas and across levels. Texts at each level can be mixed and matched according to the needs of a particular class. Or, the entire program of texts can be used to provide a comprehensive program of language instruction.

While they provide a full program for intensive courses, the *Interactions Access, Interactions* and *Mosaic* texts can also be used with semi-intensive and non-intensive courses. Different books can be used in combination, or an individual text can be used, as each book stands alone and can be used independently.

Guidelines for Levels and Student Placement

The test bank in this manual includes placement tests for *Interactions* texts. Placement tests are also available for the *Mosaic* texts. As these tests are meant only to place students within the *Interactions/Mosaic* course levels, they have not been normed against standardized tests such as the TOEFL. Teachers are encouraged to use the tests to place students whenever possible. When practical considerations make it impossible to administer the placement tests, the following chart can be used to evaluate students. It provides descriptions of the levels of students as they correspond to the *Interactions Access, Interactions,* and *Mosaic* texts. The descriptions are based on descriptions developed by the Interagency Language Roundtable for use in

various entities of the U.S. government. These levels are appropriate for ESL settings. See below for more information on EFL settings.

No Proficiency
- May know a few words or phrases but is essentially unable to function in spoken or written English

Low-Beginner
Interactions Access
- Can understand and produce a minimal amount of conversational English, enough to handle basic courtesy or travel situations
- Can read very simple written statements using very high-frequency vocabulary
- Can write limited, practical English, but cannot express more than elementary statements or paragraphs

High-Beginner
Interactions One
- Can understand and participate in familiar, predictable conversations, but has difficulty sustaining a conversation of any length or depth
- Can read simple authentic material about familiar topics
- Can write simply about a limited number of topics

Low-Intermediate
Interactions Two
- Can understand and converse about day-to-day topics and areas of special interest, but has difficulties with lengthy or sophisticated exchanges
- Can read non-technical material and some specialized work- or profession-related material with good comprehension, but reads slowly and somewhat hesitantly
- Able to write with some fluency about a range of familiar, day-to-day topics

High-Intermediate

Mosaic One

- Can understand spoken English in most day-to-day settings involving familiar topics, but may still have difficulties with unfamiliar ideas or information

- Can participate in conversations covering a range of topics, and although errors may be frequent, they usually do not interfere with meaning

- Able to read a variety of authentic material with good speed and comprehension, but still has difficulties with more specialized or lower-frequency vocabulary

- Able to write about topics of personal interest, as well as about a variety of familiar topics, but still has difficulties with vocabulary and grammatical accuracy

Low-Advanced

Mosaic Two

- Comfortable in most conversational and professional- or work-related settings, but may still have problems understanding spoken English, especially in rapid or heated discussions

- Can participate with ease in conversations and discussions on a wide range of topics, but may have fossilized errors in spoken English and may lack the range of vocabulary needed for complex situations

- Can read authentic material about a variety of topics with a high degree of comprehension and speed, but may have problems with both speed and understanding when dealing with complex material on unfamiliar topics

- Can write well about familiar topics, specialized topics of personal interest, and areas of expertise, but may have difficulty dealing with complex or unfamiliar topics

High-Advanced

- Can understand, speak, read, and write English with a high degree of fluency and accuracy

- Operates at a sophisticated level in English but has occasional problems, especially in terms idioms, pronunciation, and cultural awareness

Appropriate Age and Academic Levels

Interactions Access

Survival and conversational themes. Each text is controlled, limiting the material to high-frequency, highly applicable vocabulary and structures.

Sample themes: Neighborhoods, Cities, and Towns, Friends and Family, Food and Nutrition

Appropriate for: lower secondary, upper secondary, post-secondary, adult, and institutes

Interactions One

Survival and conversational themes. Each text is controlled, limiting the material to high-frequency, highly applicable vocabulary and structures.

Sample themes: Getting around the Community, Housing and the Family

Appropriate for: Secondary, post-secondary, adult, and institutes

Interactions Two

Begins with conversational themes using more basic structures, vocabulary, and skills and then starts the transition to more complex topics and material.

Sample Themes: Education and Student Life, Business and Money, The Media, Prejudice, Tolerance, and Justice

Appropriate for: Secondary, post-secondary and adult, corporate, university, institutes

Mosaic One

Progresses from more conversational to more academic language and topics, making the transition from basic to complex structures, vocabulary, and skills.

Sample Topics: Relationships, Health, High Tech, Low Tech, Crime and Punishment

Appropriate for: Upper secondary, post-secondary and adult, corporate, university, institutes

Mosaic Two

Designed for functionally competent students who need to refine their command of English and who want a challenge. The texts offer a rapid review of more basic material and then give in-depth study of complex skills, structures, and vocabulary.

Sample topics: Language and Learning, Mysteries Past and Present, The Mind, Breakthroughs, The Arts

Appropriate for: Post-secondary and adult, corporate, university, institutes

Hours of Class and Homework

With the exception of the grammars, the texts offer between forty and sixty hours of instructional material each, depending on the amount of homework assigned. The grammars offer sixty to ninety hours of instruction material, depending on homework assigned and classroom activities used. In the grammars, one topic roughly corresponds to material for one or two class periods. An abundance of material is given in each text so that teachers can have the opportunity of picking and choosing, focusing on some areas while omitting others of less relevance to the students. Using all texts at a given level offers you over 250 hours of instructional materials to choose from.

Using the Texts in Combination and/or for Shorter Courses

Each *Interactions Access, Interactions,* and *Mosaic* text offers sufficient material for a semester-length course. For shorter courses, teachers can cover most chapters while omitting material within the chapters. Alternatively, entire chapters may be omitted, depending on the needs of the class. Generally following the order of the texts is recommended, however, as each text progresses in difficulty and sophistication.

In terms of using texts in combination, the various books at a level complement but do not duplicate each other. When one teacher is using two or more texts, the combining of material will obviously be easier. If two or more teachers at a given level are using the texts some planning will be necessary. While the texts are highly coordinated, the topics of each chapter do not correspond strictly across the program, and chapters in some texts will take longer than chapters in others.

Classroom Management

(Skill specific information can be found in the introduction to each text)

Teachers, especially language teachers, play many different roles. At different times, they are counselors, advisors, experts, facilitators, etc. One of their most crucial roles is that of a manager. Those who are not good managers are often not very successful overall. Therefore, it is extremely important that teachers learn good classroom management techniques.

Amount of Material and Pacing of the Course

Many teachers feel they must complete every page in a book because the students have paid for it. Sometimes it is possible to do every single exercise and activity, but usually it is not. Likewise, different philosophies exist on how much we as teachers should try to accomplish. Here are some thoughts on how much to cover and how quickly. More specific suggestions are given later in this manual.

Less is Better?

Our students often have very different needs, interests, and life situations. They learn at different rates. And they often reach the point of saturation (where they just cannot take in any more information) at different times. Therefore, many experienced teachers believe that it is useless to try to cover "everything." Rather, it's best to do a good, thorough job with less material, while allowing students to work at a pace that is comfortable for them, that suits their styles and speed of learning, and that fits with their personal schedules. The belief is that a deeper, clearer understanding of fewer items or issues is better than a superficial (or no) understanding of more items or issues.

If you follow this belief, then be quite selective in choosing the *Interactions Access* material to cover. Keep careful watch on your students, looking for areas of strength and weakness that will help guide your teaching. Use the progress tests as pretests to help you find those areas that need the most attention. Tell the students from the very start that they may not complete the book, but that is not something to worry about. The course will focus on issues of greatest necessity for that particular group.

Remember, though, that going more slowly can sometimes make for boring classes. Be prepared, then, to use some of the extra material with your faster-paced students. Make sure that those at the top end of the class are also challenged. You can give them additional assignments and you can include them as discussion leaders, activity coordinators, and so on.

More is Better?

An unavoidable reality for us as teachers is that many of our students need to make great improvement in their language skills but have very little time in which to do so. For some, your particular class may be the only one they will have time to take. For this reason, other experienced teachers feel that it is imperative to make the most of limited time, to cover as much as possible in order to address all the diverse needs and interests in a given class. It's felt that the only way to "give something to everyone" is to cover a great deal of ground. Perhaps more importantly, it's believed that repeated exposure in small doses to a wide variety of language is most successful. Making a rapid survey of various grammatical structures, for example, may be more successful than spending a longer time studying and practicing a limited number of structures.

If you follow this belief, then plan to cover as much material as possible, while not worrying whether each student has understood everything. Keep your in-class work moving as quickly as possible, do not spend time on long explanations, give your students ample time to practice, and assign as much homework as possible. In any event, you will never be able to cover all aspects of the English language in one course, but you can plan to highlight many or most key elements, depending on the length of your course.

Teaching Versus Teaching Students How to Learn

Whether you plan to cover less or more, you will never be able to cover everything. You can, however, help students to become more independent as learners and to continue their own work long after you have left them. Whenever possible, give your students help and advice on how to approach a reading or an exercise or a situation where they must listen and/or respond. Use as many of the tips from later in this manual and suggestions within the texts themselves, and combine them with your own experience from teaching and learning. Try to give your students ways of remembering more easily, encourage them to be willing to experiment and take chances with the language, guide them toward more and more self-correction, get them to ask for help or clarification, help them build confidence in their own abilities. Ultimately, the goal of your and any language class is to help the students become independent learners and communicators.

Lesson Planning

There are many different ways and levels of planning lessons. Some teachers feel that they must plan everything down to the minute. Others consider that they have "planned" the lesson if they know the grammar structure to be taught or the title of the reading selection they are going to be discussing. These are the two extremes of the lesson-planning continuum and neither is ideal.

The ideal is neither over-planning or under-planning. Every teacher should be familiar with the material to be covered and should have approximate time allotments for each part of the lesson. Yet, the plan should be flexible enough to allow for the unexpected. The "unexpected" is often what makes a particular day "come alive."

During a lesson, teachers need to be looking for opportunities to make the language and the classroom come alive for the students. Perhaps there has been an event which has captured everyone's attention and students want to talk about it, rather than complete the grammar exercise you had planned. Perhaps a piece of writing reveals a structure that is in need of immediate review. Teachers must be ready to take advantage of these opportunities and necessities of the moment. The most important point is balance, the balance between structure and flexibility. A lesson plan should be a flexibile framework rather than a rigid structure.

English Only Classrooms?

Many teachers are concerned about the relative amounts of English and the student's native language that should be used in the classroom. This is particularly troubling in EFL situations where monolingual classes are the rule. The most important point to consider when deciding on English vs. native language is the ultimate goal of the students. For example, are most of your students studying English because they are required to do so and must pass a grammar-based exam at the end of the year? If so, you probably are dealing with students with little or no motivation and can expect little cooperation in an English-only classroom. In that situation, try to concentrate on making the class lively and fun before worrying about using the native language. Perhaps you are teaching a class of highly motivated business people who expect to travel to the United States in the near future. Then you are justified in insisting on as much English as possible. You still may get some resistance because the students feel insecure, but you can probably get the other students to help you with the protesters.

For those of you who would like to start using more English in your classrooms, here are some tips:

- Start small. If you have a class of beginners, teach them some classroom phrases. (Open your book. How do you say _____ in English? etc.) Always say these commands in English and insist that they use English for these simple phrases, too.

- Try to explain new vocabulary in English, but give yourself a time limit. If you can't explain in one minute (two minutes at lower levels), then translate. Without a time limit, you can get sidetracked and end up never finishing your lesson.

- Keep English-English dictionaries in the classroom (picture dictionaries at the lowest levels). They will help you avoid going straight for the translation. Having dictionaries handy will also help students get in the habit of consulting them.

- If you are a competent speaker of your students' native language, don't try to counsel students in English. Trying to talk about a student's problems in English will probably only add to his or her distress.

- If you are not a native speaker of English, don't worry that you aren't "good enough" to speak English in the classroom. You know more English than your students. If they spoke as well as you do, they wouldn't need to be in your class. Even if you aren't a perfect model, you can do them a valuable service by getting them used to speaking. Those who are interested can improve as they continue to study.

Student-Centered Classrooms

A student-centered classroom is one in which the teacher is not the center of attention. While some activities are best carried out with the attention of all the students focused on the teacher, many other activities lend themselves to pair and group work.

Pair Work

Pair work is very effective for a variety of exercises and activities. It also maximizes the amount of time each student is able to speak during a given class. In addition, in many, many cases, two heads really are better than one! Specific suggestions for pair work appear later in the manual, but some general guidelines are as follows:

- Use pair work for all types of peer feedback and evaluation. An obvious example is in writing classes, where students can give each other comments and suggestions for improving drafts of compositions. Another example is with written assignments, such as for grammar, where students can compare homework before it is handed in.

- Pairs work well for completing exercises in class—again grammar exercises, for example. Students can also drill each other or quiz each other on vocabulary, verb forms, spelling, and so on.

Group Work

One of the thorniest classroom management issues is that of group work. Theorists keep encouraging it for very good reasons but teachers, particularly those in EFL settings, often have problems implementing it in their classrooms. The reasons vary. Teachers complain that their classes are too large, that it takes too long to set up, that the students speak their native language to each other rather than English, and even that colleagues and school administrators complain about noise and a disorganized, disruptive atmosphere.

These complaints are often valid, but many can be dealt with by teachers who are determined to make pair and group work a regular part of their classes. First of all, even in large classes where desks cannot easily be moved, a group of four can be formed by students in two rows pushing their desks close together and every other row turning around to face those behind them. If you cannot move the desks, students should be encouraged to sit in different places every day, so that they work with different people.

Setting up group work can take a while, especially in the beginning when students are not familiar with the activity. However, if you use two or three methods consistently, students will soon learn the routine and get themselves organized easily and efficiently. When you are doing pair work, don't always just have students work with the person closest at hand or someone of their own choosing. You can divide the number of students in the class by two and have them count off up to that number twice. Then both eights, both thirteens, and so on work together. Groups can be formed in the same way. To get two or three teams, simply have them count off one, two or one, two, three and group the students of the same number together.

The problem of students speaking their native language rather than English is a difficult one. Pair and group work requires cooperation on the part of your students. If they do not cooperate, it won't work. However, you can try to gain the cooperation of the majority by demonstrating that the activity is important.

There are several ways to do this. First of all, when the students are doing group work, you should be circulating, monitoring the activity and being available to offer help when necessary. This will show students that what they are doing is important to you. This is particularly crucial in some EFL situations where group work is rarely done in any subject area and students are therefore inclined not to take the task seriously. When group work is a new concept to students, teachers should not take group work time as an opportunity to grade papers or even work with students who need special help. After students understand that group work is integral to the learning process, teachers can feel free to loosen control a bit. Another way of demonstrating the importance of group and pair work tasks, is by asking at least some of the groups or pairs to report on their activity.

Other colleagues and especially school administrators who are opposed to anything but a teacher-centered classroom can be especially difficult to deal with. Some teachers have had success by anticipating the problem and discussing their new ideas with administrators and colleagues before they try them out. Enlisting the aid of another language teacher is often helpful in trying to change attitudes. In addition, teachers have sometimes invited administrators into their classrooms to see for themselves how the activities work. Noise level need not be a problem if you talk to colleagues in neighboring classrooms before you try any activity that you think may disrupt other classes. Again, student cooperation is a must. If students enjoy group work and, in our experience, most students do, you can tell them that if things get out of hand, the activity will be suspended. In addition, in large classes, a small bell or a whistle will probably be more effective at getting the students' attention than shouting over the noise.

When giving group work, then, be sure to do the following:

- Make sure that the instructions are very clear. Often when there is a lot of confusion and talking in the native language, it is because students are unsure what is expected of them.

- Make sure that everyone in the group has a specific role to play and that each understands that all should and must participate. Roles in effective groups can include the following: moderator (the person who keeps everything going), time-keeper (the person who watches that the work is being completed in the specified time and who also detects when one person talks too much or another not at all), recorder or secretary (the person who takes any notes), the reporter (the person who will report back to the whole class or to the teacher), and so on.

- Always have some extra work ready, because invariably one or two groups will finish well before the others.

Do not give up on group work, even if things seem a bit disorganized at first. It will be very beneficial to your students' language development once you start doing it on a regular basis. It will also help you and your students to realize that they need not be totally dependent upon you and can actually learn with and from each other.

Error Correction

Most people hate to make mistakes. It's embarrassing, especially if your mistake is noticed by others. This is as true in the classroom as it is outside in the world. Unfortunately, this attitude is harmful to the learning process. Making mistakes is an important and positive part of learning a language. Students learn how a language works by experimenting and receiving feedback on their errors. Therefore, errors are fundamental to progress.

Why? Because, as with any skill, if you are not working at the point of your maximum ability, your work is not as effective as it could be. If your class isn't making any errors, the students are probably not working up to their ability. They're most likely continuing to use language that is comfortable for them, rather than stretching to expand their knowledge. The ideal is to have students working a bit above their current language ability. If you go too far above their level, you will get nothing but errors, which can be extremely demotivating and frustrating to both teach and students.

In addition to showing you that your students are working at the right level, errors are valuable because they guide your teaching. Correct answers show you what the students know. But, as a teacher, it is far more important for you to know what they do not know. Errors are signals for pinpointing their misunderstandings.

At the *Interactions Access* level, students have only a basic knowledge of English, so you can expect many errors. Obviously, you won't have perfect, errorless production in speaking or writing, and you will need to give feedback. Class by class, you will have to decide how to handle this.

The most critical point is that error correction should never embarrass students and that the teacher's objective should be to point out the error while helping to build their self-confidence. One useful, non-threatening technique is for teachers to simply collect errors, either in student homework, or as students are working in groups. Then part of a class period can be devoted to examining and correcting class errors and no one need know who actually made them.

Another key issue is when to correct errors and when to ignore them. The decision should be made based on the objective of the activity. If the activity demands a high degree of accuracy (pronunciation drills, grammar close exercises), then errors should be pointed out. If, however, the objective is fluency, then some errors should be tolerated and others noted for explanation later on. At this level, fluency is a major goal, so it is best not to interrupt while students are communicating. Constant correction is not only demoralizing but also very disruptive to a student's train of thought.

Across levels, a good rule of thumb for correction is to focus on high-frequency errors or errors that interfere with understanding, especially at lower levels, and to put more emphasis on polishing at higher levels.

Homework

Some students are studying English full-time and have no other major responsibilities. Other students may have jobs, families, and a variety of obligations that do not leave them much free time. Depending on the nature of your course and the type of student in your class, you may or may not be able to assign homework and realistically expect the students to complete it.

Hopefully, you will be able to assign homework, because class time may be the only time that students have to speak and as much class time as possible should be reserved for interactive communication. If you are able to assign and count on homework, try to do the following:

- Assign as homework work that students do at different speeds and generally do alone. Reading and writing are the two obvious examples. Of course, you may want to do in-class timed readings, and you may want to read aloud to your students, but if possible, other reading should be done outside of class time. Likewise, many writing activities can be done in class, but others should be completed outside whenever possible.

- Assign realistic amounts of homework. If your students are taking numerous subjects, you cannot expect them to spend most of their time on English. However, if English is an important part of their program, it should have equal weight (and hopefully equal time) with other work.

- Make agreements or contracts with your students regarding homework and hold them to the agreements. If all agree to certain "rules" and know the consequences, then your class will run more smoothly. A terrible class for any teacher is when many or most students come unprepared. So, set rules and enforce them.

Testing and Evaluation

Testing is always a difficult issue to address, and as with other issues involved in education, various philosophies exist. Some feel that students need the incentive of tests to help them study, while others feel that tests produce so much anxiety that they are always counter-productive. This manual offers a variety of progress tests. Depending on your program, you may or may not choose to or be required to use them.

Interactions Access: A Communicative Grammar

Philosophy

Interactions Access: A Communicative Grammar is for beginning to high-beginning level students. The book introduces the most common basic structures in English. It uses everyday contexts to give students practice and multiple opportunities for applying the structures in their own speaking and writing.

Sequencing

The text is organized by structure and by theme. The first several chapters concentrate on key structures (the verb *be*, present tenses, and some modal auxiliaries) while building a core of high-frequency vocabulary through contexts such as neighborhood life, shopping, friends and family, and basic health care. Later chapters introduce a wider range of structures and vocabulary through contexts such as North American history and geography, nutrition, and global issues. The beginning chapters are closely controlled for structures and vocabulary, while the later chapters offer a wider range of exercises and activities involving more vocabulary.

Timing and Pace of the Course

In ESL settings, you should be able to cover most of the text in 50–60 class hours if you assign homework. In EFL settings, you will most likely need 75–90 class hours. In general, each chapter can be covered in five to eight teaching hours if you use some exercises as homework and select only some of the activities.

Depending on the level of your group, the first few chapters may be review. If so, go through these chapters more quickly. If not, take time in the first few chapters to practice the structures well and to expand the students' vocabulary. Then, you may want to move more quickly through later chapters.

You may choose to teach the chapters in a different order than in the text. However, vocabulary is controlled in the early chapters, most structures are recycled periodically, and the chapters are designed to progress in difficulty. So, while it's not absolutely necessary, we recommend following the general progression of the text. Of course, you can omit topics or whole chapters as necessary.

Chapter Organization

Each chapter has four major topics, and many of these have sub-topics. The fourth topic of Chapters Five and Ten is review. Charts and general reference material are at the back of the book. Each topic follows a sequence of (1) contextualized introductions of the grammatical structures, (2) grammar explanations, (3) exercises for practice, and (4) activities for less-controlled applications. Here are more detailed explanations of the parts of each chapter, with some tips for using them. Many specific tips are given with the Teaching Tips and Answer Key section below. Of course, each teacher has his or her own style, and many other possibilities exist for using this text.

1. *Setting the Context*: The opening to each grammar topic includes the following:

    *   *Opening Artwork and Previewing the Questions:* Each topic opens with a brief introduction, questions, and artwork that help to introduce the theme of that section.

    *   *Passage or Conversation:* Each topic opens with a short selection. They include examples of the structure(s) to be covered and set the theme of the section.

    *   *Discussing Questions:* Several questions or statements follow the reading selection. In early chapters, these are primarily "true" or "false" items. In general, students must understand, but don't have to produce, the vocabulary or structures involved. In later chapters, the *Discussion*

Questions require more thought and involvement. In many cases, students will need to give their own opinions or explanations.

Teaching suggestions: When you are beginning the class period or beginning new material, warm-ups are an effective way for getting your students to focus on English and getting them involved in the themes and structures to be covered. We have included the artwork, questions, and reading selections as contextualized warm-ups at the beginning of each topic to help your students focus on the material coming up in that section.

The various passages and conversations can serve many purposes. They can be used as the introduction to structures, or you can save them for follow-up after you have practiced the structures. You can use them as homework assignments, as silent readings, as listening comprehension exercises, or as dialogues between students. You can read the material aloud, or you can have a student or students read it. You can ask students to role-play many of the conversations, too. In all cases, the material shows students the structures *in context.*

Some teachers consistently use the introductory art and reading selections, and others do so only sometimes. You can always substitute your own warm-ups, especially through personalized questions or passages that target the new structures but that use real-life situations, local places, or students' names, for example.

2. *Grammar Explanations:* All grammar topics and sub-topics have boxed examples of the structures and explanatory notes when necessary. Early charts include a minimum of explanation so that the students don't become overwhelmed by the teacher talk that is common in detailed grammar rules. As students progress, though, the book offers them more explanation, especially in later chapters. General reference charts are in the back of the book.

Teaching suggestions: Keep your explanation of rules as brief and as simple as possible. Give a short explanation and examples (from the text or your own) and then ask students to give other examples. In some cases, you may want to

give examples, only—avoiding any detailed explanation. As you do exercises and activities, more questions may come up, and you can always go back to the grammar charts or give additional explanations.

The text gives examples, primarily, and only brief explanations. We have purposely avoided giving much explanation in *Interactions Access* because much of the vocabulary involved in grammar explanations is not particularly useful to students at this level. At the higher levels in the *Interactions* and *Mosaic* texts, much more explanation is included.

3. *Exercises:* The text has over two hundred exercises. In each section, they progress from more controlled to less controlled, from single-structure practice to more cumulative practice. The exercises include both tradition and innovative types, and many can be done as either speaking or writing exercises.

Teaching suggestions: Most exercises can be used in a variety of ways: as whole class work, pair work, small group work, or homework. Some exercises are specifically for pairs or groups of three, however, and some are specifically for oral practice. Longer exercises are best assigned as homework, or they can be used in class with two students working together to complete one paper. See the following section for specific tips on working with exercises.

Two other features of the text are cultural notes, which periodically accompany exercises, and progress checks, which are cumulative review exercises:

- *Cultural Notes:* All chapters have two or more notes to give extra information on various topics covered in exercises. These notes are often facts or figures about the U.S. and Canada.

- *Checking Your Progress:* Every other chapter (Ch. 2, 4, 6, 8, and 10) includes a progress check. These are short, objective exercises that cover material from two chapters. You can use these as quizzes, or you can use them as regular exercises.

4. *Using What You've Learned:* Each grammar topic includes a section called *Using What You've Learned.* This section offers you one or

more language activities that help put into use the structures covered in that topic. Early activities are limited in scope, while later ones involve much more thought and participation from the students. In all, the text offers you well over one hundred language activities to choose from. The activities are varied: from role-plays and games to presentations and compositions. Some are individual activities, some are for pairs, some are for small groups, and some are for the whole class. Certain activities are more controlled, but, in general, many are quite open-ended.

Teaching suggestions: While the activities in this text are designed to help the students use the target structures, this will not happen all the time. Many times, students will use other structures, instead. Also, the students may end up changing the activity as they go; they may produce something quite different from what you had expected.

If the students are being productive, if they are actively communicating, don't be concerned. The goal of any activity is to spark communication, so don't worry if the communication varies from the original idea. If the students are not being productive, however, you must lead them back to the original ideas. The students themselves should try to be responsible for this, too.

Helping students to become responsible participants in pairs and groups takes time, but with practice students can work well together. For the first two or three activities in your class, take time to talk about the purpose of pair or group work: to give each student more time and opportunities to use the language in more natural ways. Talk about the importance of cooperating, of giving everyone opportunities to participate, and about being productive. Activities can be a lot of fun, but their purpose is serious. It is each student's chance to experiment with language, just as we do in the real world.

It may take several attempts before you find good combinations of students. Some students will work well together, but others won't. Some will try to dominate, and others won't participate at all. Some will think that activities are "silly" and won't help them. Work with your students, then, to find the best combinations and the best approaches. For more information on pair and group work, see both the beginning of the manual and later parts of this section.

Two important issues in teaching apply to your work with both exercises and activities—personalizing and correcting:

Personalizing: The text includes a blend of personal questions with impersonal or academic material. However, no text can reach every interest, so personalize the exercises and activities whenever you can. Substitute names of local places and people. Draw from current news stories, TV programs, and movies. Above all, include information on your own students' interests, hobbies, or careers. Personalizing always helps stimulate the students' interest and is a great way to motivate your class.

Correcting Oral and Written Work: Students at this level are trying to become somewhat fluent in spoken English. It's very frustrating for many, then, to be corrected constantly. Yet, almost all students will want and need some correction. In speaking, perhaps the best way is to let students finish their ideas before correcting. Don't interrupt constantly. Then try to give the students two or three useful corrections. If you give numerous corrections, the student may feel quite discouraged and probably won't remember any of them. Try to focus your correction on mistakes that interfere with understanding or mistakes that the student should be capable of correcting. When a student knows the right way but doesn't yet use it, oftentimes several corrections from you will help that student to begin to self-correct.

In terms of written work, be stricter. Written English is more formal than spoken English, and mistakes are less acceptable. Correct all written exercises. In compositions or any creative writing, though, do not correct every single error (unless there are only a few). Focus on mistakes that interfere with understanding, are the result of carelessness, or are related to structures that you have recently covered.

Teaching Tips and Answer Key

Introduction

pp. xiii-xiv: Introduce yourself to the class, using the expressions on p. xiii: "My name is . . . ; I am from . . . ; I am . . . ; My native language is . . ." Then go around the room and ask each student "What is your name?" If you can, make a brief note for each in order to remember all the names.

Now, have the students go around the room in a chain, asking the person to the left, for example. Student A asks Student B; Student B answers and then asks Student C; Student C answers, and so on.

After this, have the students look at the map. Repeat the information about yourself: "I am from . . ." Then, go around the room asking the students "Where are you from?" After each, say "You are from . . . (Japan); that means you are . . . (Japanese) and your native language is . . ." Note: If all students are from the same country, skip this part and go right into the pair work below.

Next, write the questions on the board and then ask students to work in pairs. Have them take turns asking and answering. They can use the drawing at the top of p. xiv as a model. Give them 3–4 minutes total. As they talk, circulate a little and try to learn a bit about the speaking level of the class. Then reconvene the class and introduce Chapter One.

Chapter One: Neighborhoods, Cities, and Towns

Chapter One covers many basic structures and useful words and expressions: the verb *be* (statements, questions, and negatives), singular and plural nouns with accompanying spelling rules, adjectives, articles, prepositions, some pronouns, and expressions with time and weather. The contexts include a young woman's arrival in the U.S., life in different parts of the U.S., and descriptions of many cities, both in the U.S. and in other parts of the world.

You will probably want to spend at least four or five class hours on this chapter, even if it is review for your class. Most of the parts of speech (the basic building blocks of language) are covered here, and a great deal of useful day-to-day vocabulary is included.

Topic One

This section focuses on introductions and basic descriptive language—primarily adjectives with the verb *be.* It's meant to help you and the students get to know about each other while practicing and / or reviewing basic, useful vocabulary.

p. 2

Setting the Context: Have students turn to p. 2. Point to the picture and ask the prereading questions: "Where is the young woman? Is she happy?" Let the students answer in phrases ("New York" "No"), but encourage them to say more if they can. Let 4–5 students offer answers.

Then read the passage aloud to the students. Let them follow in the book if they want. Read somewhat slowly and carefully. Then point out the "Discussion Questions." Say that these are "true or false, true or not true, correct or false." Make sure students understand the idea of "true / false." Then ask students to reread the passage silently and make their own choices of "true" or "false." After the students finish, reread the passage aloud, this final time a little more quickly. Then read the statements aloud, one by one. Ask students for the answers. Try to correct the false statements.

Discussion questions, Answers: 1. T   2. F   3. F   4. T

p. 3, Chart A

Before students look at Chart A, write the personal pronouns on the board:

I   We
You _____ from _____.   You _____ from _____.
He
She   They
It

Model the first person: *I am from (the United States).* Then try to get the other forms of *be* from a variety of students (7–9 different ones). Change the country whenever necessary to make true statements. Use this to see if the majority of the class already knows the forms of *be*. Then, have students look at the chart. Read the examples aloud, one by one. Perhaps have the class repeat chorally. Then look at the expressions below. Read the examples aloud (and have students repeat). Finally, go around the room once again, pointing to individual students or to pairs of students. (One student can begin, and you can be the second, to model the pattern). Ask the first student "Where are you from?" When the student answers ("I am from Japan / Korea / etc."), you continue: "He / she is from Korea. I am from the United States." Then point to another student to continue: "Our teacher is from the United States. I am from . . ." Now point to two students from the same country, if possible. Elicit ". . . We are from . . ." Try to get 10–12 responses.

p. 3, Ex 1

Say to the class, "Now let's learn about Mariko." Ask students to read the exercise silently and then to complete the answers, silently, as quickly as possible. Then read the passage aloud to the class, pausing for each blank. Either have students call out the answers, or point to individuals to give the answers. You may want to assign this to be written out as homework, also.

Answers: 1. am   2. am   3. am   4. are
5. are   6. is   7. is   8. is   9. are
10. are   11. is   12. is

Extension Activity

Look at the vocabulary from Ex. 1. Ask questions about new expressions: "What's an exchange student?" "What's a trip?" "What's a tour?" "What's excited mean?" (Or: "What's the opposite of excited?" "Bored") "What's nervous mean?" "What's the opposite of large?" "Small / little" "What's the opposite of crowded?" "Empty."

To help with understanding, draw simple drawings, e.g., for an exchange student—a simple world map with stick-figure students with arrows pointing Japan-US, France-US, Mexico-US; for a trip, movement on the map from one city to another and another (Draw a little car with arrows). Also pantomime: excited—bored, nervous—calm, etc. Whenever possible, work with both synonyms and antonyms.

p. 3, Ex. 2

Have students write this silently first. Then go around the room and call on students for answers. Go through the exercise 2–3 times if necessary so that each student has a chance to do an item.

Answers: 2. is; is Mexican   3. are; are Korean   4. are; are French   5. is; is Syrian   6. is; is Indonesian   7. are; are German

p. 4, Ex. 3

If you do Ex. 3 immediately after Ex. 2, do not let students prepare silently. Go through the exercise, again calling on individuals. Do the exercise 2–3 times if necessary so that each student has a chance to do an item.

Answers: 2. is; She is   3. is; He is   4. are; They are   5. is; She is   6. is; He is
7. are; They are

Note: At this point, you may want to pause from the exercises and go to Act. 1, p. 11.

p. 5, Chart B

If your students don't know the contractions of *be*, go through this chart step by step. Otherwise, you can refer the students to it and simply read the examples.

For a full presentation of the chart, write the long forms on the board and draw lines linking the subject and verb:

I'm = I am from Spain.

Have students repeat each contracted sentence after you.

p. 5, Ex. 5

Read the paragraph aloud to the class as the students read along silently. Then, have the class rewrite the paragraph, using contractions. Finally, have several students read the new version aloud.

Answers: Hi! I'm Carlos, and I'm from Mexico. I'm a student in Chicago, but I'm in New York on a tour. My brother Gabriel's here in New York too. He's on vacation. We're very excited about our trip. New York's wonderful! It's big, crowded, and interesting. Some people on our tour are afraid of the city. They're nervous—especially Mariko. She's very nice, but she's always lost and confused. Not Gabriel and me! We're in love with New York.

Note: At this point, you may want to do Act. 2 from p. 11. This will give you a writing sample for your class, too. You can let students use Ex. 5 as a model.

p. 6, Chart C

If you used the Introduction, your students have already practiced a few questions. Go through all the forms with the class and then continue directly with Ex. 6.

p. 6, Ex. 6

Have students work in pairs and you can circulate to listen to them. For more practice, you can have them do the exercise two or three times with different partners. Students can answer "Yes" or "No," but you can also encourage them to give longer responses.

Answers: 1. Yes 2. No 3. Yes 4. No
5. Yes 6. Yes 7. open 8. open

p. 7, Chart D

Take some time with this chart. You may want to assign it in advance as homework, too. You can read the questions and a student can give the answers. Then, you can have students work in pairs to practice asking and answering. Finally go on to Ex. 7.

p. 7, Ex. 7

You can assign Ex. 7 as homework or you can give students several minutes in class to write questions for these answers. Then, go over the possible questions and have students practice the exercise in pairs.

Questions: 2. Where are you from? 3. How old are you? 4. Who is your friend? 5. Where is she from? 6. Where is she right now?

Note: At this point, you can take a break from the exercises and move to Act. 3, pp. 11-12.

pp. 8–9, Ex. 8

You can do part of this exercise with the class so that all students understand what to do and then assign the rest for homework. First, look at the picture in Item 1. Then model the example: "This exercise is about New York City. Parts of New York City are beautiful." Then call on a student or ask for a volunteer and say "How about clean'?" Elicit: "Parts of New York City are clean." Continue with "safe." Then say "Not all of New York is beautiful. Parts of New York are ugly" (from Item 2). Ask for a volunteer to use the word "dirty" and another "dangerous."

At this point, you can stop and ask students to cover the pictures and words. Ask them "What's the opposite of beautiful? (Ugly) What's the opposite of dirty? (Clean) What's the opposite of safe? (Dangerous)."

Continue in this pattern through as much of the exercise as you want to do with the whole class. Then assign the rest for homework.

Answers: 1. Parts of New York are clean. Parts of New York are safe. 2. Parts of New York are ugly. Parts of New York are dirty. Parts of New York are dangerous. 3. Buildings in New York City are large. Buildings in New York City are modern. 4. Buildings in New York City are small. Buildings in New York City are old. 5. New York City is crowded. New York City is noisy. 6. New York City is peaceful. New York City is quiet. 7. Some New Yorkers are poor. Some New Yorkers are unhappy. Some New Yorkers are unfriendly. Some New Yorkers are upset. 8. Some New Yorkers are rich. Some New Yorkers are happy. Some New Yorkers are friendly. Some New Yorkers are relaxed.

You can do part or all of Ex. 9 in class as a continuation of Ex. 8, or you can assign it for homework. To be sure that the students understand the vocabulary, you can pantomime the sensations or emotions.

Answers: 2. Mr. Park and Mr. Kim are tired. 3. Benny is bored. 4. Carlos and Gabriel are excited. 5. Hassan is thirsty. 6. Gunter and Elizabeth are hungry.

Extension Activity

If your class enjoys pantomiming, you can continue the idea of Ex. 9 with more adjectives. You and/or the students can pantomime the following: angry, worried, upset, hot, cold, exhausted, sick, feverish, and so on. The rest of the class can guess the feeling or sensation. As a help, write the words on index cards or small pieces of paper, in advance, and pass them out to student volunteers.

p. 10, Chart F

Ask the students to look at the top of the chart, and review the questions with *What*. Ask each question to two different students and elicit the appropriate answer. Then model the questions *What is . . . like?* You can substitute a class member's name for the first question: "What is Ali like?" or "What is Susanna like?" You can substitute the name of your own town for New York City, also.

Either before or after you have done this exercise, you can ask students in the class if anyone has been to the cities listed. If so, have them give additional descriptions. After you do this exercise, you can go directly into Act. 4, p. 12, where students have a chance to talk about their own hometowns. You can also have them describe important cities in their area or country.

Answers: 1. A: What is New York like? B: It's large and very busy. 2. A: What is San Francisco like? B: It's beautiful. 3. A: What is Cairo like? B: It's crowded but very interesting. 4. A: What is Los Angeles like? B: It's modern but polluted. 5. A: What is Rome like? B: It's old and beautiful but very expensive. 6. A: What is Minneapolis like? B: It's safe and clean.

7. A: What is Rio de Janeiro like? B: It's fun. 8. A: What is Paris like? B: It's beautiful and interesting.

pp. 11-12

Using What You've Learned: You can do some or all of these activities when you finish Topic One, or you can intersperse the activities (as noted above). If you choose to intersperse them, Act. 1 is good to do during the first two or three days of class, as a warm-up at the beginning or at the end of a class. Act. 2 is a good follow-up to Ex. 5. Act. 3 can be used for added practice after Ex. 7, and Act. 4 as added practice after Ex. 8 or 10.

Act. 1

Help the students one more time in learning each other's names and countries. Say "Now let's see. Who knows all the names and countries in our class?" Point to one student and say ". . . is from . . . S/he is . . ." Then have that student continue, speaking about the person to his or her right or left. Continue around the room. Finally, ask for a volunteer: "Can anyone tell all of the students' names and countries?" Try to get several volunteers to do this. Then, do it yourself.

Note: Activities such as these at the very beginning of a course help to set the tone and create a friendly, open atmosphere in a short time. The sooner the students feel comfortable with you and with each other, the sooner they will be willing to open up, share ideas, and make a few mistakes. Knowing each other's names is a good first step in that direction.

Act. 2

You can do this as in-class writing or as homework. If you do it in class, you can set a time limit of 10–15 minutes. This will give you a sample of "on demand" writing for your group. For this first composition, you may want to give a few comments only and not correct heavily. You can also separate students into small groups for 5–10 minutes and let them share (saying, not reading) the information from their composition.

Act. 3

With a creative group, this activity can be a lot of fun. To help students generate ideas, you can suggest names of politicians, sports figures, movie stars, and so on.

Act. 4

This activity works well with groups of four. Give students ten minutes to gather their information. Then mix students from different groups and let them share the information they've collected.

Note: If you do most of the activities in this section, your students should be on the way to getting to know each other and feeling comfortable. In later sections, you may choose to do fewer activities, but at the beginning of a course, several "ice breakers" help a great deal in creating a friendly, open classroom environment.

Topic Two

This topic covers a wide variety of nouns, including jobs and professions and commonly-used nouns for people, places, and things. It begins work on spelling of both regular and irregular plurals, and it covers possessive adjectives. Negative forms of be are introduced, also. All of these are introduced within the context of jobs and daily life, primarily in smaller towns.

p. 13, Setting the Context

Ask the class to look at the picture and try to describe it. Ask what is in the picture and try to elicit as many nouns as possible. Set up the contrast of "large city" and "small town," and then read the passage aloud for the class. Complete the questions that follow and then answer any questions on vocabulary.

Discussion questions, Answers: 1. Gary 2. farmer   3. small   4. happy

p. 13, Cultural Note

If your class is interested, you can expand on this culture note by asking questions such as "Is there a lot of farming / Are there a lot of farmers in your country (region, etc.)?" Try to elicit types of farming if possible (cattle, dairy, vegetables, grains, etc.).

p. 14, Chart A

Before looking at the chart, you can introduce indefinite articles by saying (and writing on the board) "I am a teacher. I am an English teacher." Then ask several students "What am I?," eliciting the responses "You are a teacher. You are an English teacher." Underline or highlight a and an. Then mention another teacher ("John is a teacher"). Finally, combine the sentences: "John and I are teachers. John and I are English teachers."

Now read through Chart A with the class and continue with Ex. 1.

p. 14, Ex. 1

This exercise works well when first done in pairs and then reviewed with the whole group.

Answers: 13—a nurse's aide; 14—a plumber; 6—a computer programmer; 12—a nurse; 5—a carpenter; 10—an English teacher; 4—a businesswoman; 11—a musician; 7—a dentist; 16—a student; 9—an engineer; 3—a bus driver; 15—a secretary; 8—a doctor; 2—an auto mechanic

p. 15, Ex. 2

You can continue with the class working in pairs. Have the pairs do Ex. 2, orally and in writing, and then go over the answers orally with the whole class.

Answers: 1. Soo Young is from Korea. She is a student.   2. Alfonso is from Colombia. He is an engineer.   3. Andrea is from Argentina. She is a doctor.   4. Nancy is from the United States. She is an airline flight attendant.   5. Centa and Werner are from Switzerland. They are teachers. 6. Tomoko and Akiko are from Japan. They are computer programmers.   7. Isabelle and Pierre are from France. They are factory workers.   8. Daniel and Ben are from Hong Kong. They are auto mechanics.

p. 16, Chart B

Go back to your examples for Chart A and use the words *teacher / teachers* as a starting point. Add several more nouns the class is familiar with and ask students for the plural: pen / pens, book / books. Use four or five nouns that add only *-s*. Now have the class look at the chart and explain that some nouns have different spellings for the *-s* ending. These spelling rules should be memorized.

p. 17, Ex. 3

Do this exercise both in speaking and in writing. You can have students write first, or you can do it orally first. You can also have students quiz each other in pairs.

> Answers: 1. men   2. women   3. babies
> 4. boys   5. churches   6. potatoes
> 7. toys   8. farms   9. cities   10. wives

p. 17, Ex. 4

This exercise should be written first and then read aloud. You can have students work individually or in pairs. It can also be assigned as homework.

> Answers: 1. places   2. animals   3. cows
> 4. horses   5. chickens   6. ducks
> 7. geese   8. children   9. pets   10. dogs
> 11. cats   12. mice   13. wives
> 14. gardens   15. flowers   16. vegetables
> 17. carrots   18. onions   19. tomatoes
> 20. potatoes   21. things   22. families

p. 17, Culture Note

Depending on your group, you may want to use this opportunity to introduce a lot of vocabulary covering plants and animals—both domesticated and wild. You can set up two or three categories (farm animals, fruit, vegetables, grains, wild animals, etc.) and ask students to research a bit on their own countries or regions. They should try to get three to four entries for each category and bring pictures, if possible, to show the class.

p. 18, Chart C

You can introduce negatives with *be* by again using the familiar examples "I am a teacher. John and I are teachers." Add to these "I am not a student. John and I are not students." Then go over Chart C with the class.

p. 18, Ex. 5

You can have students do Ex. 5 in pairs and then go through the exercise orally with the class. You can expand on this exercise by highlighting a few of the antonyms (fast-slow, large-small), and then asking the class (or the pairs) to suggest more.

> Answers: 2. isn't   3. isn't   4. isn't
> 5. aren't   6. 'm not   7. aren't

p. 18, Ex. 6

Make sure that students understand that the sentences in Ex. 6 are NOT true. Using the negative will make them true. Then have students write the exercise individually. After they've finished, have them work in pairs to practice the various negative forms orally.

> Answers: 1. Gary is not a businessman. Gary's not a businessman. Gary isn't a businessman.   2. He is not from a large city. He's not from a large city. He isn't from a large city.   3. The White House is not in New York. The White House's not in New York. The White House isn't in New York.   4. It is not near the United Nations building. It's not near the United Nations building. It isn't near the United Nations building.   5. New York is not a quiet city. New York's not a quiet city. New York isn't a quiet city.   6. It is not near Los Angeles. It's not near Los Angeles. It isn't near Los Angeles.   7. You are not from England. You're not from England. You aren't from England.   8. I am not tired of grammar. I'm not tired of grammar.

p. 19, Ex. 7

This exercise can be done individually or assigned as homework and then reviewed orally with the whole class.

> Answers: (1) 1. isn't   2. isn't   3. isn't
> 4. 's   5. is   6. is   7. is
> (2) 1. 're   2. 're   3. isn't   4. isn't
> 5. aren't   6. are   7. is
> (3) 1. is   2. 'm   3. 'm   4. 'm not
> 5. 'm   6. is   7. isn't   8. 's

p. 19, Chart D

Students have already been passively exposed to many of the possessives, especially in telling their names, so the chart should need little introduction. Read through it with the class and then go directly to Ex. 8, 9, and 10.

p. 20, Ex. 8

Do this exercise with the whole class.

Answers: 3. Our   4. We   5. My
6. your   7. you   8. His   9. She
10. Their   11. Its   12. It

p. 20, Ex. 9 and 10

You can have students do these exercises individually or in pairs, and then go over them with the entire class. Likewise, you can assign them as homework, and then review them orally.

Ex. 9, Answers: (1) 1. Our   2. Our
(Its=Big City)   3. our (its=Big City)
4. Our   5. We   6. Our
(2) 1. I   2. My   3. My   4. I   5. My
6. my

Ex. 10, Answers: 1. Their   2. they
3. She   4. her   5. her   6. his   7. he
8. His

p. 21, Using What You've Learned

This activity is a natural written follow-up to Ex. 9 and 10. You can assign the story as homework and then have students tell the stories to each other, or vice versa.

Topic Three

This section focuses on time and weather with the verb *be* and appropriate adjectives.

p. 21, Setting the Context

Have the students turn to p. 21. While the students look at the picture, ask them the prereading questions (a weatherperson, the weather is not nice except in Hawaii). Then, read the passage aloud slowly. Point out the "Discussion questions" and make sure the students understand the idea of completing sentences. Then, ask the students to reread the passage silently and make their own choices for completing the sentences. Next, reread the passage

aloud, this time more quickly. Then read the statements aloud, one by one. Ask the students for their completions.

Discussion questions, Answers:
1. 24   2. rainy   3. foggy   4. closed
5. snowy

p. 22, Chart A

Say to the class, "We're talking about the weather. What's the weather today, here?" Then (if there are students from different countries in the class) ask, "What's the weather like in your country/city today?" Try to get 5 or 6 answers.

Then, on the left side of the blackboard, write the question, "What's the weather today?" and ask for other ways to ask the same question. Write "What's the weather like?" and "What's it like outside?" (and other correct responses students give) underneath the first question. Then, ask how to answer the question. Write different answers on the right side of the board, e.g., "It's beautiful, It's terrible (rainy, cold, chilly, snowy, warm, cloudy, hot, humid)." Explain any words such as chilly and humid that the students do not understand.

Finally, read Chart A with the students.

p. 22, Ex. 1

Direct the students to the two weather maps. Ask a few questions: "What's the weather in Denver today? Is it warm in Montreal? Is it sunny in San Francisco?" Then, do the exercise aloud by calling on students individually.

Answers: 1. Madison, Wisconsin is sunny, breezy, and warm.   2. Denver, Colorado is cloudy, rainy, and cool.   3. Miami, Florida is hot and humid.   4. Montreal, Quebec is cold and cloudy.   5. Tucson, Arizona is very hot and dry.   6. Boston, Massachusetts is cold and snowy.   7. New Orleans, Louisiana is warm and breezy.
8. St. Louis, Missouri is cold and rainy.
9. San Francisco, California is foggy and cool.   10. Toronto, Ontario is very cold and windy.

Note: At this time, you can take a break from the exercises and move to Act. 1, p. 26, if you wish.

p. 23, Chart B

Have the students look at p. 23. For fun, tell them that you have lost your memory and that they have to help you. Then, ask the questions in the chart to the class as a whole ("What time is it?" etc.). They can answer chorally. Next, draw some clocks on the board with different times, e.g. 8:05, 8:10, 8:15, 8:30, 8:45, 8:50, 9:00 and ask students what time it is.

pp. 23–24, Ex. 2

Have students do this exercise in pairs. The students alternate answering questions. Then, go over the answers with the class as a whole, but now the teacher asks the appropriate question before each answer.

Answers: 1. It's eight fifteen. It's quarter after (past) eight. 2. It's fifteen minutes to five. It's quarter to five. It's four forty-five. 3. It's twelve o'clock. It's (twelve) noon. It's (twelve) midnight. 4. It's Monday. 5. It's Thursday. 6. It's Saturday. 7. It's March 18th. 8. It's July 25th. 9. It's August 20th. 10. It's two ten. It's ten minutes after (past) two. 11. It's six fifty. It's ten minutes to seven. 12. It's eleven twenty-five. It's twenty-five after (past) eleven.

p. 25, Chart C

Begin by talking about yourself. Give the same information as is in Chart C, but about yourself. (This works better if you say that your birthday is today. Also, it's often funny to "lie" about the year you were born. If you are 50, say, "I was born in 1980!") Then, ask a few students some questions about yourself to elicit the correct use of *in, on, at* as shown in Chart C: "Was I born in the afternoon or at night? What month was I born in? When is my birthday? What date is my birthday on? Is my birthday party in the afternoon or at night? What time is the party? How long is the party?"

p. 25, Ex. 4

Have students do this exercise in pairs and then review the answers with the whole class. To do this, the teacher can read the sentences, pausing at the blanks for the students to chorally provide the answer or an individual student can read an entire sentence. If there is any confusion, the teacher should repeat the correct answer.

Answers: 1. on; at 2. on; at 3. on; at 4. on; on; at 5. on; at

p. 26, Ex. 5

Follow the ideas for Ex. 4.

Answers: 1. on 2. at 3. in 4. from 5. to 6. in 7. from 8. to 9. at 10. On 11. at

p. 26, Ex. 7

Follow the ideas for Ex. 4.

Answers: 1. In 2. In 3. from 4. to 5. on

p. 26, Ex 8

Follow the ideas for Ex. 4.

Answers: 1. to 2. at 3. in 4. On 5. On 6. at 7. On

Note: At this time you could go directly to Act. 3, p. 27.

pp. 26-27, Using What You've Learned

You can do some or all of these activities when you finish Topic Three, or you can intersperse the activities (as noted above). If you choose to intersperse them, Act. 1 goes well after Ex. 1; Act. 2 is a good follow-up to Ex. 3; Act. 3 should be done after Ex. 8.

Topic Four

This section focuses on how to talk about cities using *there is/are*, and appropriate prepositions.

pp. 27–28, Setting the Context

Have the students turn to p. 27. While the students look at the picture and the drawing, ask them the prereading questions (Canada is NOT a state in New England! Boston is the major city).

Then, read the passage aloud slowly. Point out the "Discussion questions." If necessary, review the concept of "true/false." Then, ask the students to reread the passage silently and make their own choice of "true" or "false." Next, reread the passage aloud, this time more quickly. Then read the statements aloud, one by one. Ask the students for the answers. Have them try to correct the false statements.

> Discussion questions, Answers: 1. False (Boston is on the East Coast.) 2. False (Boston is the capital of Massachusetts.) 3. True 4. True 5. False (There are many parks in Boston.)

pp. 28–29, Chart A

Begin by talking about the city you are all in. Ask the class some questions that will elicit *there is(n't)/are(n't)*, e.g., "Is there a museum in this city? Where is it? How many schools are there? Is there a police station nearby?" etc. Write some examples on the board. Be sure to show when the singular and plural are used and how contractions and the negatives are formed. Then, have the students look at Chart A.

p. 29, Ex. 1

Tell the students that they have taken a quick look at Boston. Now they are going to examine some other important cities in the U.S. (This may be done in pairs or orally as a class.)

> Answers: 2. are 4. are 5. is 6. is 7. is 8. are

p. 30, Ex. 2

This may be done in pairs or orally as a class.

> Answers: 3. aren't 4. aren't 5. aren't 6. aren't 7. isn't 8. isn't

p. 31, Chart B

Write the last sentence from Ex. 2 on the board: "There isn't any snow in Houston." Below the sentence, write the *yes/no* question: "Is there any snow in Houston?" Do the same thing with a plural, e.g., "There are many cable cars in San Francisco. Are there many cable cars in San Francisco?" Then, have students look at Chart B.

p. 31, Ex. 3

Begin this exercise with a brief discussion of New York. Ask the students what the most important city in the U.S. is. Eventually, tell them that many people believe that New York is. Explain that New York has many parts but that the center of the city is an island called Manhattan. This exercise is designed for pairs.

> Answers: 1. A: Is there a subway in Manhattan? B: Yes, there is. 2. A: Are there many tunnels? B: Yes, there are. 3. A: Are there four rivers around Manhattan? B: No, there aren't. 4. A: Is there a bridge to the Statue of Liberty? B: No, there isn't. 5. A: Are there many ferries to Manhattan? B: Yes, there are. 6. A: Is there a train station in Manhattan? B: Yes, there is. 7. A: Is there a large park? B: Yes, there is. 8. A: Is there a zoo in Central Park? B: Yes, there is. 9. A: Are there many museums in Manhattan? B: Yes, there are. 10. A: Is there an airport in Manhattan? B: No, there isn't. 11. A: Is there an airport in Brooklyn? B: No, there isn't. 12. A: Is there an airport in Queens? B: Yes, there is.

Note: At this time you could go directly to Act. 1, p. 36.

p. 32, Chart C

Begin by asking the students a series of questions that will elicit *in, on, at*, e.g., "Do you live in an apartment or a house? Which street is your apartment (house) on? What is the exact address? Which city is your apartment (house) in? Which state, which country? Is the city on an ocean or river?" Then, have the students quickly read Chart C.

p. 32, Ex. 4

This exercise is best done in pairs or small groups.

> Answers: 2. at   3. at   4. on   5. at
> 6. at   7. on

Note: At this time you could go directly to Act. 2, p. 36.

---

p. 33, Ex. 5

Tell the students that so far we have only looked at U.S. cities, but now we will talk about important cities around the world. This exercise can be done in pairs, small groups, or as a class with the teacher calling on individual students.

> Answers: 1. Paris is in France.   2. Geneva is in Switzerland.   3. Tokyo is in Japan.
> 4. Chicago is on Lake Michigan.   5. San Francisco is on the Pacific Ocean.
> 6. Buenos Aires is in Argentina.   7. Miami is on the Atlantic Ocean.   8. Cairo is on the Nile River.

p. 33, Ex. 6

Do this exercise in pairs or small groups.

> Answers: 1. Santa Barbara isn't in Oregon. It's in California.   2. The Cascade Mountains aren't in Arizona. They're in Washington.   3. Reno isn't on the Pacific Ocean. It's in Nevada.   4. Vancouver and Edmonton aren't in Washington. They're in Canada.   5. (True) Los Angeles is on the Pacific Ocean.   6. Seattle isn't on the Columbia River. It's on Puget Sound near the Pacific Ocean.   7. Phoenix and Tucson aren't in Nevada. They're in Arizona.
> 8. (True) The Grand Canyon is in Arizona.

Pronunciation Notes: Vancouver = /van COO ver; Edmonton = /ED mon ton/; Phoenix = /FEE nix/; Tucson = /TOO san/

---

p. 34, Chart D

You can introduce this by talking about where different family members are at the moment, e.g., "Where's my father? Right now my father is at the bank." "Where's my brother? He is at home." "Where's my sister? My sister is downtown." Write these sentences on the board underlining *at the bank, at home*, and *downtown*. Then, show the students Chart D.

p. 34, Ex. 7

This exercise is designed to work as a chain.

> Possible answers: 1. Where's Anne? She's at home.   2. Where's Carlos? He's downtown.   3. Where's Jack? He's at the museum.   4. Where's Fred? He's at work.
> 5. Where's Jane? She's over there.
> 6. Where's Lucy? She's in class.
> 7. Where's Rick? He's at the post office.
> 8. Where's Sandy? She's at the store.
> 9. Where's Mary? She's at the movies.
> 10. Where's Laura? She's at church.

p. 35, Ex. 8

Explain the concept of "homesick." Ask if any of them is (or has ever been) homesick. Then, say they are going to learn about Akiko, a young woman who is living away from home. Do this exercise in pairs or small groups and review the answers as a class. You can also assign this as homework and then go over it in class.

> Answers: 1. is   2. it's   3. is   4. Her
> 5. is   6. My   7. is   8. at   9. in   10. at
> 11. at the   12. There   13. On   14. am
> 15. is   16. it's   17. is   18. are   19. on
> 20. are   21. I   22. in   23. In
> 24. sunny   25. am

Note: At this time you could go directly to Act. 3, p. 36.

---

p. 36, Using What You've Learned

You can do some or all of these activities when you finish Topic Three, or you can intersperse the activities (as noted above). If you choose to intersperse them, Act. 1 goes well after Ex. 3; Act. 2 is a good follow-up to Ex. 4; Act. 3 should be done after Ex. 8.

Chapter Two: Shopping—A National Pastime?

The theme of this chapter is shopping in a variety of contexts. The grammar focus of this chapter is on the present continuous tense. As it is still early in the course, you should plan to spend the same number of hours on this chapter as on Chapter One.

Topic One

pp. 38–39, Setting the Context

Ask the students to looking at the picture of two friends shopping. Ask the question, "What are they looking for?" Write the answers on the board. If students do not know the vocabulary, this is a good time for you to help them. An easy way to indicate synonyms is to write an equal sign (=). Vocabulary includes *gift=present, purse= pocketbook*. You can ask other simple questions. "Are they shopping for a child or an adult? A man or a woman?"

Then, follow the suggestions for the opening dialogue for Chapter One, or for a change, have the students, in groups of three, begin by trying to read the dialogue. Circulate while the students read to give assistance with pronunciation. Anticipate that students will have problems with the following: special (Spanish speakers will tend to put an *es* sound at the beginning.); gift (be sure that the vowel is a short sound); suit /soot/; blouse /blows/; purse (the /er/ sound is difficult for Asian students). Next, ask for volunteers to read aloud. This is a good time to focus on pronunciation of difficult words.

p. 38, Discussion questions

You can have students work in pairs asking and answering the questions. Then, to give students a sense of security, ask the questions to the whole class to check answers. Students will probably not know the meaning of "outfit." You can explain by giving examples and pointing at the outfits of students in the room: a skirt and blouse / a jacket, blouse and pants, etc. until students understand that it means clothes that go together.

> Answers: 1. Yes./ Yes, they are.
> 2. Clothes for a job interview./ Something serious. / She's thinking about something serious. / She's looking for clothes for a job interview.   3. A gift. / A birthday gift for his mother. /He's looking for a birthday gift for his mother.   4. Yes, she is. / Yes, she's going to the birthday party.

p. 39, Chart A

Write the chart on the board or use an overhead transparency. Point out that the present continuous tense is made of two verb forms. Ask students to supply the *-ing* form of other verbs, for example, *talk, speak*, etc. Cover the board or transparency and quiz the students on the correct form of the verb "to be," for example, *it (is), you (are), they (are)*, etc. Next point out the contraction forms. Have the students practice the contractions by writing them. Call out "I." Students should write "I'm." Continue by calling out the forms in random order. After each one, write the correct form on the board, pronounce it and have the students repeat. In this way they will get immediate feedback and they will practice writing and pronunciation. Spanish speaking students will need to be careful with the pronunciation of "it's." Write "it's" and "eats" on the board and model the difference between the long and short vowel. This is also a good time to write homonyms on the board and point out that there are words in English that sound the same, but have different pronunciation and meaning: *you're/your, they're/there*.

p. 40, Ex. 1

> Answers: are you looking; My friend is looking; I'm shopping; I'm looking; I'm trying; I'm looking; we're having; Cristina is coming

p. 40, Ex. 2

> Answers: 2. are playing   3. are taking   4. are looking   5. are shopping   6. is going   7. is listening   8. is reading

p. 41, Chart B

Using the board or the overhead, point out that these question forms are made by changing word order. Practice the affirmative answers after you present them by calling out a few questions in random order and having the class call out the correct answer. You may want to avoid confusion by presenting one form of the negative first (*he isn't/she isn't* etc.) and have the students practice speaking or writing (as suggested in Chart A) before presenting the other contraction forms (*he's not/she's not* etc.). Students may ask which form is more common. You can tell them that both forms are equally common.

p. 41, Ex. 3

Suggest that, in each pair, students change roles so that both have practice asking and answering.

Answers: 1. Yes, he is. 2. No, he isn't. / No he's not. (He's reading a newspaper.) 3. Yes, they are. (Point out that "Yes, they're" is not correct.) 4. No, they aren't. / No, they're not. They're playing on a see-saw. 5. No, he isn't. / No he's not. (He's walking and listening to music.) 6. Yes, he is. (Point out that "Yes, he's" is not correct.) 7. No, she isn't. No, she's not. (She's taking a walk with her mother.)

p. 42, Chart C

On the board or an overhead transparency, underline, point or highlight to show that two independent clauses can be joined by and. Note the comma. While it is true that the comma is sometimes not used in a short sentence, it is easier for students to apply the rule all of the time.

p. 42, Ex. 4

Students must write this exercise. This is a good exercise to assign for homework. Check the exercise carefully. Students often tend to capitalize the pronoun in the second independent clause after and.

Answers: 1. Gloria is looking for some new clothes, and the salesperson is helping her. 2. Cristina is buying a gift, and Fernando is

looking for a birthday card. 3. Mrs. Gomez is having a birthday, and Miguel is planning a party for her. 4. We're going to a restaurant tonight, and our teacher is paying for the dinner. (You can have a laugh together on this one. This is a good place to introduce the word "joke" if students do not know it.) 5. I'm _____ after class, and my friends are _____ (answers vary). 6. I'm _____ this weekend, and my friends are _____ (answers vary).

p. 43, Chart D

On the board or an overhead transparency, underline the parts of the pairs of sentences that are the same. Then, cross out the words that are repeated and can be deleted. Example: I'm ~~spending a lot of money~~. My brother is spending a lot of money. Show that when you combine the clauses with *and*, you can use the form of the verb "be" and "too." Write another example on the board, for example, My friend is learning English fast. I'm ~~learning English fast~~. Follow the same process of crossing out *and* using *too*. Continue giving examples until you feel that most of the students understand.

p. 43, Ex. 5

Assign this as pair work if the students had difficulty with the examples above. Two heads are better than one and students teach each other well. Be sure to check this assignment carefully to make sure that students don't use contractions.

Note: In Item 6, if students do not know what a "mall" is, explain by naming malls in your community as examples. If malls do not exist in your country, draw an oval or rectangle on the board. Make squares around it to illustrate shops and restaurants. Write in the names of some stores that are familiar to your students. Have them suggest others. Then draw a parking lot around it.

Answers: 2. is too 3. am too 4. are too 5. am too 6. are too 7. is too 8. is too 9. are too.

p. 43, Chart E

On the board or an overhead transparency, show the question word *what* and the question word order previously practiced.

p. 44, Ex. 6

This exercise should be done orally in class with students working in pairs. First, model the examples. Ask "What is the little boy doing?" The class can answer, "He's playing." Then point to the picture of the girls riding and point to the class, or an individual student. Mime a question mark. The class or the student should read the question. Then point at the class again or an individual student to indicate an answer is required.

Circulate around the room as the students work so that you can hear what they are having difficulty with. Also, students who may hesitate asking a question in front of the entire class may feel more comfortable asking you directly. It is a good idea to check the answers next as a whole class so that the students feel that the teacher has corrected them. You can do this quickly in two minutes by asking the class as a chorus to call out the question. You can immediately repeat it, correcting if necessary. Then indicate that the class should call out the answer. Again, you should repeat the correct answer. An alternate way of verifying the answers is to have the students write the exercise done orally in class as homework. You should only do this if the exercise is difficult for the class or if you feel they need more writing practice.

Pronunciation Note: sweater /sweter/; listening (be sure students don't pronounce the /t/).

Answers: 1. What is (What's) s/he doing? S/He's trying on a sweater.   2. What is (What's) he doing? He's buying gifts. 3. What's is (What's) he doing? He's writing a check.   4. What are they doing? They're resting.   5. What are they doing? They're waiting for the bus.   6. What is (What's) he doing? He's listening to music.

p. 45, Ex. 7

Answers: What is the man carrying? He's carrying gifts (packages). / What are the children doing? They're playing ball./What is the (old) man drinking? He's drinking water (soda, cola, etc.). / What is the man eating? He's eating a sandwich (bread). / What is the woman reading? She's reading a magazine. / What is the man (boy) riding? He's riding a bicycle (bike).

pp. 45–46, Chart F

On the board or an overhead transparency, use the chart to show that there are other ways to form questions with *What* to ask for more specific information. Students may not know the meaning of "wool." If someone in the room is wearing a sweater of wool, you can go over and touch it and contrast it to the cotton of another student's shirt. An alternate way is to draw a sheep on the board and indicate cutting the wool and then mime knitting a sweater.

pp. 46–47, Ex. 8

Have two students volunteer to read the example dialogue or divide the class in half for a choral reading. Make sure that the students understand that Gloria is preparing for a job interview. You may expand the activity by asking if any students have gone on a job interview. Ask what they wore. Note that there are two correct spellings for the color *gray/grey*.

Preview the vocabulary for the dialogues. You can do this by having students repeat after you. For each word, check for meaning by asking students to point to or say an example, or you can ask for a synonym or antonym. Potential pronunciation difficulties include: casual /kazual/; elegant (stress on the first syllable); special (stress on the first syllable); clothes (only one syllable/final consonant is /z/; shoes (final consonant is /z/ not /s/); suit /soot/; party (contrast with potty); work (contrast with walk); kind (long vowel).

Here are some synonyms and antonyms. Synonyms: casual = not formal = informal; elegant = formal; inexpensive = cheap. Antonyms: casual/elegant or formal; inexpensive/expensive; warm/cool

You may also want to explain the U.S. sizing system. Most dictionaries have a chart. However, it is probably sufficient for students to simply know that there is a different system. Answers in this exercise will vary.

p. 48, Act. 1

The stories will vary from pair to pair or group to group. Students should be encouraged to be creative in this kind of exercise and to experiment with language for communication without worrying about accuracy. Circulate around the room to help students who have vocabulary questions and to help stimulate groups who are having difficulty producing a story. You can help by asking *yes/no* questions to get the students started.

Students will be interested in hearing other versions of the story. You can manage the sharing by having one person from each group report to the entire class, or by rotating a reporter from each group to another group to retell the story.

p. 48, Act. 2

This should be a fun activity and a meaningful context for expanding vocabulary related to clothing. In a very large class, there can be several bags of names to accommodate groups rather than the entire class.

p. 48, Act. 3

This activity is similar to Act. 1. For variety you can have the students produce the story orally as a group and then for homework have them write the story.

Extension Activity

Have students tell or write about their own favorite birthday party, either real or imagined. It is always important for students to relate what they are learning to personal experience. The sharing of personal stories will also create a higher interest level for the class.

Topic Two

p. 49, Setting the Context

You can introduce the dialogue by writing on the board: "spend money" and "save money." Ask for a show of hands of how many students in the class like to do each. You should include yourself as well. Then ask the prereading questions. Present the dialogue as you see fit: as a reading, as a listening exercise with books closed, with students reading in pairs, with the teacher reading one part and the class reading the other, or with two parts of the class reading chorally.

p. 49, Discussion questions

Just as you vary presentation of the dialogue, you should vary presentation of the discussion questions: you can ask the class a question and have students respond chorally or call on individual students for response, or you can have students ask and answer in pairs or small groups.

> Answers: 1. No./ No, she isn't./ No she's not. 2. No./ No, they aren't. No, they're not. 3. No./ No, she isn't./No, she's not. 4. Yes./ Yes, they are.

p. 50, Chart A

The spelling rules in this chart are straightforward. Students will benefit from mastering them as early in their English studies as possible.

p. 50, Ex. 1

> Answers: Are you buying; I'm not spending; Are you saving; Peter and I are saving; We're not going; we're not eating; are you looking for; We're looking for; We're not buying; I'm not saving; I'm spending

pp. 50–51, Ex. 2 and 3

These exercises require practice and application of the rules presented in Chart A. They can be assigned for homework, or assigned for class work either individually or in pairs.

Ex. 2

> Answers: 2. shopping 3. studying 4. buying 5. resting 6. making 7. using 8. running 9. paying 10. taking 11. eating 12. sleeping 13. getting 14. driving

Ex. 3

Answers: 2. is writing; is using   3. is making   4. is drawing; is cutting   5. is sleeping
6. is studying   7. is looking   8. is riding; is
running   9. sitting; watching

p. 51, Chart B

Students are introduced here to the negative
forms of the present continuous tense, including the
two contraction forms. As suggested with the charts
in Topic One, it is better to have students focus on
one column of the chart at a time. You can check for
comprehension as you go along by asking the class
to supply the negative forms for other verbs in random order. Example: You say, "They/study" and the
class can call out, "They are not studying."

p. 52, Ex. 4

If students are having difficulty, you can have
them do the exercise first orally and then in writing.
Be sure to check that students are putting the apostrophe in the right place in the contractions.

Answers: 1. She isn't buying new clothes.
2. He's not using a credit card.   3. They
aren't spending money.   4. We aren't eating in restaurants.   5. It isn't working.
6. You're not driving the car often.

p. 52, Ex. 5

As always, be sure that students understand the
example when assigning an exercise.

Answers: 1. They're not eating in restaurants.   2. They're not driving the car very
often.   3. They're not buying new clothes.
4. They're not making long-distance phone
calls.   5. They're not going to movies.
6. They're not using credit cards.

p. 52, Chart C

Point out the similarity between the use of *and*
and *but*. Show that the pattern is the same, including the use of the comma, but that the meaning is
different. You can do this by reading the pairs of
sentences and asking if the situations are the same or
different. Note that students may not know what a
"tie" is. You can explain by mime or a simple picture on the board. Be sure that students are using a
long vowel sound.

p. 53, Ex. 6

This exercise must be assigned as a writing exercise. Check that students are not capitalizing the
pronouns (except "I") in the second independent
clause. Also be sure that students are putting the
commas before *but* rather than after.

---

*Note: Students may not understand
"coworkers" in Item 1. You can explain
simply by naming other teachers in your
school as examples of your coworkers. You
can also explain that "co" is a prefix that
means "together." Elicit other examples of
words with the same prefix such as "cooperate" or "codirector."*

Answers: 1. My coworkers are going out to
lunch, but I'm eating a sandwich from
home.   2. Our friends are driving a lot
these days, but Donna and I are taking the
bus.   3. Our friends are seeing a lot of
new movies, but Donna and I are renting
videos.   4. Joe is spending a lot, but
Donna is saving her money.   5. Jane is
buying a new winter coat, but Donna is
using her old one.   6. Mary is using her
credit card, but Donna is paying in cash.

p. 53, Ex. 7

Before doing this exercise, you may want to go
over some vocabulary. Students may not understand
"food coupons" in Item 6. Explain that they are discount certificates from the manufacturers. They are
a common and popular way of reducing grocery
bills in the United States. In Item 7 "specials" means
items that have a special discount for a very limited
period of time. Also note that some items in this
exercise can easily be in the simple present tense. For
now, limit the students to the present continuous for
practice.

Answers: 1. is   2. are doing   3. is riding
4. am   5. too   6. are using   7. are shopping   8. are trying   9. is   10. are saving
11. are getting

p. 54, Culture Note

To illustrate the American interest in finding "bargains," cut out examples of special offers or discounts from American magazines or newspapers that you have.

p. 55, Act. 1

The example about long-distance calls may need some explanation. Most telephone companies in the United States offer different rates for telephone calls made at different times and on different days. The most expensive time to call is on weekdays during business hours (typically 9 A.M. to 5 P.M.). If you have a shy or hesitant class, you can start this exercise off by modeling your own list. As in other exercises where groups produce different answers, it is important to build into the exercise an opportunity to share answers with the entire class or from group to group.

p. 55, Act. 2

Answers will vary. You can follow up the oral group exercise by having students write the sentences with *and* and *but* for homework.

Topic Three

p. 55, Discussion questions

These questions also help familiarize students with different testing formats by practicing true/false questions.

Answers: 1. T   2. T   3. F   4. F

pp. 56–57, Ex. 1

This exercise gives students experience reading a map and answering in a true/false format. Be sure that students understand the example and also that they correct the false statements.

Answers: 1. F ~~Fast Food Burgers~~ Max-Mart 2. T   3. F ~~Grandma's Cookies~~ Your Pet Store or Max-Mart   4. T   5. T   6. F ~~to the left of~~ to the right of OR ~~Family Furniture~~ Discount Drugs (is to the left of Max-Mart)   7. T   8. F ~~to the right of~~ to the left of OR ~~Famous Fashion~~ Grandma's Cookies   9. T

Extension Activity

Have students make their own true or false statements and have other students answer them. They can either use the map of the mall provided or make their own mall map.

p. 57, Ex. 2

Answers: 2. between   3. across from 4. next to / to the right of   5. between 6. next to / to the left of   7. across from

p. 57, Chart B

The pattern *There is/ There are* is a very useful pattern for students to master early in their studies.

p. 58, Ex. 3

Students are asked first to work with vocabulary already introduced in other exercises and then to create their own sentences. By focusing on familiar vocabulary and verb forms, they can also practice a new pattern.

Answers: 1. listening   2. carrying   3. talking   4. sitting   5. reading   6. playing (Original sentences will vary.)

p. 59, Ex. 4

Answers: 1. There is a dog barking. 2. There are three cats meowing.   3. There is a monkey climbing a ladder.   4. There is a fish swimming in the water.   5. There is a mouse sitting in a cage.   6. There are two rabbits eating lettuce.

p. 59, Chart C

This chart presents two contrasting rules for students to learn and apply.

pp. 59-60, Ex. 5

Students will learn a lot about the customs and holidays in the United States. There are many references to weather. Point out that the weather referred to in this exercise is typical of the northern part of the country. You can expand this exercise by having students compare and contrast each statement to their own country.

Answers: 1. It; it; There   2. There; it; it
3. There; it; it   4. It; it; There   5. It; It;
There   6. There; it; it   7. There; it; it
8. There; it; it   9. It; It; There   10. There;
it; it   11. It; It; There   12. It; It; There

p. 60

*Culture Note: You can explain that most
people in the United States do their own
yard work, including raking leaves in the
fall and shoveling snow in the winter.
Nowadays, snow blowers and leaf blowers
(machines to reduce the amount of physical labor) are also very common.*

p. 60, Setting the Context

Introduce the topic by asking students what
news station they like to watch. You can even ask if
they have a favorite newscaster. Students have
already been introduced to the definition of "mall."
You may also need to explain that there are three
kinds of "skiing": water skiing, cross-country skiing, and down-hill skiing. Depending upon the location of the class, you can ask students to explain
which kinds of skiing they have done and where.
Alternately, pictures from magazines or sketches on
the board can also clarify this.

p. 61, Chart A

The best way to explain prepositions is by
demonstrating with objects or with students. For
example, you can hold a book above a student's
head and ask, "Where is the book?" Perhaps a student will already know the answer and call out,
"Above Jose." If nobody knows, you can then supply the word. Remember that some students are
visual learners and will learn best in this way. Other
students will learn best by manipulating objects into
the different positions. Others will need to read and
write the words as well. Be sure to ask for all of the
opposites and similar words.

p. 61, Act. 1

Answers will vary. Encourage students to
be creative and funny by giving an example.

p. 61, Act. 2

You can use this activity as a group discussion
activity, or have students prepare and memorize a
2–3 minute talk on the topic to present to the class.
Class "speeches" can become boring if you do not
give listeners an active role. An easy way to do that
is to ask one or two comprehension questions after
each presentation.

p. 61, Act. 3

Students typically enjoy preparing role plays
and then performing for the class.

Topic Four

p. 62, Setting the Context

The TV program from Topic Three continues.
Be sure that students understand what a "lottery" is
and that the "jackpot" is the biggest prize or grand
prize.

p. 62, Discussion questions

Answers: 1. lottery tickets   2. winning /
spending money / buying a big house or a
new car

p. 63, Chart A

You may want to point out that in casual speech
the pronunciation is /gonna/. Be sure that students
understand that this is not a written form.

p. 63, Ex. 1

Answers: there's going to be; are you
going to buy; I'm going to win; They're
going to pick; I'm going to change

p. 63, Ex. 2

Answers: 1. Jack to going to get a Rolls-
Royce.   2. Jack to going to take a long
trip. 3. Jack to going to buy presents for
his family and friends.   4. Jack to going to
give money to charity.   5. Jack to going to
build a new house.   6. Jack to going to
send his children to a good university. (In
the United States there are many universi-
ties and some are very expensive.)

p. 63, Culture Note

Legalized gambling is limited and restricted in the United States. Las Vegas, Reno, and Atlantic City in New Jersey have the most famous casinos. Some Native American Indian Reservations also permit casinos and gambling. Many states have individual lotteries.

p. 64, Chart B

Students often feel that using the word *to* twice may be wrong. With a lot of practice applying these rules, they should soon develop a high level of accuracy.

p. 64, Ex. 3

Answers: 1. She's going to go to the bank.
2. She's going to go to the post office.
3. She's going to go to home.   4. She's going to go there.   5. She's going to go to school.   6. She's going to go to work.
7. She's going to go to the movies.
8. She's going to go to the museum.
9. She's going to go downtown.   10. She's going to go to the beach.

p. 64, Chart C

As suggested with previous charts, begin by presenting the long form, then present one contraction form before presenting the second.

p. 65, Ex. 4

The word *anymore* will be new to most students. Explain that it is used to contrast something that was true in the past but is not true in the present.

Answers: 1. Jack's not going to drive his old car anymore. He's going to buy an expensive sports car.   2. Jack's not going to work anymore. He's going to quit his job.   3. Jack's not going to stay home anymore. He's going to take a trip around the world.   4. Jack's not going to do housework anymore. He's going to hire a cleaning service.   5. Jack's not going to wear his old clothes anymore. He's going to buy designer suits.   6. Jack's not going to use credit cards anymore. He's going to pay in cash.

p. 65, Chart D

This chart presents a question pattern previously practiced with the *going to* pattern.

p. 65, Ex. 5

Answers will vary.

p. 66, Chart E

Be sure to point out that a comma is not generally used with *because*. This is different from the coordination with *and* and *but* as previously practiced. This is the first introduction to subordination.

p. 66, Ex. 6

Answers: 1. I'm looking for a suitcase because I'm going to take a trip.   2. I'm looking for a nice dress because I'm going to have a party.   3. I'm looking for ice skates because I'm going to take skating lessons.   4. I'm looking for a French dictionary because I'm going to study French.
5. I'm looking for yarn because I'm going to knit a sweater. (Be sure that students don't pronounce *knit* with a /k/; it should be /nit/.)   6. I'm looking for fabric because I'm going to make a skirt.

p. 66, Ex. 7

Answers: 1. is   2. is not working   3. is sitting   4. is talking   5. are not listening
6. are dreaming   7. are going to take / are taking   8. are going to travel / are traveling   9. are going to visit   10. are going to go / are going   11. is shopping
12. is not happy   13. is tired   14. is dreaming

p. 67, Act. 1

As with other exercises of this type, encourage students to be creative. You can have listeners from other groups take notes during the reports.

p. 67, Act. 2

Another way to do this exercise is to select several "fortune tellers" and place them around the room. Students can go from one to the other asking questions about their own future. It will be fun for each student to compare the answers from the different "fortune tellers."

pp. 67–68, Checking Your Progress

The format of this progress check is similar to some parts of the TOEFL.

Answers: Part 1—1. b 2. c 3. a 4. b
5. c 6. c 7. a 8. b 9. b 10. c

Part 2—1. It's 2. are 3. planning 4. to the 5. on 6. to 7. across from 8. there 9. a 10. and

Chapter Three: Friends and Family

In this chapter, students are introduced to the simple present tense. They will practice spelling and pronunciation rules and adverbs of frequency. Question forms and negative statements with the simple present tense are different from the formation of the present continuous tense as practiced in the previous chapter. In this chapter, students will practice command forms and a number of verb plus infinitive combinations. After sufficient practice with the simple present tense, students will contrast usage with the present continuous tense. The content focus for this chapter is the family. Students will read and talk about the changes in family structure in the United States, and will have the opportunity to examine the family structure of their own culture.

Topic One

The focus is on the formation of the simple present tense with the irregular verbs *have* and *do* and spelling and pronunciation rules.

pp. 70–71, Setting the Context

Students read about three different families: a large traditional family, a small family, and a single-parent family. New vocabulary may include "single-parent family" and "chores."

Discussion questions

Answers: 1. F 2. F 3. T 4. T 5. F

p. 72, Chart A

This is the first introduction to the irregular third person singular form. Be sure that students are pronouncing *has* with a final /z/ sound rather than a /s/ sound.

p. 72, Ex. 1

Answers: 1. have; has 2. have; have; have; has 3. have; have; has; have

p. 73, Chart B

This chart presents the third person singular form *does*. Be sure that students pronounce the final consonant /z/. The chart and following exercise present a number of useful expressions for vocabulary expansion. You can assign this chart and exercise for homework. Students should be encouraged to ask about new vocabulary in the following class. You can easily explain new vocabulary by miming or giving examples like "errand means going to the bank, going to the cleaners, going to the post office," etc. It is important for students to develop the confidence that they can learn English through English, and that they do not always need to consult a dictionary for a translation.

p. 73, Ex. 2

Answers: 1. does 2. does 3. do 4. do 5. do 6. does 7. does 8. does 9. do

p. 74, Chart C

This chart presents the regular verb *work* with the third person *s* along with time expressions and the first rule for use of the tense. In this case the *s* is pronounced /s/.

p. 74, Ex. 3

Answers: 1. works 2. works/work 3. work 4. works 5. works 6. works

p. 74, Culture Note

You may want to have a brief discussion about the kind of part-time jobs that American and Canadian high school students have: baby-sitting, working in a fast food restaurant, working in a shop or movie theater or doing yard work. You can compare this to the students' own cultures. It is interesting to point out that because of the American school year, students also have almost three months during the summer vacation to work full-time. Camp counselor is a common summer job for high school and university students.

p. 75, Chart D

Because this chart focuses on pronunciation, you should present the chart in class with the students repeating after you. Be sure that students are also pronouncing with the correct number of syllables. All of the verbs presented in this chart are one syllable with the exception of *listens*.

p. 75, Ex. 4

This exercise may be difficult for students because they are asked to focus on sound rather than spelling.

> Answers: lau_gh_s (pronounced as /f/), wor_k_s, slee_p_s, ha_t_es, ro_b_s, nee_d_s, cal_l_s, co_m_es, listen_s, tour_s, lo_v_es, pla_y_s, se_e_s

pp. 75–77

It is essential for Ex. 5–9 that students first write the exercise and then have practice reading aloud to focus on the pronunciation. The exercises continue to develop characters introduced in this unit and provide the context to explore current North American culture and lifestyles.

p. 75, Ex. 5

> Answers: 1. Rose eats breakfast.   2. Rose drinks a cup of tea.   3. Rose walks to school.   4. Rose works hard at school.
> 5. Rose thinks a lot about the future.
> 6. Rose wants a job at a newspaper.

p. 75, Ex. 6

> Answers: 1. Mrs. Somma prepares breakfast.   2. Mrs. Somma drives to the train station.   3. Mrs. Somma arrives at work at 10:00 A.M.   4. Mrs. Somma comes home at 6:00 P.M.   5. Mrs. Somma cleans at night.   6. Mrs. Somma stays up late.

p. 76, Chart E

Students are asked to focus on spelling rules and pronunciation. Be sure that students are pronouncing with the correct number of syllables. You can indicate syllables by tapping out the rhythm on a desk or the board. Pay particular attention to the pronunciation of *says* as students have difficulty: *say* /say/ *says* /sEz/.

p. 76, Ex. 7

> Answers: (1) 1. studies   2. spends
> 3. plays   4. enjoys   5. hates
> (2) 1. works   2. stays   3. says   4. tries
> 5. has   6. worries   7. buys

p. 76, Chart F

This chart presents more spelling and pronunciation irregularities. As mentioned before, be sure that students are pronouncing the correct number of syllables.

p. 77, Ex. 8

Point out that in this context (Item 2), *fix* is a synonym to *prepare* or *make*.

> Answers: 1. pushes   2. fixes   3. washes
> 4. kisses   5. watches   6. does   7. goes
> 8. relaxes

p. 77, Ex. 9

This exercise is more comprehensive than the previous four exercises.

> Answers: 1. has   2. get   3. fixes   4. buy
> 5. makes   6. plays   7. tries   8. does
> 9. watches   10. enjoys   11. kisses

p. 78, Act. 1

This is an excellent activity, but will take some time to do properly. Have students write their family paragraph for homework. You may suggest a minimum number of sentences (five). Have one student read his/her paragraph while the other person listens and asks any questions of clarification. It is important that the listener not see the paragraph. Then s/he should repeat the paragraph as a dictation. Finally, the students should check for accuracy. Students should then reverse roles.

p. 78, Act. 2

Make sure that students first create a sentence for each check in the chart. Example: "Rose does the cooking. Everyone does the cleaning." For the personal chart, students have not yet practiced the question forms, so you cannot expect them to ask questions.

p. 79, Act. 3

Answers will be open.

p. 79, Act. 4

This can be a very interesting exercise if all students do in fact have photographs. You may suggest that students who don't have a photograph make a drawing. Of course, this exercise will not work if students see each other's work in advance. To avoid that, and to heighten the mystery, you may request that this assignment be submitted in a sealed envelope.

p. 79, Act. 5

This exercise will be especially interesting if it is near holiday time and if there are people in the class from different countries.

Topic Two

This is a difficult and important topic. Students will learn adverbs of frequency and the formation of questions and negative statements with the verb do. Plan to spend a little extra time on this topic to make sure that students master it before moving on.

pp. 79–80, Setting the Context

The monologue is presented from a child's point of view and with appropriate language. You can help students understand the title by explaining that *tough* means difficult. You may also need to explain *upset* (angry and sad at the same time) and *either* (not one/not the other).

p. 80, Discussion questions

Answers: 1. F 2. F. 3. F. 4. F

Note: You may want to have a class discussion to discover how many "neat" and how many "messy" people there are. Ask, "Who was responsible for cleaning your room when you were a child?"

p. 80, Chart A

This chart presents an easy-to-understand explanation of the adverbs of frequency. You can anticipate that students will have difficulty with word order with adverbs of frequency and point that out now.

pp. 80–81, Ex. 1

Answers are open. Check word order carefully.

Extension Activity

You could make a chart on the board illustrating how many people always, usually etc. get up early.

p. 81, Chart B

Students need to understand that the verb be often follows a different pattern. This is true with word order with adverbs of frequency.

p. 81, Ex. 2

Answers will vary.

p. 81, Chart C

Highlight the word order of *who* and the verb, and the short answers using some form of the verb *do*.

p. 82, Ex. 3

This exercise will be challenging. Note that answers will vary.

Questions: In your family, who usually repairs things. In your family, who usually fixes breakfast? In your family, who usually does laundry? In your family, who usually cleans the house? In your family, who usually takes out the garbage? In your family, who usually pays the bills? In your family, who usually waters the plants? In your family, who usually makes dinner?

p. 82, Chart D

This chart presents the negative form of sentences both in the long form and the contraction. This chart and the following exercises are crucial. Before going on to the following exercises, you may want to ask students to supply the forms for different verbs. First focus only on long forms. Call out a person and a verb and the students can call out the form. Example: "we/ have homework tonight" "We do not have homework tonight." After practicing in a substitution form of several verbs, practice the contractions in the same way.

pp. 82–83, Ex. 4

Check that students put the apostrophe in the correct place.

> Answers: 2. True   3. doesn't; True
> 4. don't; True   5. doesn't; True
> 6. doesn't; False   7. don't; True   8. don't;
> True. Students who speak Chinese will, of
> course, answer in the affirmative.

p. 83, Ex. 5

> Answers will vary. Students should be
> interested in sharing answers. You can ask
> students to do this on a piece of paper so
> that you can collect and correct it.

p. 83, Chart E

This chart looks easy, but is very important. This is the introduction to forming *yes/no* questions with the verb *do*.

pp. 83-84, Ex. 6

This is the first exercise of the "information gap" type. While students do not have different information, they have different questions. Exercises of this type will be less effective if not done correctly, so you should spend some time explaining the directions. Use two students as a model. Select students who are not shy and who should not have a problem understanding and providing the correct answer. Have them sit face to face. Demonstrate that they are each looking at different charts by pointing at one student and saying, "Student A." Hold up the book for the class to see and say, "Chart A." Do the same with Student B. Then have Student A read the first question and have Student B answer. Next, have Student B read the question and have Student A answer. Students should see that listening and understanding is an important part of this exercise. Answers will vary.

p. 84, Chart F

Students will continue practicing *yes/no* questions as in Chart E, but now will add adverbs of frequency and *how often*. Be sure that students do not pronounce the /t/ in *often*.

pp. 84-85, Ex. 7

> Questions and Answers: 1. How often
> does he clean the apartment? He cleans
> the apartment every week.   2. How often
> does she put toys away? She puts toys
> away every night.   3. How often does he
> make dinner? He makes dinner once or
> twice a week.   4. How often does he
> wash the dishes. He washes the dishes
> every day.   5. How often does she do the
> watering? She does the watering once a
> week.   6. How often does he make long-
> distance calls? He makes long-distance
> calls four or five times a day.

p. 85, Act. 1

Assign the questions to write for homework. You may want students to write them on a piece of paper if you plan to correct them. Questions and answers will vary.

p. 85, Act. 2

If no Americans are available, students can interview other students studying English in another class.

Topic Three

The focus is on commands and a first introduction to the verb and infinitive pattern.

p. 86, Discussion questions

> Answers: 1. F   2. T   3. F   4. T

p. 87, Chart A

This chart illustrates affirmative and negative commands and the *Let's* pattern in affirmative and negative form. Be sure that students understand the first pattern is for telling someone else to do something, and the second pattern is for suggesting that you do something together.

As suggested for previous charts, it may be helpful to conduct a short substitution drill to be sure that students understand. Example, say "Talk" and students say "Don't talk."

p. 87, Ex. 1

> Answers: Turn off the TV; let's do the
> homework; let's set the table.

p. 87, Ex. 2

Students may have problems with pronunciation of *fight* in Item 7: /fait/.

Answers: 3. Clean 4. Wash 5. Comb
6. Do 7. Don't fight 8. Don't be
9. Don't watch 10. Wash or Do

p. 87, Ex. 3

Answers: 1. Let's clean your room.
2. Let's make your bed. 3. Let's take out the garbage. 4. Let's do the laundry.
5. Let's read your assignment. 6. Let's practice your grammar exercises.

p. 88, Culture Note

If you want, you can model different intonation patterns that make a difference in meaning. For example, "Please do your homework" can sound sarcastic, polite or threatening.

p. 88, Chart B

In the future, students will have to learn a lot of verb plus infinitive, verb plus gerund and verb plus gerund or infinitive patterns. This chart presents eight common verb plus infinitive combinations that will be useful for students at this level.

pp. 88-89, Ex. 4

You can have students do this orally only. If you feel that students need more practice, have them do it orally in class and then have them write it for homework (or vice versa). Students may have pronunciation problems with *build* /bIld/ and *bridges* /brIgEz/

Answers: 1. She wants to live in Paris. She wants to be an artist. 2. He wants to work very hard. He wants to build bridges.
3. They want to open a restaurant. They want to become famous chefs. 4. She wants to be very rich. She wants to have lots and lots of money. 5. They want to be police officers. They want to stop drug dealers.

pp. 89–90, Ex. 5

Encourage students to elaborate on the short answers as in the example. If students do not understand "Monopoly," you can explain that it is a classic board game about buying and selling land, houses and hotels.

Questions and Answers: 1. Do you know how to make Chinese food? Yes, I do. No, I don't. 2. Do you know how to bake a cake? Yes, I do. No, I don't. 3. Do you know how to iron? Yes, I do. No, I don't 4. Do you know to play Monopoly? Yes, I do. No, I don't 5. Do you know how to dance? Yes, I do. No, I don't. 6. Do you know how to use a computer? Yes, I do. No, I don't. 7–12. open.

pp. 90–91

Assign Ex. 6 and 7 for homework. Students can then focus on the pronunciation in class.

p. 90, Ex. 6

Answers: 1. to do; to study; to help 2. to do; to cut; to clean; to relax

pp. 90–91, Ex. 7

Answers: 1. to see 2. to find 3. Call
4. to baby-sit 5. to play 6. to do 7. Do
8. go 9. to help 10. to do 11. to see
12. stay 13. rent

p. 91, Act. 1

Possible commands: Please study pages 92–100. Please print two copies of this letter. Please be careful. Please give me your tickets. Please give this medicine to Mr. Smith.

p. 91, Act. 2

The ideal result from this exercise would be to have the class actually carry out some of the suggestions.

p. 92, Act. 3

Answers will vary.

Topic Four

Students can review simple present and present continuous tenses by now contrasting usage and students will learn object pronouns.

pp. 92-93, Setting the Context

You can assign this passage as a homework reading, or you can have students close their books and listen as you read. In that case you can also ask the discussion questions as listening comprehension questions.

Discussion questions, Answers: 1. F   2. T
3. F   4. F

p. 93, Chart A

You may want to call out different adverbs of frequency and words that mean "now" such as "at the moment," "today" and "right now" and have students call out "present continuous tense" or "simple present tense."

pp. 93–94, Ex. 1

This is a true information gap exercise and can only be effective if students follow the instructions by looking only at the one chart that they are working with. Take the time to clarify the instructions. (See pp. 83–84, Ex. 6.) This is a challenging exercise. If students have difficulty, repeat the exercise with new partners the following class period. You can also divide the class in half and have half of the class look at chart A and respond chorally and the other half of the class can look at chart B.

Questions and Answers: What is Sally doing now? She's sleeping./ What does Sally do every Monday morning? She baby-sits./ What does Sally do every Saturday night? She works at a movie theater. /What is Sam doing now? He's smoking a cigarette. /What does Sam do every Monday morning? He works at McDonald's. /What does Sam do every Saturday night? He goes out with friends./ What is John doing now? He's eating a snack./ What does John do every Monday morning? He plays tennis./ What does John do every Saturday night? He stays home./ What is Jane doing now? She's taking a nap./ What does Jane do every Monday morning? She works in a hospital./ What does Jane do every Saturday night? She visits her family.

p. 94, Ex. 2

You can assign this for homework. If you want to collect it, be sure to ask students to write on a piece of paper. Answers will vary.

p. 94, Chart B

This chart presents thirteen nonaction verbs that do not appear in present continuous tense. Preview the chart by explaining the concept (the notes column of the chart) and have the students read the examples for homework.

p. 95, Ex. 3

Answers will vary. Encourage students to answer "Yes, I do" or "No, I don't," and then elaborate.

p. 95, Ex. 4

Questions will vary.

p. 96, Chart C

Students will learn several expressions with *have*.

p. 96, Ex. 5

Answers: 2. am having   3. have   4. have
5. am having   6. has   7. has

p. 97, Chart D

This chart presents object pronouns and reviews subject pronouns and possessive adjectives. If you reproduce the chart on the board or have an overhead transparency, you can practice different forms by covering or erasing them.

p. 97, Ex. 6

Answers: 2. her   3. them   4. us   5. him
6. it   7. her/him   8. them   9. them

p. 98, Ex. 7

Answers: 1. is   2. love   3. always have
4. knows   5. understands   6. lives
7. means   8. don't see   9. have   10. like
11. always tells   12. sometimes feel   13.
is   14. miss   15. feel   16. am

pp. 98–99, Ex. 8
  Answers: (1) 1. She   2. her   3. me   4. she
  5. them   6. her
  (2) 1. my   2. it   3. it   4. me   5. we
  6. our   7. we
  (3) 1. my   2. me   3. me   4. us   5. he
  6. him

p. 100, Act.
  Refer students to Ex. 7 and 8 for models. Assign for homework. You can have students memorize their paragraphs and tell them to a group or the entire class.

Chapter Four: Health Care

Chapter Four covers many important modal auxiliaries. The context is health care, which includes such areas as diet, exercise, illness, medicine. Plan to spend approximately one hour per topic, in other words, four hours for the entire chapter.

Topic One

In this section we learn about physical fitness and kinds of exercise. The modal auxiliaries *can* and *can't* are introduced as are questions with *when*, *where*, and *how*.

pp. 102–103, Setting the Context
  Have the students turn to pp. 102–103. While the students look at the drawing, ask them the pre-reading questions. Then, choose a more advanced student and read the dialogue together. The teacher should take the father's part. Next, have students answer the "Discussion questions" in pairs. Finally, ask the class to give the answers aloud.

Discussion questions
  Answers: 1. His father is overweight.
  2. No. He is embarrassed because he looks fat.   3. It doesn't seem like he will start exercising.

p. 103, Chart A
  Before looking at the chart, ask the students, "Do you think the father can run fast? Do you think he can eat a lot of potato chips?" Then write the following sentence on the board: "He can eat a

lot of potato chips." Ask the students to identify the subject (He) and the verb (can eat), and underline them. Write other pronouns above and/or below *He*, showing how the verb does not change. Then, ask the students if you can say "He can eat<u>s</u>." Make the point that *can* is a modal auxiliary and that verbs that follow modal auxiliaries are always followed by simple verbs. Then, write "He cannot run fast" on the board. Again identify the subject and verb and ask the students if there is another way to make *can* negative. Write *can't* under *cannot*. Finally, have the students look at Chart A.

p. 104, Ex. 1
  Have students underline the uses of *can* and *can't* individually. Then, go over the sentences they have found with the whole class.

p. 104, Ex. 2
  Have students do this exercise in pairs.

Note: You may want to pause at this point and do Act. 3 (p. 107). It can also be done after Ex. 3 or 4 or at the end of Topic One.

p. 104, Chart B
  Begin by asking various students questions with *can*, e.g., "Can you run ten miles? Can you swim a mile? Can you sleep in a chair?" Then write "He can sleep in a chair" on the board. Ask the students to identify the verb and underline *can sleep*. Then show them that to make a simple *yes/no* question, all you have to do is move the modal auxiliary (*can*) to the front of the sentence. Then write the short answers ("Yes, he can; No he can't") to the right of the question. Finally, direct the students to Chart B.

p. 104, Ex. 3
  This exercise is designed for pairs.

  Answers: Every question should begin with *Can you* plus the phrase in each item.
  Students answer with either "Yes, I can" or "No, I can't."

p. 105, Ex. 4
  This exercise can be done in pairs or small groups. Review the answers by calling on individual students.

Answers: 1. He can play soccer, but he doesn't know how to play American football.   2. She can skate, but she doesn't know how to ski.   3. They can swim, but they don't know how to dive.   4. They can canoe, but they don't know how to sail.   5. She can speak Russian, but she can't speak Japanese.

p. 105, Chart C

Ask a student if he can go to the movies tonight. Then write "Can you go to the movies?" on the board. Then ask him (her) when he can go and write *When* on the board before "Can you go to the movies?" changing the capital C to a small c. Finally, show the students Chart C, making the point that the question word (*When, Where*) comes at the beginning of the sentence followed by *can*.

p. 106, Chart D

Begin by asking several students a question with one of the structures in Chart D, e.g., "How far can you walk in a day? How fast can you drive on the freeway? How long can you hold your breath?" Then, write the three questions on the left side of the board and three of the answers on the right side. Finally, have the students read Chart D.

p. 106, Ex. 5

This exercise can be done in pairs or small groups.

Answers: 1. How far can you run?
2. How fast can you ride your bicycle?
3. How fast can you ski?   4. How long can you hold 100 pounds?   5. How far can you throw a football?   6. How far can you swim?

p. 107, Using What You've Learned

You can do some or all of these activities when you finish Topic One, or you can intersperse the activities (as noted above). If you choose to intersperse them, Act. 1 and 2 should follow Ex. 5. Act. 3 is good after Ex. 2, 3, or 4.

Topic Two

In this section doctors and the use of medicine are explored. The grammatical focus is the modal auxiliaries *would* and *could*.

p. 108, Setting the Context

Have the students look at the picture at the top of the page while you ask them the prereading questions (He has a toothache. He is calling a dentist's office). Then, with a student read the dialogue aloud for the class. Finally, ask them the discussion questions aloud.

Discussion questions

Answers: 1. He has a toothache.   2. No, he can't.   3. His appointment is at 4:45.

p. 109, Chart A

Begin by asking the students a group of questions with *could*, e.g., "Could I ask you a question? Could we work together? Could I have a ride home?" Then, write one of these questions on the board and solicit possible answers from the students, writing a few to the right of the question. Make sure the students realize this is a question in the present (not the past) tense. Finally, have them look at Chart A.

p. 109, Ex. 1

Do this exercise aloud with individual students providing the answers or have the students do it in pairs.

Answers: 1. Could I make a dental appointment, please?   2. Could I make an appointment with a doctor, please?
3. Could I talk with a nurse, please?
4. Could I have some aspirin, please?
5. Could I get a prescription, please?
6. Could I talk to a pharmacist, please?

p. 110, Chart B

Introduce the information in the chart the same way as in Chart A.

p. 110, Ex. 2

Do this exercise with the whole class, having individual students ask you the questions. Respond with appropriate answers. (This exercise may also be done with pairs.)

> Answers: 1. Could you help me, please? 2. Could you give me some information, please? 3. Could you fill this prescription for me, please? 4. Could you explain these instructions, please? 5. Could you tell me the meaning of this word, please?

Note: You may want to pause at this point and do Act. 1 (p. 112).

---

p. 111, Chart C

Say to the class, "I'm sick and I would like a lot of things. I would like some medicine, I'd like to see a doctor, I'd like to take the day off. You're also sick. Tell me some things you would like." Then, write one of the sentences on the board and ask the students to identify the verb (*would like to _____*). Mention that *would* is a modal auxiliary and write the other pronouns above and/or below *I*. Ask if it's OK to say, "He would like<u>s</u> . . . " and then "Why not?" (because modal auxiliaries are always followed by simple verbs). Then, show the students the contracted forms (*I would = I'd* etc.) Finally, have the students look at Chart C.

p. 111, Ex. 3

This may be done in pairs or with the whole class.

> Answers: 1. I would like to buy some cough syrup. 2. I would like to make an appointment with Dr. Cruncher. 3. I would like to talk to the receptionist. 4. I would like to take some vitamins. 5. I would like to get an appointment with Dr. Freud.

p. 112, Chart D

Ask the class some questions with *would you like*, e.g., "Would you like to have a million dollars? Would you like to have a wife (husband)? Would you like to have three wives (husbands)?" etc. Then write "I would like to have . . ." on the board and ask them to identify the modal and the rest of the verb. Next, ask how to form a *yes/no* question and write the question, "Would you like . . . ?" underneath the sentence. Finally, go over Chart D with the students.

p. 112, Ex. 4

This exercise is designed to be done in pairs.

> Answers: Each question begins with *Would you like to* followed by the phrase that is given. The responses will vary.

pp. 112-113, Using What You've Learned

You can do these activities when you finish Topic Two, or you can intersperse the activities (as noted above). If you choose to intersperse them, Act. 1 goes well after Ex. 2. Act. 2 is best after Ex. 4.

Topic Three

In this section we learn about emergency situations and practice the modal auxiliaries *should*, *must*, and *have to*.

pp. 113-114, Setting the Context

While the students look at the drawing, ask them the prereading questions. Then, read the passage aloud slowly. Have the students reread the passage silently and answer the discussion questions. Finally, go over the answers with the class.

p. 114, Discussion questions
Answers: 1. F 2. T 3. T 4. F

p. 114, Chart A

Direct a series of sentences with *should* toward individual students, e.g., "Ricardo, you look tired; you should get more sleep. Martin, your hair is messy; you should comb it." Then, write one sentence with *should* on the board. Point out that *should* is a modal auxiliary and show how when other pronouns are used, the verb doesn't change. Also, elicit from the students how the negative is formed. Finally, go over Chart A with the students.

p. 114, Ex. 1

Students may do this individually or with a partner. Go over the answers with the whole class.

pp. 114–115, Ex. 2

Say "We've just seen some of the things that drivers like Misha should and shouldn't do. Now let's look at some other situations and discuss what people should and shouldn't do." Students begin individually or in pairs. Then, in small groups they compare their answers.

> Possible answers: 2. shouldn't; shouldn't (You should wait for help); shouldn't. You should call the fire department. 3. shouldn't; should; should. She should be careful about what she eats. 4. should; shouldn't. He should learn all the safety rules.
> 5. shouldn't; shouldn't; should; should. She should follow her doctor's advice.

Note: You may want to pause at this point and do Act. 2 (p. 120).

---

p. 115, Ex. 3

This exercise is design for partners. Go over the answers with the whole class.

> Answers: 1. You should call for medical . . .
> 2. If possible, you should check the victim .
> . . 3. You should not move the victim . . .
> 4. If a rescue is necessary, you should move a victim . . . 5. You should check for breathing. 6. You should give artificial . . . 7. You should control bleeding.
> 8. You should not give food or drink . . .

p. 116, Chart B

You may introduce this chart in a way similar to the way you introduced Chart A, p. 114.

pp. 116-117, Ex. 4

Have students work individually or with a partner. Then, they should join a small group to compare answers.

> Answers: 1. a. the landlord must keep . . .
> b. . . . must provide . . . c. . . . must not enter . . . d. . . . must make repairs . . .
> e. . . . must rent to people . . .
> 2. a. you must use a car seat . . .
> b. . . . must bring your license . . .
> c. . . . must keep your car . . . d. must not drive with six . . .

> 3. a. you must not leave them alone . . .
> b. . . . must use car seats . . . c. . . . must not leave medicine . . . d. . . . must get immunizations . . .

p. 117, Ex. 5

This exercise works best with pairs.

> Answers: 2. b 3. a 4. b 5. a 6. b
> 7. a

p. 118, Chart C

You may introduce this chart in a way similar to the way you introduced Chart A, p. 114.

p. 118, Ex. 6

Introduce this exercise by saying "There are many rules about driving, many things that you must or must not do." Students may do this exercise individually or in pairs.

> Answers: 1. Misha has to pay . . . 2. You have to drive . . . 3. You have to obey . . .
> 4. Young children must sit . . . 5. You have to read . . . 6. Children have to . . .
> 7. Your landlord has to . . . 8. Your landlord has to put . . .

p. 119, Chart D

The students now know that *must* and *have to* can have the same meaning, so the concept of *must not* and *don't have* to having different meanings is not easy for them.

Begin by eliciting things you must not do when driving, e.g., "You must not drive over 65 miles per hour on the freeway. You must not drink and drive. You must not read a newspaper (and drive at the same time)." On the board, write "You must not drive over 65 mph." Underline *must not* and ask what it means (It is prohibited or not allowed). Then ask "Can I say, you must not drive over 50 mph on the freeway"? Try to get them to give you *don't have to* instead of *must not* and write the sentence "You *don't have to* drive over 50 mph" on the board. Have the students identify the verb and then ask what *don't have to* means (It is not necessary, but it is allowed.) Next, go over Chart D. You may have to put several more examples on the board before all the students understand.

p. 119, Ex 7

Students should work in pairs or small groups.

Answers: 1. don't have to   2. must not
3. must not   4. don't have to   5. don't
have to

pp. 119–120, Using What You've Learned

You can do some or all of these activities when
you finish Topic Three, or you can intersperse the
activities (as noted above). If you choose to intersperse them, Act. 1 is best after Ex. 7. Act. 2 is good
after Ex. 3.

Topic Four

In this section we continue to explore physical
fitness. The grammatical focus is the modal auxiliary *might*, the simple future tense with *will*, and the
coordinate conjunction *or*.

pp. 121-122, Setting the Context

Begin Topic Four as you have with introductory
dialogues, e.g., Topic Two, p. 108. However, here
there are characters in the conversation. Choose a
different student for each part.

Discussion questions

Answers: 1. Alfonso is hurt. His left leg is
hurt.   2. No, they aren't. They're going to
call 911.

p. 122, Chart A

Introduce Chart A in a way similar to the way
you introduced Chart A, Topic Two, p. 114.

p. 122, Ex. 2

This exercise can be done by calling on individual students or as pair work.

Answers: 1. It might snow.   2. She might
be sick.   3. He might have a fever.   4. She
might be on a diet.   5. He might be a
vegetarian.   6. She might be homesick.

---

*Note: You may want to pause at this point
and do Act. 2 (pp. 126-127).*

---

p. 123, Chart B

Give the students several examples of short
clauses with *might* joined by *or*, e.g., "I'm tired of
working. I might watch TV, or I might take a nap."
Then write two sentences on the board, e.g., "He
might watch TV. He might take a nap." Ask the students how many sentences these are (two) and how
to make these into one sentence. Put a comma and
or between the sentences. Then change the capital H
in the second part of the sentence. Finally, go over
Chart B with the students.

p. 123, Ex. 3

This exercise is best done in pairs before you
review the answers with the whole class.

Answers: 1. He might exercise . . . , or he
might watch TV.   2. He might stay home,
or he might hang out . . .   3. She might
eat . . . , or she might have some potato
chips.   4. She might try . . . , or she might
watch . . .   5. He might play . . . , or he
might try another . . .

---

*Note: You may want to pause at this point
and do Act. 1 (p. 126).*

---

p. 124, Chart C

Tell the students to imagine that they are doing
very poorly in class. This is because they always
come late, they never do their homework, and they
don't study for tests. Then ask them what they will
do to improve the situation. Try to elicit, "I will
come on time, I will do my homework, I will study
for tests."   Write "I will come on time" on the
board. Underline the verb and ask what kind of verb
will is. (It is a modal auxiliary.)   Then, below, write
"I won't come late" and ask them what *won't*
means. Mention that *will* and *won't* are often used
in promises. Then, go over Chart C with the class.

p. 124, Ex. 4

This exercise can be done in pairs, small groups, or with the whole class.

Answers: 1. I promise I will eat . . .
2. I promise I will get . . .   3. I promise I won't go . . .   4. I promise I will get . . .
5. I promise I won't watch . . .   6. I promise I will read . . .   7. I promise I will do . . .   8. I promise I won't call collect.

Note: Act. 3 and/or Act. 4 (p. 127) may be done at any point after this.

p. 125, Chart D

Write "I will do the laundry" on the board. Ask the students how to make a *yes/no* question and then below, write "Will you do the laundry?" Then, ask the students to place *When* in front of the question. Next, write *Where* below *When*. Finally, go over Chart D with the whole class.

p. 125, Ex. 5

Have students do this exercise in pairs.

Answers: 1. Will you call me . . . ? Of course. I promise I will.   2. Will you take care . . . ? Of course . . .   3. Will you have a good time? Of course . . .   4. Will you be careful? Of course . . .   5. Will you remember all of us? Of course . . .
6. Will you keep in touch? Of course . . .

p. 125, Ex. 6

Students may do this individually or in pairs.

Answers: 1. work   2. get   3. teach
4. do   5. like   6. like   7. is   8. keeps
9. is   10. don't get   11. need
12. want   13. will   14. be   15. will come   16. will register   17. will be
18. won't be   19. will see

pp. 125–126, Ex. 7

Students may do this individually or in pairs.

Possible answers: 1. can   2. can / should / must   3. Could   4. would   5. Would
6. should / must   7. will   8. won't / can't   9. will

pp. 126–127, Using What You've Learned

You can do all of these activities at the end of Topic Three, or you can intersperse them. If you choose to intersperse them, Act. 1 would go well after Ex. 3. Act. 2 is good after Ex. 2. Act. 3 and Act. 4 can be done anytime after Ex. 4.

pp. 128–129, Checking Your Progress

Students should work individually on this; however, it is helpful for them to check their answers in pairs or small groups.

Answers:
Part 1—1. c   2. a   3. c   4. c   5. a
6. a   7. a   8. d   9. a   10. a

Part 2—1. my   2. live   3. calls   4. is
5. working   6. retire   7. usually works
8. hates   9. to spend   10. might
11. doesn't have to   12. has to

Chapter Five: Men and Women

Chapter Five introduces the past tense in statements and questions with both regular and irregular verbs. Topic Four is a review of the first five chapters of the book. The context throughout the chapter is men and women in society. Plan to spend at least one hour per topic, in other words, at least four to five hours for the entire chapter.

Note that there will be a change in the *Instructor's Manual* beginning in this chapter. Answers are given for all objective exercises, and some teaching suggestions are given, but with less detail than before. Chapters One to Four of the manual include detailed suggestions for the presentation of passages, dialogues, charts, exercises, and activities. If you have questions on how to present a topic in Chapter Five, please refer to a similar passage, dialogue, chart, exercise, or activity in the earlier chapters.

Topic One

In this section we meet Christine, who tells us about how her parents met and eventually decided to marry. The grammatical focus is on the simple past tense with the verb *be*; questions and the uses of *there was/were* are also explored.

p. 132, Discussion questions
 Answers: 1. F 2. T 3. F 4. F 5. T

p. 134, Ex. 1
 This exercise may be done individually, in pairs, or with the class as a whole.

 Answers: 1. were 2. was; was 3. was; was 4. was; was; wasn't; was
 5. weren't; was; was 6. were; was; was
 7. wasn't; was; was 8. was; was
 9. weren't; were

p. 135, Ex. 2
 This exercise should be done in pairs.

 Answers: 1. Yes, he was. 2. Yes, they were. 3. No, she wasn't. 4. No, they weren't. 5. Yes, he was. 6. No, she wasn't.

p. 135, Ex. 3
 This is an extension of Ex. 2 and should be done in pairs.

pp. 136–137, Ex. 4
 This exercise may be done individually, but it seems to work best in pairs.

 Answers: 1. Where were Robert and Catherine? 2. Where was Robert from?
 3. Who was from New York? 4. How old was she? 5. How old was he? 6. Who was Scandinavian? 7. Where was her family from? 8. Who was Protestant?
 9. What was she? 10. When were they married?

p. 138, Ex. 5
 This exercise may be done individually, in pairs, or with the class as a whole.

 Answers: 2. were 3. were 4. weren't
 5. was 6. was 7. were 8. wasn't

p. 138, Act.
 This activity works best if it is done after you finish Ex. 5.

 A follow-up homework assignment could be to have each student write a paragraph about his or her own family. It is then interesting to compare this with the essay written by the partner. It should demonstrate how good of a listener each student is.

Topic Two
 In this section Christine describes what happened to her parents when World War II started. The grammatical focus is on the past tense but now with regular verbs; in this context, spelling, pronunciation, and affirmative and negative statements are explored.

p. 140, Discussion questions
 Answers: 1. They went to war. 2. They went to work. 3. They did not want to go back to their places in the home. (They continued working outside the home.)

p. 141, Ex. 2
 This exercise should be done in pairs.

 Answers: 1. Before World War II, most women washed the clothes.
 2. . . . most women ironed the clothes.
 3. . . . most women folded the clothes.
 4. . . . most women cleaned the house.
 5. . . . most women watched the children
 6. . . . most women cooked the meals.
 7. . . . most women listened to their husbands.

pp. 142-143, Ex. 3
 This exercise may be done individually, but it works best with students in pairs or small groups.

 Answers: 2. joined; hugged; kissed; went
 3. stayed; cleaned; watched 4. washed; folded; fixed 5. needed; worked; helped
 6. worked; learned; liked 7. stayed; listened; waited; talked 8. joined; arrived; stayed 9. loved; hated; ended; returned

p. 144, Ex. 4
 This exercise may be done individually or in pairs.

 Answers: 1. Robert didn't work as a pilot. He worked as a doctor. 2. He didn't serve for nine years. He served for five. 3. He didn't receive twelve awards. He received three. 4. He wasn't a general. He was a captain. 5. He didn't love the military. He hated it.   6. He didn't have brown eyes and blue hair. He had blue eyes and brown hair.   7. He wasn't five feet, two inches. He was 6 feet, two inches.   8. He didn't weigh 210 pounds. He weighed 180 pounds.

pp. 145-146, Ex. 5
This exercise should be done in pairs.

Answers: 1. Did Catherine (your mother) have a lot of experience? No, she didn't. 2. Did she have brown hair and brown eyes? Yes, she did.   3. Did she weigh 210 pounds? No, she didn't. (She weighed 110 pounds.)   4. Was she (your mother) married? Yes, she was.   5. Did she (your mother) have children? No, she didn't. 6. Did she like her job? Yes, she did. 7. Was she eighteen years old? No, she wasn't. (She was 21.)   8. Did she live in New York? Yes, she did.

Note: You may want to pause at this point and do Act. 1 (p. 159).

p. 147, Ex. 6
Students may do the questions individually, but after they are finished, put them in pairs to have them ask and answer the questions. The student who is answering should close his/her book.

Answers: 1. Who joined the army? 2. How long was he in the navy? 3. What was he? (What did he do?) 4. Who(m) did he help?   5. Where did he work?   6. What was difficult but interesting?   7. What did he enjoy?   8. What was terrible?   9. What did he hate? 10. Who(m) did he miss?   11. Who(m) did he write almost every night? 12. What lasted for four long years?

p. 148, Using What You've Learned
You can do Act. 1 when you finish Topic Two, or you can do it after Ex. 5. Act. 2 should be done after at the end of Topic Two.

Topic Three
In this section we learn more from Christine about what her parents did during the war. The grammatical focus is on the coordinate conjunction so, the modal auxiliary verb *could*, and the expression *had to*.

p. 149, Discussion questions
Answers: 1. Christine's mother (Catherine) had to earn money because her father (Robert) was gone.   2. No, she didn't. 3. She realized that she could do the work as well as or even better than most men. 4. She began to enjoy it when she realized that she could do the work as well as or even better than most men.

p. 150, Ex. 1
This may be done individually or in pairs. In number 1 be sure to point out that the noun (not the pronoun) should begin the sentence.

Answers: 1. My mother didn't have . . . , so she used the bus . . .   2. The bus was . . . , so the ride to work . . .   3. There was a lot . . . , so she worked . . .   4. She needed . . . , so she worked . . .   5. It was very . . . , so she didn't like . . .   6. Later she became . . . , so she liked the work . . . 7. No one lived . . . , so she sometimes felt . . .   8. She wanted to be . . . , so she decided . . .

pp. 150-151, Ex. 2
This exercise works best with students in pairs.

Answers: 2. My mother was lonely, so she wrote to my father a lot.   3. My dad hated the navy, so he wanted to come home as soon as possible.   4. My mother worked for a car company, so she helped build cars.   5. My father was a surgeon, so he helped save lives.   6. The navy needed surgeons, so it (they) asked him to stay. 7. My mom became a supervisor, so she started to make more money. 8. My mother was tired of taking the bus, so she bought a used car.

p. 151, Ex. 3

This may be done individually or in pairs.

pp. 152–153, Ex. 4

This may be done individually or in pairs.

Possible answers: 2. could; couldn't
3. could; couldn't   4. could; couldn't
5. could; couldn't   6. could; couldn't

Note: You may want to pause at this point and do Act. 1 (p. 154).

---

p. 153, Ex. 5

This may be done in pairs or with the class as a whole.

Answers: 1. They had to learn to live together.   2. He had to find a new job.
3. They had to visit many relatives.
4. They had to decide about having children.

p. 154, Using What You've Learned

Act. 1 may be done at the end of Topic Three or after Ex. 4. Act. 2 should be done after you finish Topic Three.

Topic Four

In this section we learn about the lives of Christine and her brothers as adults. Topic Four is a review of the grammar in Chapters One to Five.

p. 155, Discussion questions

Answers: 1. F   2. F   3. F   4. F   5. T

p. 156, Ex. 1

This exercise may be done individually, but it works best if done in pairs or small groups.

Answers: 1. in   2. was; at; on   3. were; on; at   4. had; in   5. were; at   6. had; in   7. robbed   8. walked; at   9. with; from; to   10. In; was   11. was; in.
12. will be; from (for); to

p. 156, Ex. 2

This exercise may be done with students working individually or in pairs.

Answers: 1. When did the robbery happen?   2. Who walked in the front door?
3. How old was he?   4. Who(m) did he talk to?   5. What did he hand her?
6. What did the note say?   7. What did he show her?   8. Who gave him the money?

p. 157, Ex. 3

This exercise works best with students working in pairs or in small groups.

Answers: 2. on the bridge.   3. next to (on the side of)   4. on top of   5. in front of
6. over the demonstration   7. next to the man   8. between two horses   9. next to each other   10. next to

pp. 157–158, Ex. 4

This exercise should be done with students working in pairs.

Answers: 1. . . . , but   2. because
3. . . . , so   4. . . . , but   5. because
6. . . . , so   7. because   8. because
9. . . . , but   10. . . . , so   11. . . . , but
12. . . . , but   13. . . . , so   14. . . . , but

pp. 158–159, Ex. 5

This exercise should be done with students working in pairs.

Answers: 1. I; her; She   2. I; them (him / her); They (he / she)   3. your; My; your
4. We; us   5. Our; it   6. she; him   7. it; you; it   8. I; them   9. My; their   10. I; me   11. they; them   12. Our; their

pp. 159–160, Ex. 6

This exercise may be done with students working individually or in pairs.

Answers: 1. am   2. were   3. was
4. was   5. started   6. were   7. didn't finish   8. dropped out   9. didn't drop out   10. received   11. were   12. graduated   13. moved   14. live / are living
15. work / are working   16. has
17. work   18. likes   19. makes

20. want   21. am   22. am going to (will) look

p. 160, Ex. 7
This exercise can be done with students working individually, in pairs, or in small groups.

Answers: 1. can 2. can 3. can 4. must (has to) 5. must (has to) 6. must (has to) 7. must (has to)

pp. 160-161, Using What You've Learned
Since this is a review section, Act. 1 and 2 may be done at the end of the topic or anywhere before. Act. 3 may be done either at the end of the topic or after Ex. 6.

Chapter Six: Native Americans and Immigrants

Chapter Six continues with the past tense. The primary focus is irregular verbs. After finishing this chapter, students should be comfortable with the past tense with regular and several irregular verbs. The context throughout the chapter is the people (Native Americans and immigrants) of North America. Plan to spend approximately one hour per topic, in other words, four hours for the entire chapter.

Note that Chapters One to Four of this manual include detailed suggestions for the presentation of passages, dialogues, charts, exercises, and activities. If you have questions on how to present a topic in this chapter, please refer to a similar passage, dialogue, chart, exercise, or activity in the earlier chapters.

Topic One
In this section how Native Americans first came to North America is discussed. The grammatical focus is the past tense forms of some irregular verbs; too and either are also presented.

p. 165, Discussion questions
Answers: 1. F   2. F   3. T 4. T   5. F

pp. 165–166, Ex. 1
This exercise may be done with students working individually or in pairs.

Answers: 3. began   4. didn't (did not) begin   5. became   6. didn't become 7. froze   8. didn't freeze   9. ate 10. didn't eat   11. went   12. didn't go

pp. 166-167, Ex. 2
This exercise can be done individually, but it works best with students in pairs or small groups.

Answers: (1) 1. were   2. were   3. ate b. Yes, there were. c. They ate caribou.

(2) 1. began   2. became   3. froze 4. ate   5. froze   6. had a. The weather began to change. b. They usually ate grass. c. It froze.

(3) 1. began   2. froze   3. became 4. became a. It froze.   b. It became an ice bridge.

(4) 1. went   2. came   3. came 4. walked   5. were a. They went across the bridge. b. The hunters came after the caribou because they needed food.

(5) 1. came   2. went   3. were a. Many thousands of Indians probably came to America. b. They went to all parts of the continent. c. Yes, they did.

p. 169, Ex. 3
This may be done with students working individually or in pairs.

Answers: 3. The Cherokee had many leaders and the Creek did too.   4. The Cherokee couldn't write and the Creek couldn't either.   5. The Cherokee were a large tribe and the Creek were too. 6. The Cherokee were hunters and the Creek were too.   7. The Cherokee didn't have only one leader and the Creek didn't either.   8. The Cherokee weren't farmers and the Creek weren't either.   9. The Cherokee became traders and the Creek did too.   10. The Cherokee smoked tobacco and the Creek did too.   11. The Cherokee didn't have alcoholic drinks and the Creek didn't either.   12. The Cherokee aren't rich now and the Creek aren't either.

Note: You may want to pause at this point and do Act. 2 (p. 171).

pp. 169–170, Ex. 4

Students should go around the room individually asking each other the questions and recording the answers. However, they should work in pairs or small groups to share the information they have gathered when they start to write the sentences.

pp. 170–171, Ex. 5

Answers: 1. went   2. went   3. hunted
4. learned   5. traded   6. were   7. had
8. loved   9. were   10. did   11. came
12. arrived   13. was   14. pushed
15. forced   16. wanted   17. were
18. were (are)

p. 185, Using What You've Learned

Act. 1 should be done at the end of Topic One. Act. 2 may be done at the end of Topic One, or it could follow Ex. 4.

Topic Two

In this section the experience of one immigrant from Europe to the U.S. is examined. At the same time, the past tense forms of more irregular verbs and tag questions are presented.

p. 173, Discussion questions

Answers: 1. F   2. F   3. T   4. F   5. T

p. 174, Ex. 2

This can be done individually, in pairs, or with the class as a whole.

Answers: 2. grew up   3. found   4. didn't find   5. didn't get   6. got   7. spoke
8. didn't speak   9. left   10. didn't leave
11. brought   12. didn't bring

pp. 174–176, Ex. 3

This can be done with students working individually or in pairs.

Answers: (1) 1. got   2. had   3. left
4. stayed   5. came   b. He got married to Nina in 1918. c. He left Italy in 1918.

(2) 1. got   2. brought   3. got   4. went
5. was   a. He got on the boat on September 20, 1921. b. He brought one bag of clothing and some food. c. He got to the U.S. on October 5th. d. He left Ellis Island two days later (October 7th).

(3) 1. was   2. had   3. spoke   4. spoke
5. was   6. helped   7. found   a. No, he wasn't. He was excited. b. No, he didn't. He had only a little money. c. No, he didn't. He spoke only a few words of English. d. He spoke Italian.

(4) 1. began   2. didn't know   3. worked
4. spoke   5. helped   a. He didn't know much about construction. b. Yes, they did. c. They taught him English.

(5) 1. went   2. went   3. brought
4. found   5. was   6. grew up   7. spoke
8. learned   9. wasn't   10. were   a. He brought them to America in 1926. b. No, they didn't. They found a house. c. They grew up in New York. d. No, they didn't. They spoke Italian at home.

Note: You may want to pause at this point and do Act. 2 (p. 178).

p. 177, Ex. 4

This can be done with students working individually or in pairs.

Answers: 2. weren't you?   3. didn't you?
4. didn't you?   5. isn't he?   6. doesn't she?   7. don't you?   8. don't I?
9. didn't you?   10. can't I?

p. 177, Ex. 5

This can be done with students working individually or in pairs.

Answers: 2. was she?   3. did she?
4. did you?   5. did you?   6. were you?
7. can you?   8. do you?   9. do I?   10.
are you?

p. 177-178, Using What You've Learned

Act. 1 should be done at the end of Topic Two. Act. 2 may be done at the end of Topic Two or after Ex. 3.

Topic Three

In this section immigration from Asia to the U.S. is examined. The past tense forms of more irregular verbs, along with *even though* and *used to*, are presented.

p. 179-180, Discussion questions

Answers: 1. F   2. T   3. F   4. F   5. T
6. F

p. 180, Ex. 1

This exercise should be done with students working individually.

Answers: became; began; brought; came; did; ate; found; froze; got; went; grew up; had; had to; knew left; spoke

p. 181 Ex. 2

This may be done with students working individually or in pairs.

Answers: 1. Even though Dung . . . , he didn't   2. Even though Dung liked . . . , he wanted . . .   3. Even though Dung's relatives . . . , he moved . . .   4. Even though his English . . . , he got . . .   5. Even though Dung worked . . . , he made . . .
6. Even though Dung couldn't . . . , he entered . . .   7. Even though he was . . . , he continued . . .   8. Even though classes . . . , he did . . .

p. 181, Ex. 3

This may be done with students working individually or in pairs.

Answers: 2. Even though the Indians . . . , they (the Indians) were able . . .   3. Even though Tony came . . . , he left . . .
4. Even though Tony was . . . , he (Tony) never learned . . .   5. Even though Rene had . . . , she really wanted . . .   6. Even though Dung wants . . . , he can't find . . .
7. Even though Dung is working, he still goes . . .   8. Even though Dung enjoys . . . , he gets homesick . . .

p. 181, Ex. 4

This may be done with students working individually, but it works best in pairs.

p. 182, Ex. 5

This may be done with students working individually, in pairs or with the class as a whole.

Possible answers: 1. Now he eats hamburgers every night.   2. Now he walks around Santa Barbara.   3. Now he speaks English all day.   4. Now he plays baseball.
5. Now he works all day.   6. Now he visits his relatives in L.A.

p. 183, Ex. 8

This may be done with students working individually or in pairs.

pp. 183-184, Ex. 9

This may be done with students working individually, in pairs or small groups.

Answers: 1. Was   2. did   3. cost
4. was   5. cost   6. is (was)   7. didn't buy   8. did   9. got   10. had
11. bought   12. paid   13. needed
14. does   15. did   16. spend   17. got
18. costs   19. was   20. paid   21. Are
22. have to   23. am not   24. do
25. want

p. 184, Act.

This activity can only be done after Ex. 8 and 9 have been completed.

Topic Four

In this section one man's decision to immigrate to the U.S. illegally is explored. The grammatical focus is the past tense forms of more irregular verbs and reported speech.

p. 186, Discussion questions
Answers: 1. T   2. F   3. F   4. T   5. F

p. 186, Ex. 1
This may be done with students working individually.

Answers: became; began; bought; brought; came; cost; did; ate; found; froze; got; went; grew up; had; had to; knew left; paid; spoke; spent

p. 187, Ex. 2
This may be done with students working individually or in pairs.

Answers: 2. didn't hear   3. didn't know
4. knew   5. said   6. didn't say

pp. 187–188, Ex. 3
This may be done with students working individually, but it works better in pairs.

Answers: 2. . . . life was hard in his village.
3. . . . it was difficult to enter the U.S.
4. . . . everyone in the U.S. was rich.
5. . . . jobs were easy to find. 6. . . . all Americans lived in nice houses. 7. . . . many Mexicans became rich in the U.S.
8. . . . they got good salaries.
9. . . . Americans didn't worry about money. 10. . . . you could make a lot of money in the U.S.

p. 189, Ex 5
This may be done with students working individually or in pairs.

Answers: 2. didn't give   3. didn't lend
4. lent   5. saw   6. didn't see

p. 189, Ex. 6
This may be done with students working individually, but it is better with students in pairs or small groups. You can assign it in advance and then go over it orally.

Answers: 1. had   2. lent   3. bought
4. gave   5. was   6. could   7. said
8. was   9. was   10. arrived   11. was
12. bought   13. went   14. was
15. said   16. was   17. knew   18. was
19. agreed   20. gave   21. paid   22. left
23. went   24. was   25. saw   26. could
27. crawled   28. was   29. saw
30. walked

p. 190, Act.
This activity should not be done before Ex. 6 has been completed.

pp. 190–191, Checking Your Progress
Students should work individually on this; however, it is helpful for them to check their answers in pairs or small groups.

Answers: Part 1: 1. b   2. d   3. b   4. a
5. d   6. c   7. b   8. d   9. a   10. a

Part 2: 1. had   2. go   3. stay   4. leave
5. could   6. said   7. got   8. either
9. Even though   10. knew

Chapter Seven: Work and Lifestyle

Chapter 7 introduces the past continuous tense in affirmative, negative and question forms. Topics Three and Four contrast the past continuous tense with the simple past tense with the use of *when* and *while*. The context throughout this chapter is on work and lifestyles with an emphasis on immigrants.

Note that Chapters One to Four of this manual include detailed suggestions for the presentation of passages, dialogues, charts, exercises, and activities. If you have questions on how to present a topic, please refer a similar passage, dialogue, chart, exercise, or activity in the earlier chapters.

Topic One

This section covers affirmative statements in the past continuous. The verbs are practiced through the story of a young immigrant to the U.S. The reading introduces Monique, a young immigrant from Haiti seeking a better life through education and career development in Miami, Florida and New York City. The section looks at what she was doing at various stages.

p. 194, Discussion questions

Answers: 1. Five years ago./ Monique came to Miami five years ago.
2. dishwasher/in the kitchen at Mercy Hospital./ She was a dishwasher at Mercy Hospital.   3. at Mercy Hospital/ She is working at Mercy Hospital.

p. 195

Culture Note: Ask students how may jobs their parents had in their working careers.

p.195, Ex. 1

This exercise can be done individually or in pairs.

Answers: was living; were all working; was working; was also attending; was learning; was washing

p. 195, Ex. 2

This exercise can be done individually or in pairs.

Answers: 1. She was living in a small apartment in Miami five years ago.   2. Her relatives were all working and paying the bills together five years ago.   3. She was improving her life five years ago.   4. She was learning a lot of new things five years ago.   5. She was thinking about her future five years ago.

pp. 195–196, Ex. 3

This exercise can be done individually or in pairs.

Answers: 1. Monique was living in Miami five years ago.   2. Monique's relatives were living together last year.   3. Our class was studying Chapter Seven (Chapter Six) last week.   4. We were speaking English yesterday.   5. I was living in (name of student's city) last year.

p. 196, Ex. 4

This exercise can be done individually or in pairs.

Answers: (1) 1. was working   2. was planning

(2) 1. was living   2. was trying   3. was dreaming

(3) 1. was studying   2. was inventing   3. was calling   4. were trying   5. was taking

p. 196, Ex. 5

This exercise should be done individually first and then shared in pairs or small groups. Answers will vary.

p. 197, Ex. 6

This exercise can be done individually or in pairs. It can be assigned in advance and then reviewed orally.

Answers: (1) 1. was reading   2. was sending   3. was also becoming   4. am working/ 'm working   5. am writing/ 'm writing   6. am helping/ 'm helping

(2) 1. were looking   2. were applying   3. were feeling   4. are running/ 're running   5. are doing/ 're doing   6. are thinking/ 're thinking   7. are hiring/ 're hiring

p. 198, Act. 1

This activity should be done in small groups. Answers will vary.

p. 198, Act. 2
This activity should be done individually. Answers will vary.

Topic Two
This section covers negative and question forms of the past continuous. It begins with a dialogue, which is an interview with Monique.

p. 200, Discussion questions
Answers: 1. F 2. F 3. F

p. 200, Ex. 1
This exercise can be done individually or in pairs.

Answers: 1. Monique wasn't earning a lot of money. 2. Monique wasn't studying French. 3. At first, Monique wasn't getting good tips. 4. Monique and her relatives weren't living in New York. 5. Our class wasn't studying Chapter Nine last week. 6. We weren't speaking Chinese in class yesterday.

pp. 200–201, Ex. 2
Have students write this exercise individually and then take turns reading it to a partner.

Answers: I wasn't having; wasn't earning; wasn't making; wasn't having; wasn't excited

pp. 201–202, Ex. 3
This exercise can be done individually or in pairs.

Questions: 2. Was Monique making a lot of money? 3. Was Jean Paul having fun? 4. Were Monique's relatives all working hard? 5. Were Monique's relatives living in Miami? 6. Were you studying hard last night? 7. Were you speaking your native language in English class?

p. 202, Ex. 4
This exercise can be done individually or in pairs.

Answers: 1. No they weren't./Yes, they were. 2. Yes, s/he was./No, s/he wasn't. 3. No, I wasn't./Yes, I was. 4. Yes, I was./No, I wasn't. 5. Yes, I was. /No, I wasn't 6. Yes, I was./No, I wasn't.

p. 203 Ex. 5
This exercise can be done individually or in pairs.

Answers: 2. What 3. Who 4. Where 5. How/When 6. When/Why 7. How/Why 8. Why/When 9. Who 10. How much

pp. 203–204, Act. 1
This activity can be done in pairs or small groups. Answers will vary.

p. 204, Act. 2
Be sure that students are looking at different charts.

Answers: Student A: Haiti; $1,000; nobody; $1,000

Student B: Mike; $1,500; Haiti; $800

p. 205, Act. 3
Answers will vary. You can post the articles on the board or duplicate them in a newsletter for the entire class to read.

Topic Three
This section introduces *while* and the contrast between past continuous and simple past forms. The grammar is practiced within the theme of Jean Paul's move to New York City and his job making deliveries by bicycle.

p. 207, Discussion questions
Answers: 1. No./No, he wasn't. 2. In New York. /His cousin was living in New York. 3. Delivering mail by bicycle. 4. His old girlfriend./He saw his old girlfriend.

p. 208, Ex. 1
This exercise can be done individually or in pairs.

Answers: While, was becoming, was having, While, was earning, was having

p. 208, Ex. 2
This exercise can be done individually or in pairs.

Answers: 2. she 3. they 4. he 5. he

p. 208, Ex. 3

This exercise can be done individually or in pairs.

Answers: 1. While Jean Paul was working in New York, he wasn't studying. 2. While Monique was working at the hospital, she was saving money. 3. While Jean Paul was living in New York, Monique was living in Miami. 4. While Monique was making friends in Miami, Jean Paul was making friends in New York. 5. While we were studying Chapter Three, we were talking about friends and families.

p. 209, Ex. 4

This exercise can be done individually or in pairs.

Answers: 2. saw 3. went 4. was crossing 5. was making 6. took; ran

p. 209, Ex. 5

This exercise can be done individually or in pairs.

Answers: 1. While Monique was working, she got a phone call from Jean Paul. 2. While Jean Paul was talking, Monique was crying. 3. While Jean Paul was telling about the accident, Monique was writing notes. 4. While Jean Paul and Monique were talking, the operator asked for more money. 5. While Jean Paul was saying good-bye, he said he was OK.

pp. 209-210, Act 1

Students will work in pairs. Be sure that they each look at only one chart.

Answers: What was Monique doing at ____ yesterday? At 7:30, she was sleeping. At 10:00, she was getting up. At noon, she was studying. At 5:00, she was going to work. At 6:00, she was starting work. At 7:00, she was working. At 10:00, she was taking a break. B: What was Jean Paul doing at ___? At 7:00, he was going to work. At 7:30, he was making his first delivery. At 10:00, he was taking a break.

At noon, he was eating lunch. At 5:00, he was making his last delivery. At 6:00, he was going home. At 7:00, he was eating dinner. At 10:00, he was watching a movie with his girlfriend.

pp. 210–211, Act. 2 and 3

Answers will vary.

Topic Four

This section introduces *when* and continues the contrast of simple past and past continuous forms within the context of another immigrant's story about making a better life.

p. 212, Discussion questions

Answers: 1. A mechanic/ He's a mechanic. 2. At a Gulf service station. He works at a Gulf service station. 3. A letter./He got a letter from his father. 4. He felt excited/happy/nervous.

p. 212, Ex. 1

This exercise can be done individually or in pairs.

Answers: when, was doing (past continuous) arrived (simple past); when, turned (simple past), saw (simple past), when, were shaking (past continuous), picked up (simple past), when, was beating (past continuous), opened (simple past)

pp. 212–213, Ex. 2

This exercise can be done individually or in pairs.

Answers: 1. While 2. When 3. When 4. When 5. While 6. When

p. 213, Ex. 3

This exercise can be done individually or in pairs.

Answers: 1. When Rismani's Service Station became successful, the brothers bought a second service station. 2. When Al's daughter entered college, Al was working seven days a week. 3. When Al's daughter graduated from college, Al was working six days a week. 4. When the Rismani's bought another service station, Al's daughter became a manager. 5. When Al's son entered college, Al was working five days a week.

p. 213, Ex. 4

This exercise should first be done individually, and then shared in pairs or small groups. Answers will vary.

p. 214, Ex. 5

This exercise can be done individually or in pairs.

Answers: 1. went 2. was sleeping
3. worked 4. was working 5. was fixing
6. was fixing

p. 214, Ex. 6

This exercise can be done individually or in pairs.

Answers: 1. was 2. was working
3. understood 4. liked 5. was 6. were getting

pp. 214-215, Ex. 7

This exercise can be done individually or in pairs.

Answers: (1) 1. was dreaming 2. saw
3. loved 4. was making 5. was working
6. is 7. is living 8. arrived 9. is helping

(2) 1. was living 2. was not 3. decided
4. felt 5. is 6. owns 7. is earning
8. is not working/doesn't work 9. has

(3) 1. was working 2. was saving 3. was working 4. bought 5. is not working/does not work 6. own 7. are living/live
8. are managing/manage

Chapter Eight: Food and Nutrition

This chapter focuses on count and noncount nouns with the use of *some, any, much, many how much/many, a little, a lot, a few*. The context is food and nutrition.

Note that Chapters One to Four of this manual include detailed suggestions for the presentation of passages, dialogues, charts, exercises, and activities. If you have questions on how to present a topic, please refer to a similar passage, dialogue, chart, exercise, or activity in the earlier chapters.

Topic One

This section begins the topic of nouns with work on count nouns, plurals, and related structures. The reading introduces the topic of diet and eating habits. Students will have the opportunity to explore American eating habits and compare them to those in their own countries.

p. 219, Discussion questions

Answers: 1. Go to supermarkets. Answers will vary. 2. Answers will vary.
3. Answers will vary.

p. 220, Ex. 1

This can be assigned for homework or done in class individually or in pairs.

Answers: 2. women 3. parties 4. children 5. oranges 6. boxes 7. radios
8. babies 9. geese 10. wives
11. churches 12. apples 13. mice
14. loaves 15. cherries 16. dishes
17. men 18. tomatoes 19. shelves
20. feet

pp. 220–221, Ex. 2

This exercise must be done in pairs with students looking only at their own pictures. Answers provided here are for alternating questions. You may wish to have both Student A and Student B ask all of the possible questions.

Answers: 1. Linda, do you have any grapes? No, I don't have any. 2. Mark, do you have any frozen dinners? No, I don't have any. 3. Linda, do you have any oranges? No, I don't have any.
4. Mark, do you have any potatoes? Yes, I have some. 5. Linda, do you have any onions? No, I don't have any. 6. Mark, do you have any bananas? Yes, I have some. 7. Linda, do you have any canned tomatoes? Yes, I have some. 8. Mark, do you have any carrots? Yes, I have some.

9. Linda, do you have any peas? Yes, I have some. 10. Mark, do you have any apples? Yes, I have some.

p. 222, Ex. 3

This exercise needs to be done in groups. Here are the questions. Answers will vary.

Possible Answers: 1. How many eggs do you eat each week? 2. How many apples do you eat each week? 3. How many glasses of milk do you drink each week? 4. How many cookies do you eat each week? 5. How many avocados do you eat each week? 6. How many salads do you eat each week? 7. How many ice-cream cones do you eat each week? 8. How many bags of potato chips do you eat each week? 9. How many bottles of beer do you drink each week? 10. How many cups of coffee do you drink each week? 11. How many bowls of rice do you eat each week? 12. How many oranges do you eat each week? 13. How many hamburgers do you eat each week? 14. How many cans of soda do you drink each week? 15. How many sandwiches do you eat each week?

p. 222, Ex. 4

This exercise can be written individually and then checked orally in pairs or as a whole class.

Answers: 3. an 4. a 5. an 6. an 7. an 8. a 9. a 10. an 11. a 12. a

p. 223, Ex. 5

This exercise can be done in pairs. Be sure to have the students working orally. You can also assign this as homework and then go over it orally.

Answers: 1. a 2. X 3. an 4. an 5. an 6. X 7. X 8. X 9. a 10. a 11. X 12. a 13. X 14. a 15. a 16. a 17. an 18. X

p. 223, Ex. 6

This exercise can be done in pairs. Be sure to have the students working orally. You can also assign it in advance and then go over it orally.

Answers: 1. some 2. any 3. an 4. any 5. some 6. a 7. a 8. some 9. any 10. a

p. 223, Act. 1

This activity can be done in pairs or small groups. Answers will vary.

p. 224, Act. 2

Students should do this out of class and report back to their group. Answers will vary.

Topic Two

Noncount nouns are introduced through more discussion of food and eating customs. The opening reading raises the topic of diet determined by religion or culture.

p. 225, Discussion questions

Answers: 1. No, they don't. 2. No, they don't. (Yes, they do. The word "some" makes both answers possible.) 3. Meat and Eggs. Some Buddhists don't eat any meat and eggs. 4. Answers vary.

p. 225, Ex. 1

This exercise can be done individually, in pairs or in small groups.

Answers: 2. C 3. N 4. N 5. C 6. N 7. C 8. N 9. N 10. C 11. N 12. C

pp. 226–227, Ex. 2

This exercise should be done in pairs with each student looking at only one shopping list. Answers here are for alternate questions. You may ask each student to ask all questions.

Answers: 1. (A) Do you need some (any) rice? (B) No, I don't need any rice. 2. (B) Do you need some (any) milk? (A) Yes, I need some milk. 3. (A) Do you need some (any) coffee? (B) Yes, I need some coffee. 4. (B) Do you need some (any) sugar? (A) No, I don't need any sugar. 5. (A) Do you need some (any) tea? (B) Yes, I need some tea.   6. (B) Do you need some (any) mustard? (A) Yes, I need some mustard.   7. (A) Do you need some (any) jam? (B) Yes, I need some jam. 8. (B) Do you need some (any) ketchup? (A) Yes, I need some ketchup.   9. (A) Do you need some (any) cereal? (B) No, I don't need any cereal.   10. (B) Do you need some (any) meat? (A) Yes, I need some meat.   11. (A) Do you need some (any) ice cream? (B) No, I don't need any ice cream.   12. (B) Do you need some (any) lettuce? (A) Yes, I need some lettuce.

p. 227, Ex. 3

This exercise must be done in small groups or as the whole class. Answers will vary. Students may not know that "dip" in number 3 means something that you can put on chips. "Onion dip," made from onions and sour cream is a classic dip.

p. 228, Act.

This activity must be done in groups. It will not work well if students are all from the same culture. In that case, you could assign each student a culture and have them go to the library to prepare the information. In class they can role play and complete the exercise.

Topic Three

Units of measurement are covered in this section, and contrast is given for count and noncount nouns. The opening reading and accompanying chart show that for some people food is taken for granted and for others it is a scarcity. Students may not know that "elderly" means older people.

p. 230, Discussion questions
Answers: 1. 3 million   2. 3,011 pounds
3. Guadalajara, Mexico   4. Yes, it is.

p. 231, Ex. 1

This exercise can be done individually, in pairs or in small groups.

Answers: a bottle; a can; a carton; a dozen; a head; a jar; a loaf; a piece; a pound

p. 231, Ex. 2

This exercise can be done individually, in pairs or in small groups.

Answers: 2. pound   3. bunches   4. jar
5. pounds/ounces   6. dozen   7. head
8. tubes   9. bars   10. bunches/pounds
11. box   12. bottle

p. 232, Ex. 3

This exercise can be done individually, in pairs or in small groups. Note that the answers can be approximate.

Answers: 1. approximately 1 gallon
2. 1 meter   3. 1 quart   4. 2 yards
5. 2 pounds   6. 1 pound   7. 3 miles
8. 64 degrees

pp. 232–233, Ex. 4

This exercise should be done with pairs.

Answers: 1. How much ice cream do I need? You need two scoops of ice cream. How much chocolate sauce do I need? You need three tablespoons of chocolate sauce. How much whipped cream do I need? You need one tablespoon of whipped cream. 2. How much spaghetti do I need? You need one quarter pound. How much spaghetti sauce do I need. You need one cup of spaghetti sauce. How much grated cheese do I need? You need 2 tablespoons of grated cheese.   3. How much bread do I need? You need two slices of bread. How much cheese do I need? You need two pieces of cheese. How much butter or margarine do I need? You need one tablespoon of butter or margarine.   4. How much bread do I need? You need two slices of bread. How much tuna do I need? You need one half can of tuna. How much chopped onion do I need? You need one teaspoon of chopped onion. How much mayonnaise do I need? You need two tablespoons of mayonnaise. How much lettuce do I need? You need one piece (leaf) of lettuce.

pp. 233-234, Ex. 5

This exercise must be done in pairs with one student looking at the ingredients card and the other looking at the recipe card.

Answers: 1. How much rice do we need? We need four cups of cooked rice.
2. How much soy sauce do we need? We need four tablespoons of soy sauce.
3. How much garlic do we need? We need two teaspoons of garlic. 4. How many onions do we need? We need one small onion. 5. How much celery do we need? We need two stalks of celery. 6. How many carrots do we need? We need two carrots. 7. How many eggs do we need? We need two eggs. 8. How much chicken do we need? We need one cup of chicken.

p. 234, Act. 1

This activity can be done in a group or as the whole class. It's a lot of fun with the entire class because remembering the list gets more and more difficult. Answers will vary.

p.234, Act. 2

Students will need to prepare this first for homework.

Topic Four

This section continues the contrast of count and noncount nouns. The opening reading explores the current North American concern with healthy diets.

p. 236, Discussion questions
Answers: 1. "Lite" food is low fat food.
2. It is not healthy to eat a lot of fat.
3. Whole milk, 2 percent, 1 percent or skim.

p. 237, Ex. 1
This exercise should be done in pairs.

Answers: 1. Do you eat a lot of fruit? Yes, I do./ No, I don't. 2. Do you eat a lot of vegetables? Yes, I do./ No, I don't. 3. Do you drink a lot of coffee? Yes, I do./ No, I don't. 4. Did you spend a lot of money last week? Yes, I did./ No, I didn't. 5. Did you get a lot of mail last week? Yes, I did./

No, I didn't. 6. Do you have a lot of American friends? Yes, I do./ No, I don't.
7. Did you have a lot of problems when you came here? Yes, I did./ No, I didn't.
8. Do you have a lot of furniture in your home? Yes, I do./ No, I don't.

pp. 237–238, Ex. 2
This exercise can be done individually, in pairs or in small groups.

Answers: 1. + -   2. + -   3. + -   4. - +
5. - +

p. 238, Ex. 3
This exercise can best be done individually or in pairs. You can assign it in advance, have pairs compare answers, and then go over it orally with the entire group.

Answers: 1. a little 2. some 3. A
4. some 5. some 6. a lot of 7. X
8. many 9. X 10. a lot of 11. a
12. a lot of 13. some 14. a few
15. much 16. a little 17. a few 18. a lot of

p. 239, Act.
This activity should be done in small groups. Answers will vary.

pp. 239-240, Checking your progress
This can be done as a quiz or a homework assignment.

Answers: Part 1: 1. b 2. c 3. a 4. d
5. c 6. a 7. c or d 8. d 9. b 10. d

Part 2: 1. wanted 2. a lot of 3. don't
4. used 5. had 6. any 7. many
8. a lot of 9. did 10. much

Chapter Nine: Travel and Leisure

Chapter Nine covers different adjective and adverb forms, particularly when they are used within comparative and superlative structures. The context throughout the chapter is travel and leisure. Plan to spend about one hour per topic, in other words, four hours for the entire chapter.

Note that Chapters One to Four of this manual include detailed suggestions for the presentation of passages, dialogues, charts, exercises, and activities. If you have questions on how to present a topic, please refer to a similar passage, dialogue, chart, exercise, or activity in the earlier chapters.

Topic One

In this section, leisure time at college is explored through the lives of two students. The grammatical focus is adjectives with *-ing* and *-ed*, *go* vs. *play*, and infinitives after the use of *It's* + adjectives.

pp. 242–243, Discussion questions,
Answer: 1. T 2. F. 3. T 4. F 5. T

pp. 243-244, Ex. 1
Students may do this individually, but it is better when they work in pairs or small groups.

Answers: 1. want 2. is 3. are 4. have
5. study 6. helps 7. is 8. is 9. have
10. likes 11. like 12. asked 13. said
14. were walking (walked) 15. changed
16. said 17. wanted 18. agreed
19. was 20. was 21. loved 22. said
23. was 24. have

pp. 244-245, Ex. 2
Students may do this individually, but it is better when they work in pairs.

Answers: 1. boring/bored 2. fascinated/fascinating; shocked/shocking
3. disappointing/disappointed; satisfying/satisfied 4. confused/confusing; excited/exciting 5. surprising/surprised; interesting/interested

pp. 245-246, Ex. 3
Students may do this in pairs, or you may do it with the class as a whole.

Answers: 1. Ms. Hansen/the students
2. Mr. Mosca/the students 3. Lou/Marilynn 4. Shehab/the result of the final exam 5. Saba/the score on the TOEFL Test 6. disappointing/disappointed
7. confusing/confused

p. 247, Ex. 4
Answers: 1. Let's go shopping. No, let's play tennis. 2. Let's go roller-skating. No, let's play chess. 3. Let's play Ping-Pong. No, let's go skiing. 4. Let's go jogging. No, let's play checkers. 5. Let's go surfing. No, let's play baseball. 6. Let's play soccer. No, let's go sightseeing. 7. Let's go dancing. No, let's play basketball. 8. Let's play soccer. No let's go walking.

p. 248, Act.
This activity should be done after Ex. 5 has been completed.

Topic Two

In this section, two tourists compare France and Italy as possible vacation destinations. The grammatical focus is on the use of *would rather* and comparative adjectives.

p. 250, Discussion questions
Answer: 1. F 2. F 3. T 4. F 5. F

pp. 250–251, Ex. 1 and 2
Ex. 1 can be done in pairs or with the class as a whole. Ex. 2 should be done in pairs.

pp. 251-252, Ex. 3
This can be done in pairs or with the class as a whole.

Answers: 1. Nice is warmer than Paris
2. Paris is noisier than Nice 3. Nice is greener . . . 4. Paris is bigger . . .
5. Nice is smaller . . . 6. Nice is closer to the ocean . . . 7. Nice is sunnier . . .
8. Paris is cloudier . . . 9. Paris is nearer to England . . .

p. 253, Ex. 4
This can be done in pairs or with the class as a whole.

Possible Answers: 1. Rome is more exciting than Florence. 2. Florence is safer than Rome. 3. Florence is more expensive . . .
4. Rome is more important . . .
5. Florence is more relaxing . . . 6. Rome is more interesting . . . 7. Rome is more

crowded . . . 8. Florence is more peaceful
. . . 9. Florence is more enjoyable . . .

p. 254, Ex. 6

This may be done with students working individually, but it is better with pairs or small groups.

Answers, Part 1: 1. better   2. faster
3. cheaper   4. safer   5. worse   6. slower
7. more expensive   8. more interesting
9. more romantic

Part 2: 1. better   2. better   4. worse
5. worse

pp. 255-256, Using What You've Learned

Both of these activities work best when they are
done after Ex. 6 has been completed.

Topic Three

In this section leisure for the middle-aged and
elderly is explored through the life of John Wilson.
The grammatical focus is adjectives vs. adverbs in
expressions with *as . . . as* and in comparatives.

p. 257, Discussion questions
Answers: 1. T   2. T   3. F   4. T   5. F

pp. 257-258, Ex. 1

Students may work on this individually, but it is
better if they work in pairs.

Answers: 2. slow/slowly   3. well/good
4. soft/softly   5. carefully/careful
6. dangerously/dangerous   7. beautiful/
beautifully   8. quietly/quiet   9. easily/
easy   10. fast/fast   11. well/good

pp. 258-259, Ex. 2

This should be done in pairs or small groups.

Answers: 1. a. John plays harder than Ben.
b. Ben plays better than John. c. John
plays worse than Ben.   2. a. Ben swims
faster than John. b. John swims more
slowly than Ben. c. Ben swims more quickly than John.   3. a. Ben skis more dangerously than John. b. John skis more safely
than Ben. c. John skis more carefully than
Ben.   4. a. Ben runs farther than John. b.
Ben runs harder than John. c. Ben runs
more seriously than John.

p. 260, Ex. 3

This should be done in pairs or small groups.

Answers: 1. fast/as fast as John
2. well/as well as John   3. carefully/as
carefully as John   4. well/as well as John
5. dangerously/as dangerously as John
6. quickly/as quickly as John   7. clearly/as
clearly as John   8. well/as well as John

p. 261, Ex. 4

This should be done in pairs or small groups.

Answers: happy as a clam, fast as the
wind, good as gold, quiet as a mouse, old
as the hills

*Note: At this point, you may want to
pause from the exercises and do Act. 2, p.
263.*

p. 261, Ex. 5

This can be done in pairs or small groups.

Answers: 2. lazy/lazier   3. well/better
4. bad/worse   5. slowly/more slowly
6. good/better   7. quickly/more quickly
8. careless/more careless

*Note: At this point, you may want to
pause from the exercises and do Act. 1, p.
263.*

p. 262, Ex. 6

This should be done in pairs or small groups. It
can also be assigned as homework.

Answers: 1. harder   2. more interesting
3. more quickly   4. more carefully
5. better   6. bored   7. boring   8. young
9. boring   10. to find   11. play
12. watch   13. go   14. to read   15. to
work   16. to play   17. bored   18. good

p. 263, Using What You've Learned

You can do some or all of these activities when
you finish Topic One, or you can intersperse the
activities (as noted above). If you choose to intersperse them, Act. 1 goes well after Ex. 5. Act. 2
should be done after Ex. 6. Act. 3 is good after
Ex. 4.

Topic Four

This section explores television as a type of leisure. The grammatical focus is superlatives with adjectives and adverbs.

p. 264, Discussion questions
Answers: 1. F   2. F   3. F   4. F   5. T

p. 265, Ex. 1
This should be done in pairs.

p. 266, Ex. 2
This should be done in pairs or small groups.

pp. 266-267, Ex. 3
This should be done in pairs.

Note: At this point, you may want to pause from the exercises and do Act. 1 and/or 2, pp. 268-269.

---

pp. 267-268, Ex. 4
Students may work on this individually, but it is better if the work is done in pairs. It can also be assigned as homework.

Answers: 1. good   2. bad   3. dirty
4. could never   5. frightened   6. was
7. shocked   8. beautiful   9. as
10. more beautiful   11. the most beautiful
12. was   13. didn't   14. was
15. husband's   16. quickly   17. believe
18. on   19. on

Note: At this point, you may want to do Act. 3, p. 268.

p. 268, Using What You've Learned
You can do some or all of these activities when you finish Topic One, or you can intersperse the activities (as noted above). If you choose to intersperse them, Act. 1 and 2 go well after Ex. 3. Act. 3 cannot be done before Ex. 6 has been completed.

Chapter Ten: Our Planet

Chapter 10 gives an overview of past participles and introduces the present perfect tense and passive voice. Topic four is a review of the last chapters. The context in this chapter is "Our Planet" and presents several global issues.

Note that Chapters One to Four of this manual include detailed suggestions for the presentation of passages, dialogues, charts, exercises, and activities. If you have questions on how to present a topic, please refer to a similar passage, dialogue, chart, exercise, or activity in the earlier chapters.

Topic One

p. 272, Prereading questions
The pictures are widely varied, but they are all of living beings.

p. 273, Discussion questions
Answers: 1. Extinction means the end of a species.   2. Answers vary.   3. Damaged beyond repair means that it cannot be fixed or changed.

p. 274, Ex. 1
This exercise can be done individually, in pairs or in small groups.

Answers: 2. convinced   3. worry   4. scare
5. frightened   6. saddened
7. endangered   8. worry   9. worried
10. concerned   11. interested

pp. 274-275, Ex. 2
This exercise can best be done individually or in pairs.

Answers: 1. Many people are worried about the large animals in Africa.   2. Lou is interested in learning about African wildlife.   3. Many zoos and nature preserves are concerned about protecting wildlife.   4. At the zoo, a little boy was frightened by the lion.   5. The little girl was excited about seeing a tiger.   6. The mother was exhausted by spending the whole day at the zoo.

p. 275, Ex. 3

You may want to assign this first for homework and then have students work in pairs or small groups. Answers will vary.

pp. 277–278, Ex. 4

This exercise can be done individually, in pairs or in small groups. Be sure that students have the opportunity to read the story aloud and not just the answers.

Answers: (1) 2. married   3. invited
4. interested   5. elected

(2) 6. drunk   7. arrested   8. hurt
9. arrested

(3) 10. upset or disappointed   11. upset or disappointed   12. interested

(4) 13. separated   14. finished
15. reelected   16. divorced

(5)17. built   18. worried   19. polluted
20. determined.

pp. 278-279, Ex. 5

This exercise can be done individually, in pairs or in small groups. Be sure that the students have the opportunity to read the story aloud and not just the answers. Note that some answers have several possibilities.

Answers: 2. concerned   3. interested
4. upset   5. reelected   6. built   7. scared
/ upset / frightened / disgusted
8. shocked / disgusted / upset / scared /
frightened   9. upset   10. determined
11. exhausted   12. closed / shut
13. arrested.

p. 280, Ex. 6

This exercise can be assigned for homework and then compared in small groups. You may wish to have each group choose one of the "sequels" to act out for the class.

p. 280, Act. 1

This activity should be done in small groups. After organizing the campaign, each group should present to the entire class.

p. 280, Act. 2

Letters will vary. You may need to assist students in locating an address to send the letters. If you have access to the INTERNET, it is likely to find a web site with an address.

Topic Two

p. 281, Discussion questions

Answers: 1. No, it isn't.   2. Because of technological advances such as the telephone and airplanes. (Note that you may want to expand this discussion.)

p. 283, Ex. 1

This exercise can best be done individually or in pairs.

Answers (listed horizontally): paid; become; put; begun; read; brought; started; choose; seen; done; study; found; speak; get; taken; learn; think; left; traveled; made; visited

p. 284, Ex. 2

This exercise can be done individually, in pairs or in small groups.

Answers: Irregular: has become, hasn't grown   Regular: have changed, have discovered, have connected

p. 284, Ex. 3

This exercise can be done individually, in pairs or in small groups. Answers will vary.

Possible Answers: 1. I have/haven't lived in
. . .   2. I have/haven't studied . . .
3. I have/haven't traveled . . .
4. I have/haven't visited . . .
5. I have/haven't tried . . .   In Item 5, explain to students that roller blading is also called inline skating.

p. 284, Ex. 4

This exercise can best be done individually or in pairs.

Answers: 2. helped   3. become
4. opened   5. given   6. brought   7. used
8. made

pp. 285-286, Ex. 5, 6, and 7

These exercises can be done in pairs or in small groups. Answers will vary.

p. 287, Act.

You may want to assign the chart for homework and then have the students report in groups. Answers will vary.

Topic Three

p. 288, Discussion questions

Answers: 1. They make global efforts to protect and improve people's lives and help people in natural disasters and in wars. 2. Answers will vary. (Note that you may want to expand this discussion.)

p. 291, Ex. 1

This exercise can be done in pairs or in small groups.

Answers: 1. was finished; is finished; will be finished   2. will be elected; was elected; will be elected   3. was given; will be given; are given   4. was repaired; is repaired; will be repaired   5. will be made; are made; will be made   6. will be done; is done; was done

pp. 292–293, Ex. 2

This exercise can be done in pairs or in small groups.

Answers: 2. was introduced   3. were developed   4. was not used   5. were discovered   6. was invented   7. was concerned   8. was interested   9. were created   10. were started   11. are located   12. are composed   13. are awarded   14. is used

pp. 293–294, Ex. 3

This exercise can be done in pairs or in small groups.

Answers: 2. was chosen   3. was born   4. was spent   5. was made   6. were taken   7. were begun   8. was held   9. was left   10. was shot

p. 294

Culture Note: You can expand to a discussion about discrimination in the United States and in the students' countries.

---

p. 295, Ex. 4

This exercise can be done in pairs or in small groups. This exercise, along with Ex. 5, can be assigned as homework and then reviewed in class.

Answers: 4. was formed   5. was located   6. was meant   7. was disbanded   8. was proposed   9. was begun   10. is located   11. is said   12. are given   13. is paid   14. is made   15. are helped   16. are discussed   17. (are) solved   18. are educated   19. are fed   20. are provided   21. will be disbanded   22. will be created

p. 296, Ex. 5

This exercise can be done in pairs or in small groups. As with Ex. 4, it can be assigned as homework and then reviewed in class.

Answers: 4. is known   5. became   6. used   7. was controlled   8. wanted   9. were not given   10. were discussed   11. bought   12. fought   13. taught   14. was given   15. was not finished   16. was faced   17. was killed   18. ended (was ended)   19. remain

p. 296, Act.

This activity can be done individually or in pairs before the group reports. Students may need to go to the library.

Topic Four

p. 298, Ex. 1

This exercise can be done individually or in pairs.

Answers: 1. is often   2. is not/isn't   3. am reading   4. think   5. are getting   6. will be   7. do not know/don't know   8. says   9. is/will be/is going to be   10. talks   11. does not look/doesn't look   12. hope

p. 298, Ex. 2

This exercise can be done individually or in pairs.

Answers: 2. has improved 3. face 4. has increased 5. have developed 6. was 7. was 8. is growing 9. are 10. needs 11. wants

p. 299, Ex. 3

This exercise should be done individually first and then reported in pairs or small groups. Answers will vary.

p. 299, Ex. 4

This exercise can be done individually or in pairs.

Answers: 1. Many people need to eat better. 2. Who can feed the hungry people? 3. Most of us don't go to bed hungry. 4. Some organizations give food to hungry people. 5. Other organizations prefer to find jobs for people. 6. We should continue to help all poor people. 7. The world will always have problems. 8. We might find better solutions.

p. 299, Ex. 5

This exercise can be done individually or in pairs.

Questions: 1. Who worked for equal rights for all people? 2. How many people marched on Washington, D.C., in 1963? 3. When did Martin Luther King, Jr., make an important speech? 4. Why did some people hate him? 5. What do more people in America have today? 6. Do all people have equal opportunity? 7. Where do many people have to live today? 8. When will all people in the world have equal rights?

p. 300, Ex. 6

This exercise can be done individually, in pairs or in small groups.

Answers: 2. much, many 3. find, to find 4. has, have 5. worry, worried 6. serious, a serious 7. is needing, needs 8. damage, damaging 9. endangering,

endangered 10. taking, taken 11. its, their 12. most largest, largest 13. because need, because people need 14. we can, can we 15. to try, try

p. 300, Act. 1

You may want students to work individually before working in groups. Answers will vary.

pp. 301-302, Checking Your Progress

You may use this as a quiz or assign it for homework.

Answers: Part 1) 1. a 2. a 3. d 4. d 5. c 6. a 7. c 8. b 9. c 10. b

Part 2) 1. frustrating 2. bored 3. tired. 4. exhausted 5. X 6. more fluent 7. easier 8. said 9. have learned 10. than

Quizzes and Examinations

The following quizzes and examinations can be used for review and summary of grammar points or as a check of problem areas. The parts of each test may be used individually or the entire quiz may be used at one time.

Each chapter has a quiz with 20 items. If you are using a system based on 100, multiply the results by five. Two cumulative tests are also included as a "mid-term" and "final." The first covers Chapters One to Six, and the second Chapters Seven to Twelve. Individual sections carry different points, but each test totals 100. The tests are divided into parts — more or less according to chapters. Parts corresponding to chapters that you haven't covered can be deleted. In that case, you would need to restructure the point system if you wish to base the tests on 100 points.

Here are some suggested steps for the presentation and use of these quizzes and tests:

- Explain that the purpose of the test is to give students an idea of how they are doing and what areas they need to work on.

- Emphasize that the tests are a learning device.

- Read the instructions for each exercise. Make sure that students understand what they are to do. Since test items are similar to exercises in the chapters, the students should be familiar with the various formats.

- Allow students time to complete the test. The quizzes are meant to be brief and on average should not take more than ten to fifteen minutes. The mid-term and final exams may take an entire class period, depending on the group.

- You can vary the conditions for the quizzes and tests. For example, while most may be done individually, at times during the course, you may ask students to work in pairs or groups.

- Try to correct the quizzes and tests as quickly as possible. For the quizzes, you may want to correct them in class after finishing in order to give rapid feedback. Discuss points that have caused students problems. Point out that, because language is not always "right" or "wrong," answers may vary in some cases. Encourage students to write the most probable answer, but allow alternative ones if they seem logical and would be accepted by a native speaker. (As an example, in some cases, the line between *going to* and *will* is clear, but in other cases, both would be equally acceptable. The same will occur with the present perfect and present perfect continuous tenses, the simple past and past perfect tenses, and so on.)

These quizzes and tests should help to provide a fairly objective view of your students' progress—in a limited area. However, such tests cannot accurately measure students' true mastery of grammar across the skill areas of reading, writing, listening, and speaking. Using quizzes or activities from any or all of the four corresponding texts of *Interactions Two* will give a much more realistic assessment of your students' mastery of English. You may also consider adding your own "communicative" sections by using oral interviews or by video-taping students and then critiquing them or by assigning written compositions that will generate the relevant grammar.

Chapter One: Quiz

Name_____   Date _____

Part 1: (20 points)

Circle the correct words to complete this letter.

Example: Andreas (is / are) my friend.

Dear Andreas,

Hi! How (is / are) you? I'm fine. I am (in / at) Maine now. Maine is a state (in / on) the
Atlantic Coast of the United States. I am living in (a / an) town called Portland with (a / an) American
family. My "family" here is very (friend / friendly). Joe is (a / an) teacher and Mary is (a / an)
accountant. They have two (childs / children). There (is / are) a son. (He / His) name is Alex. (He / His)
is 10. (There / Their) is also a daughter. (Her / Hers) name is Marina. (She's / She) seven years old. Oh,
(they / their) have a dog, too. (It / Its) name is Garth.

Today (its / it's) beautiful—sunny, warm, and breezy, but I'm not outside. I am (at / at the)
library studying. My classes (is / are) difficult, and I have to study a lot! I miss you and all my friends.

        Your friend,

        Paco

Part 2: (15 points)

Make questions for the following. Use the question word in parentheses. (15 points)

Example: (Where) _Where is Paco?_
                 Paco is in Maine.

1. (How)   _____
   Paco is fine.

2. (Where)   _____
   (Maine) is in the United States.

3. (How old)   _____
   Marina is seven years old.

4. (What . . . like) _____
   It's beautiful today.

5. (What month)   _____
   It's September.

Part 3: (15 points)

Find the mistakes and correct them. There are fifteen mistakes. (15 points)

Example: Juan has two (friendes) in the United States.   friends

1.   How old you are? I are 21 years old.

2.   Soo Young is student.

3.   Who your roommate is?

4.   New York City is noise and crowd.

5.   Are you a airplane pilot? No, I not

6.   There are two churchs in the town.

7.   In Maine there are only a few big citys.

8.   Alex was born at October 30 at the night.

9.   The library is in Second Avenue. Marina is at library now.

10.   This test am easy!

Chapter Two: Quiz

Name_____   Date _____

Part 1: (15 points)

Make the following sentences negative.

Example: Joe is working at a restaurant.
                  Joe isn't working at a restaurant. or _Joe is not working at a restaurant_.

1.   My brother is spending a lot of money.

       _____

2.   Gloria is looking for a job.

       _____

3.   They are studying in Texas.

       _____

4.   We're going to play tennis.

       _____

5.   I'm going to go to the bank.

       _____

Part 2: (15 points)

Make questions for the following answers.

Example: Is she going to go shopping? _Yes, she's going to go shopping_.

                  Where is she reading? She's reading _in the library_.

1. _____

   <u>My cousin</u> is going to move to Alaska.

2. _____

   The pharmacy is <u>next to the movie theater</u>.

3. _____

   I'm looking for a <u>wool</u> sweater.

4. _____

   She's buying <u>a jacket</u>.

5. _____

   <u>Yes, I'm spending too much money</u>.

Part 3: (10 points)

Combine the following pairs of sentences with *and* with *too*, or with *but*. (10 points)

Example: Jack is studying French. I'm studying French.
             Jack is studying French, and I am too.
             I'm using my credit card. John is paying in cash.
             I'm using my credit card, but John is paying in cash.

1.   Cristina is going to the dance. I'm going to the dance.

     _____

2.   I'm buying some clothes. My friend is just looking.

     _____

3. My coworkers are taking a vacation. I'm staying here.

_____

4. My coworkers are taking a vacation. I'm taking a vacation.

_____

5. He's going skiing. She's going to visit San Francisco.

_____

Part 4: (10 points)

Write sentences with *There is* or *There are*.

Example: dog/barking *There is a dog barking.*

1. two girls/dancing _____

2. a man/reading the newspaper _____

3. a woman/sitting on a bench _____

4. two boys/playing ball _____

5. a young man/carrying presents _____

Chapter Three: Quiz

Name_____ Date _____

Part 1: (20 points)

Find the mistakes in the following sentences and correct them.

Example: He ~~don't~~ cook. _doesn't_

1.   She kiss the children every morning before they go to school.

2.   I get up always early.

3.   In your house, who does wash the dishes?

4.   Maria not know how to cook.

5.   Reads your assignment carefully.

6.   I hate clean the house.

7.   Does he knows how to cook Chinese food?

8.   I'm not wanting a new car.

9.   John plays with him friends everyday.

10.   He's having two good friends.

Part 2:   (30 points)

Make questions or statements with the following words. You may need to add some words.

Example: set/ you/not need to/the table <u>You don't need to set the table</u>.

1.   to the movies/go/let's

     _____

2.   not/to become/want/a doctor

     _____

3.   plan/you/to become/a teacher/?

     _____

4.   he/right now/ with a friend/is talking

     _____

5.   seldom/he/studies

     _____

6.   never/she/cooks

     _____

7.   call/you/home/how often/?

     _____

8.   a mess/not make

     _____

9.   need/laundry/to do/who/?

_____

10.   a headache/has/she

_____

Chapter Four: Quiz

Name_____   Date _____

Part 1: (50 points)

Complete the following conversations by choosing the appropriate words in parentheses. (50 points)

Example: Jack (is / are) very tired.

1.   Jack: I'm very tired, but I (don't have to / must not) go to bed. I (have to / should to) do a lot

     of work before tomorrow.

     Jill: You (can / can't) do your best work if you are tired. You (has to / must) get some sleep.

2.   Jingi: Mr. Neilson, I don't have my homework. It's at home. (Will / Can) I bring it to you

     tomorrow?

     Mr. Neilson: Sorry, today is Friday. We (don't have to / must not) come to school on

     Saturdays. You (would / can) bring it on Monday.

3.   Jamie: Hey, Eva, what are you going to do tonight? (Will / Should) you go to a movie

     with me?

     Eva: I (would / could) like (go / to go) to a movie, but I have a big test soon. I (have to / can)

     study.

     Jamie: But, to do well on a test, you (must / must not) be tired. You (have to / might) relax—

     at a movie, for example. That's why you (should not / should) come with me!

     Eva: Whatever you say, Jamie!

4.   Mark: Where is Vern?

     Jan: I'm not sure. He (might / can) be at home, (or / so) he (might / is) be in school.

     Mark: When (will / would) he be here?

     Jan: He (must / has) to be here by 9:00. He (will / is) be here soon.

5.   Stella: What homework do we (have / has) to do for tomorrow? What should I

     (study / to study)?

     Bill: We (have / should) to review all of Chapter Four, but we (don't have / must not) to review

     Chapter Three. Next week, we (are going / will) to start Chapter Five.

Chapter Five: Quiz

Name_____   Date _____

Part 1: (10 points)

Change these sentences from negative to affirmative.

Example: John didn't like his job.
             John liked his job.

1.   Mary didn't want to take the bus.

     _____

2.   We didn't study that chapter.

     _____

3.   I didn't try to call you last night.

     _____

4.   The country didn't need many workers.

     _____

5.   They didn't play soccer yesterday.

     _____

Part 2: (20 points)

Circle the correct word(s) in parentheses.

Years ago, women (can't / couldn't) do many things. Most women (didn't work / didn't
worked) outside the home. They (had / had to) do everything inside the home, though. They
(cleanned / cleaned), (cookked / cooked), and (watch / watched) the children. But World War II
(change / changed) many things for women. The country needed workers, (because / so) women
(start / started) working in many kinds of jobs. Soon, there (was / were) women in factories and all
kinds of companies.

Part 3: (20 points)

Find and correct the mistakes. There are ten mistakes.

At the start of World War II, my mother were 20 years old. During the war, she works in a

factory. My father join the military. He doesn't fight. Because he were a doctor, he works in a hospital.

He like his work, but he hated the war. He dident like to see people hurt and dying. After the war, my

mom and dad move to a new house, and then they have a baby—Me!

Chapter Six: Quiz

Name_____   Date _____

Part 1: (20 points)

Write the past tense of these verbs.

1. become	_____	11. hear	_____
2. begin	_____	12. know	_____
3. buy	_____	13. learn	_____
4. change	_____	14. leave	_____
5. come	_____	15. lend	_____
6. cost	_____	16. pay	_____
7. eat	_____	17. play	_____
8. enter	_____	18. speak	_____
9. give	_____	19. study	_____
10. grow	_____	20. write	_____

Part 2: (15 points)

Change these statements to reported speech. Begin with "My friend said that." (15 points)

Example: "San Francisco is a beautiful city."
            My friend said that San Francisco was a beautiful city.

1.   "San Francisco has many beautiful places to see."

_____

2.   "Thousands of tourists go there."

_____

3.   "It costs a lot to stay in a nice hotel."

_____

4.   "You can eat great Chinese food there."

_____

5.   "It doesn't get very cold in San Francisco."

_____

Part 3: (15 points)

Find and correct the errors with verbs. There are fifteen errors.

Han is a very special person. He growed up in Vietnam during the war. Life was very difficult for Han and his family, but one thing gaved them a lot of happiness—music. Everyone in the family liked music, but Han liked it the most. Even when he was a very little boy, Han love music. He use to listen to music anytime he can. Above all, Han like the flute. When he were eight, his parents getted him his first flute. His father buyed the flute even though it is very expensive and the family need money for food. Han's father knowed that the flute could helped Han later in his life. In the end, the flute helped Han a lot. He learn to play very well, and finally he becamed a professional musician.

Chapter Seven: Quiz

Name_____   Date _____

Part 1: (10 points)

Circle the letter of the best word or words to complete the sentence.

1. Yesterday, at 6:00 I _____.
   a. studied
   b. studies
   c. studying
   d. was studying

2. She _____ at a department store.
   a. was worked
   b. wasn't working
   c. working
   d. work

3. Were you calling me? Yes, I _____.
   a. did
   b. do
   c. wasn't
   d. was

4. What were you doing when the accident _____.
   a. was happening
   b. happened
   c. happens
   d. happening

5. While Patricia was taking a nap, _____ was dreaming of a Hawaiian vacation.
   a. Patricia
   b. She
   c. her
   d. she

Part 2: (20 points)

Circle the correct answer.

1. Monique (got up/was getting up) early every morning when she (was/was being) in her country.

2. He (mailed/was mailing) a letter when he saw an old friend.

3. Peter (arrived/was arriving) in Dallas three years ago.

4. Two years ago I (started/was starting) my own company.

5. When I opened the package, I (began/was beginning) to cry.

6. While Maria was singing, her friends (held/were holding) their ears.

7. When I (saw/was seeing) the accident, I (called/was calling) for help.

8. At this time yesterday, I (studied/was studying) for the test.

Part 3: (20 points)

Write in the correct question word. In some cases more than one answer is correct.

Who   What   When   Where   Why   How   How long

1. _____ were you saying?

2. _____ was he going to the doctor?

3. _____ were you doing there?

4. _____ did you live last year?

5. _____ is he going to leave?

6. _____ was calling me?

7. _____ did you receive that package?

8. _____ said that?

9. _____ did she live in Boston?

10. _____ was the test?

Chapter Eight: Quiz

Name_____ Date _____

Part 1: (20 points)

Circle the correct word or words to complete each of the following sentences.

Example: You need (a / an) oven to bake a cake.

1.   I don't have (some / any) money to lend you.

2.   Do you need (a / any) sugar?

3.   Please buy me a (tube / head) of lettuce.

4.   Don't forget to get two (loaves / bars) of soap.

5.   (How much / How many) people did you meet?

6.   I don't have (much / many) time to talk now.

7.   Daniel has (a lot / a lot of) work to do.

8.   I don't have (much / many) furniture in my apartment.

9.   A nutritious diet includes (few / a few) pieces of fruit .

10.   Please buy six (tubes / rolls) of toilet paper.

Part 2:   (30 points)

Make a question with each of the following words.

banana   *How many bananas do you eat each week?*

coffee   *How much coffee do you drink each week?*

1.   bread _____

2.   onion _____

3.   milk _____

4.   cans of soda _____

5.   egg _____

6.   rice _____

7.   meat _____

8.   cheese _____

9.   apple _____

10.   popcorn _____

Chapter Nine: Quiz

Name_____   Date _____

Part 1: (20 points)

Circle the correct words.

Alex: There's nothing to do. I'm (bore / bored). Let's find something (interesting / interested)
           to do.

Nico: Let's (play / go) cards or let's see a movie. I heard that Star Wars 27 is very
           (excite / exciting).

Alex: No . . . I'm (tire / tired) of cards and of movies about outer space. I was really
           (disappointed / disappointing) with Star Wars 26. Especially the ending . . . The
           ending was very (disappointed / disappointing). Let's think of something else.

Nico: Alex, you know. You are never (satisfy / satisfied). You always complain.

Alex: OK, OK. What do you want to do?

Nico: Let's (go / play) bowling.

Alex: Sure! That sounds like fun.

Nico: I can't believe it! I'm really (surprised / surprised)! This is the first time you're not com
plaining!

Part 2:   (20 points)

Write the comparative and superlative forms of these adjectives.

1. bad   _____ _____   6. good   _____ _____

2. cheap   _____ _____   7. interesting _____ _____

3. easy   _____ _____   8. noisy   _____ _____

4. enjoyable _____ _____   9. relaxing   _____ _____

5. far   _____ _____   10. warm   _____ _____

Part 3: (10 points)

Complete these comparisons by adding the correct words.

    I'm not a very good athlete. My sister Ann is a much better athlete _____ I
am even though Ann is 22 and I am 20. Ann is two years _____ than I am, but she's
good at many sports. For example, I can't run very fast. Ann runs much _____ than I
run. I'm not a good swimmer. Ann swims much _____ than I swim.

    Ann is a good athlete, but the _____ athlete of the entire family is our sister
Molly. Molly is 18, so she's two years _____ than I am. I will never be able to run as
_____ as Molly runs. And I will never be able to swim or play tennis or ski
_____ well _____ she does. But I think that I have
_____ fun in sports than she does because she's so serious and I'm not.

Chapter Ten: Quiz

Name_____   Date _____

Part 1: (20 points)

Circle the correct word to complete each sentence.

Example: I am (amazing / (amazed)) at that story.

1. What do you (worry / worried) about?

2. Are you (concerned / concerning) about pollution?

3. That river is very (pollute / polluted).

4. Have you studied about the United Nations? Yes, I (do / have).

5. What is the (most long / longest) book you have ever read?

6. I brought my car to the mechanic, but it (was repaired / wasn't repaired).

7. That bridge (will finish / will be finished) next year.

8. Radium (discovered / was discovered) by Marie Curie.

9. Where (did / were) you born?

10. He is well (know / known) for his athletic ability.

Part 2: (30 points)

Make questions about the underlined words.

Example: He was born <u>in France</u>.
            Where was he born?

1. Many people in the world today go to bed hungry <u>because they don't have enough food.</u>

    _____

2. He visited the United Nations Headquarters <u>when he went to New York</u>.

    _____

3. Racism exists <u>in many countries</u>.

    _____

4. That book was written by <u>my favorite author.</u>

    _____

5. <u>Two thousand</u> people marched to the President's house.

    _____

6. <u>Someday in the future</u> we might have world peace.

    _____

7. Many people are worried about <u>whales</u>.

    _____

8. Hunters often kill animals <u>for food</u>.

    _____

9. She was living <u>in Florida</u> before she moved here.

    _____

10. I feel <u>sad</u> at the end of a course.

    _____

Answer Key, Quizzes

Chapter One

Part 1:

1. are 2. in 3. on 4. a 5. an 6. friendly 7. a 8. an 9. children 10. is 11. His 12. He 13. There 14. Her 15. She's 16. they 17. Its 18. it's 19. at the 20. are

Part 2:

1. How is Paco? 2. Where is Maine? 3. How old is Marina? 4. What's the weather like today? / What's it like today? 5. What month is it?

Part 3:

1. How old are you? I am . . . 2. Soo Young is a student. 3. Who is. . . ? 4. . . . is noisy and crowded. 5. . . . an airplane pilot? No, I'm (I am) not. 6. churches 7. cities 8. . . . on October 30 at night. 9. . . . on Second Avenue. Marina is at the library now. 10. This test is easy!

Chapter Two

Part 1:

1. My brother isn't (is not) spending. . . 2. Gloria isn't (is not) looking. . . 3. They aren't (are not) studying. . . 4. We aren't (are not) going. . . 5. I'm not (I am not) going. . . .

Part 2:

1. Who is moving to Alaska? 2. Where is the pharmacy? 3. What kind of sweater are you looking for? 4. What is she buying? 5. Are you spending too much (a lot of) money?

Part 3:

1. . . . to the dance, and I am too. 2. some clothes, but my friend. . . 3. . . . a vacation, but I'm staying here. 4. a vacation, and I am too. 5. skiing, but she's going. . .

Part 4:

1. There are two girls dancing. 2. There is a man reading the newspaper. 3. There is a woman sitting on a bench. 4. There are two boys playing ball. 5. There is a young man carrying presents.

Chapter Three

Part 1:

1. She kisses. . . 2. I always get up early. 3. . . . who washes. . . 4. Maria does not (doesn't) know. . . 5. Read your assignment. . . / Your teacher reads. . . 6. I hate to clean. . . 7. Does he know. . . 8. I don't want. . . 9. . . . with his friends. . . 10. He has two. . .

Part 2:

1. Let's go to the movies tonight. 2. I don't (Mary doesn't) want to become a doctor. 3. Do you plan to become a teacher? 4. He is talking with a friend right now. 5. He seldom studies. 6. She never cooks. 7. How often do you call home? 8. Don't make a mess. / Let's not make a mess. 9. Who needs to do laundry? 10. She has a headache.

Chapter Four

1. must not 2. have to 3. can't 4. must 5. Can 6. don't have to 7. can 8. Will 9. would 10. to go 11. have to 12. must not 13. might 14. should 15. might 16. or 17. might 18. will 19. has 20. will 21. have 22. study 23. have 24. don't have 25. are going

Chapter Five:

Part 1:

Mary wanted to take. . . 2. We studied that chapter. 3. I tried to call. . . 4. The country needed. . . 5. They played. . .

Part 2:

1. couldn't 2. didn't work 3. had to 4. cleaned 5. cooked 6. watched 7. changed 8. so 9. started 10. were

Part 3:

At the start of World War II, my mother was 20 years old. During the war, she *worked* in a factory. My father *joined* the military. He *didn't* fight. Because he *was* a doctor, he *worked* in a hospital. He *liked* his work, but he hated the war. He *didn't* like to see people hurt and dying. After the war, my mom and dad *moved* to a new house, and then they *had* a baby—Me!

Chapter Six

Part 1:

1. became 2. began 3. bought 4. changed 5. came 6. cost 7. ate 8. entered 9. gave 10. grew 11. heard 12. knew 13. learned 14. left 15. lent 16. paid 17. played 18. spoke 19. studied 20. wrote

Part 2:

1. My friend said that San Francisco had many. . . 2. . . . that thousands of tourists went there. 3. . . . that it cost a lot. . . 4. . . . that you (we) could eat. . . 5. . . . that it didn't get. . .

Part 3:

Han is a very special person. He *grew* up in Vietnam during the war. Life was very difficult for Han and his family, but one thing gave them a lot of happiness—music. Everyone in the family liked music, but Han liked it the most. Even when he was a very little boy, Han *loved* music. He used to listen to music anytime he *could*. Above all, Han *liked* the flute. When he *was* eight, his parents *got* him his first flute. His father *bought* the flute even though it *was* very expensive and the family *needed* money for food. Han's father *knew* that the flute could *help* Han later in his life. In the end, the flute helped Han a lot. He *learned* to play very well, and finally he *became* a professional musician.

Chapter Seven

Part 1:

1. d 2. b 3. d 4. b 5. d

Part 2:

1. got up; was 2. was mailing 3. arrived 4. started 5. began 6. were holding 7. saw / called 8. was studying

Part 3:

1. What 2. When / Why 3. What 4. Where 5. When / Why 6. Who 7. When / Where / How / Why 8. Who 9. How long / When / Where / Why 10. How / How long / When / Where / What

Chapter Eight

Part 1:

1. any 2. any 3. head 4. bars 5. How many 6. much 7. a lot of 8. much 9. a few 10. rolls

Part 2:

1. How much bread do you eat each week? 2. How many onions do you eat. . . ? 3. How much milk do you drink. . . ? 4. How many cans of soda do you drink. . . ? 5. How many eggs do you eat. . . ? 6. How much rice do you eat. . . ? 7. How much meat do you eat. . . ? 8. How much cheese do you eat. . . ? 9. How many apples do you eat. . . ? 10. How much popcorn do you eat. . . ?

Chapter Nine

Part 1:

1. bored 2. interesting 3. play 4. exciting 5. tired 6. disappointed 7. disappointing 8. satisfied 9. go 10. surprised

Part 2:

1. worse; worst 2. cheaper; cheapest 3. easier; easiest 4. more enjoyable; most enjoyable 5. farther; farthest 6. better; best 7. more interesting; most interesting 8. noisier; noisiest 9. more relaxing; most relaxing 10. warmer; warmest

Part 3:

1. than 2. older 3. faster 4. better 5. best 6. younger 7. fast / well 8. as 9. as 10. more

Chapter Ten

Part 1:

1. worry 2. concerned 3. polluted 4. have 5. longest 6. wasn't repaired 7. will be finished 8. was discovered 9. were 10. known

Part 2:

1. Why do many people go to bed hungry? 2. When did he visit the U.N.? 3. Where does racism exist? 4. Who(m) was that book written by? 5. How many people marched. . .? 6. When will (might) we have world peace? 7. What are many people worried about? 8. Why do hunters often kill animals? 9. Where was she living. . .? 10. How do you feel at the end of a course?

Interactions Access: Reading/Writing

Philosophy

Interactions Access: A Reading/Writing Book gives low-level academic students the skills and confidence they need to read sophisticated material, understand real-life materials written in English, and write about themselves and the world around them. The text is designed to be intellectually stimulating but not beyond the beginning student's lexical, grammatical, or syntactic understanding. The reading selections—especially in the later chapters of the book—look difficult but aren't. The level of grammar in these readings has been carefully controlled, as has the length of each reading. New vocabulary items can usually be guessed from context, and items are recycled again and again, allowing students to absorb them easily. Likewise, the writing material in this text is designed to stimulate language development while not going far beyond the students' capabilities. In each chapter, students build up to writing tasks through a series of prewriting exercises. The text includes grammar and editing support for writing and revising and offers students ample opportunities to share their work with others.

Sequencing and Pace of the Course

The text offers fifty to sixty hours of teaching material, and individual exercises and activities can range from one minute to fifteen or twenty minutes in length. Depending on your course, you may need or choose to omit individual exercises or activities or even whole chapters. Because the text progresses in difficulty and sophistication and because many items are recycled, we recommend following the general order of the text.

Chapter Organization and General Teaching Suggestions

The text consists of ten chapters, each of which has a central theme. Each chapter is divided into four parts:

Part One:

Part One opens with artwork and prereading questions that set the context for the selection that follows—a controlled nonfiction passage about the chapter theme. The prereading material forms the springboard for student discussion. It is here that students make predictions about main ideas in the reading. These predictions are crucial for active reading, so class discussion need not be limited only to the questions in the book. Since the more students think about the ideas, the more ready they will be to read and understand.

When reading, it is important that students not use a dictionary, since guessing meaning from context is one of the primary skills the text seeks to instill. Various types of context clues are introduced gradually throughout the book to help students acquire that skill. As they progress through the book, they will rely less and less on their dictionaries and become much faster and more active readers.

After reading the selection once, students should complete the various exercises and then reread the selection, this time more carefully and—if necessary—with a dictionary. The first postreading exercise helps students check their general understanding of the selection and (in later chapters) of each paragraph. Then, an exercise for guessing meaning from context is included, and some chapters contain exercises on making inferences, understanding pronoun references, noting details, and recognizing supporting material in a paragraph. Personalized exercises for pair work or small groups relate each reading to students' lives.

Part Two:

Part Two also begins with artwork that sets the tone for the second controlled reading of the chapter. This reading is generally lighter than the one in Part One and is usually fiction written in the first person. All chapters contain various exercises to help students expand their passive and active vocabulary. In addition, exercises that relate the reading to students' lives and personal experience are included. Various study skills are stressed in this section to aid students in acquiring essential skills for academic reading such as following directions, dictionary usage, and understanding paragraph organization. Some chapters contain exercises that practice skills such as finding main ideas, details, and so on.

Part Three:

Part Three contains realia such as advertisements, pages from brochures, bills, and application forms to develop scanning skills. Some of this is, of course, simplified.

Part Four:

Part Four is comprised of a brief grammar presentation box, followed by several prewriting exercises, leading up to a writing task. Editing practice follows, which includes a presentation box on some aspect of writing mechanics, a follow-up exercise on the point(s) covered, and an editing checklist for students to use to check their writing task before they share it with a partner or group. Part Four ends with a journal writing activity, where students choose a topic listed or write about a topic of their own. Note that journal writing is meant to promote fluency in students' writing, so don't be worried if these pieces are filled with errors. Encourage students to get their ideas on paper—without focusing heavily on being perfectly correct.

Teaching Tips and Answer Key
Chapter One: Neighborhoods, Cities and Towns

In Chapter One, students are introduced to some of the reading and writing skills that they will practice throughout the book.

Part One

p. 2, Getting Started

Have students use the picture to answer the two questions. (Ask students to volunteer to answer.) For Question 1, they should tell you that the city is large and not nice. For Question 2, they may give a variety of answers depending on their level of vocabulary: The problem of this city is traffic / cars / smog / too many people, etc.

Note: Make sure that students don't reach for the dictionary to look up "monster" in the title. This word is explained in the reading.

p. 3, Reading

Have students read through this passage silently. (If they read aloud, they'll focus on pronunciation instead of meaning.) You might read aloud as they read silently or play the cassette tape that accompanies the text. Have them read the four paragraphs without stopping. Some students will probably want to use a dictionary or ask you for the meaning of each new word; they may already have acquired the habit of looking up every new word and writing the translation in the margin. You should encourage them, right from the beginning, to guess meaning from context, instead. Every chapter has an exercise on this skill, and you'll notice that most new vocabulary has been carefully presented in the reading passages so that students can guess.

p. 4, Ex. 1

Give students a minute to read the two questions and circle the letter of the correct answer to each. These should be easy for most students.

Answers: 1. c   2. b

p. 4, New Words

This section contains a boxed explanation of one way to guess the meaning of new words from the context, followed by an exercise with words from the passage. These explanations are sequenced so that in early chapters the ways to guess may seem obvious; in Chapter One, for example, students learn to look for a definition of the word after *is* or *are*. Although this may seem easy to the teacher, many students are so attached to their bilingual dictionaries that it doesn't occur to them to use the context even if it is very clear. Encourage students (1) to look for meaning in the context, (2) to trust the combination of a clear context and their own ability to reason, and (3) not to worry about every new word. Have students write their answers to Exercise 2.

p. 4, Ex. 2

Answers: 1. a big, terrible thing   2. a very, very large city   3. the number of people in every square mile

p. 5, Ex. 3

This one-question exercise introduces the skill of making inferences. If students can answer this, they have understood the main idea of the reading passage and are demonstrating that they can also "read between the lines", in other words, understand something not directly stated. Have students circle the letter of the correct answer; then check their answer.

Answer: b

p. 5, Ex. 4

This exercise allows students to practice reading a chart in English and saying aloud long numbers. Before they answer the questions with a partner, have students repeat after you two or three of the numbers for which there is no question in this exercise, for example, the population of Jakarta, Indonesia in 1995: Eleven million, one hundred fifty-one thousand. In doing this exercise with a partner, they need to alternate; Person A answers Question 1, Person B Question 2, Person A Question 3, and so on. Encourage them to answer in complete sentences. For questions about population, they can answer using either the 1995 or 2000 numbers, whichever year is closer to the year in

which you use the book. Walk around the room as they do this exercise in case students need help.

Answers: 1. 29,971,000 (in the year 2000)
2. 25,354,000 (in 2000)   3. 27,872,000
(in 2000)   4. 8,985   5. 45,953   6. 79,594
7. 247,004   8. 5,956,000 (in 2000)
9. 122,033

p. 5, Writing Activity

Give students 15–20 minutes to write this letter, or assign it for homework if you're short of time. This should give students the opportunity to use some of the new vocabulary from this section of the chapter while practicing simple letter format. For this chapter, have students begin with

Dear_____,
(the name of a friend who is not from their own city) and end with

Sincerely,

+ their signature

They should write one paragraph in the body of this letter. Before they begin to write, show them paragraph form (indentation, margins) on the blackboard. You can either collect these and check them or have students exchange letters and read each other's. In either case, students should have a separate section in their notebooks in which they collect all of their writing. In this way, they can better see their own progress.

Part Two

p. 6, Making Predictions

The ability to think ahead and make predictions about a reading passage before actually reading is an important skill for all students to acquire. For this reason, there are pre-reading questions in Parts One and Two of all chapters in this book. If students do not approach reading material as "empty vessels" but instead have some expectations about it, they will understand more and retain it longer. It doesn't matter if students incorrectly anticipate information in the reading; the reading process naturally involves both confirming and adjusting prior beliefs. In this section in Chapter One, students can briefly discuss the picture with a partner, or you might ask volunteers to answer the questions. Add any questions that seem relevant. (In this case, for example, you might ask students which signs they can understand or how they know which country this is in.)

p. 6, Reading

As in Part One, have students read silently as you either read the passage aloud or play the cassette. Don't interrupt the reading to answer questions or explain anything. When students finish reading, you can either have them do the exercises that follow or see if they have any questions first. You might ask if they have questions about vocabulary. (Although there is a vocabulary building section, there is no exercise on guessing meaning from context in Part Two.) You can probably expect students to ask about the words *olive* and *sycamore*. If they do, don't simply translate these words for them or show them pictures; this is a good opportunity, instead, for you to point out what they already know from the context—that these are both trees—and tell them that they don't need to know exactly what kind of trees. The ability to accept some amount of uncertainty, like guessing meaning from context, is an important reading skill and one which you need to reinforce frequently.

p. 7, Culture Note

With this culture note, and all others in the book, you'll need to decide how your students would benefit most. You can have students discuss the information or questions with a partner, in small groups, or in the class as a whole; alternatively, you can have them write a paragraph about it in the journal section of their notebooks (see Part Four Teaching Tips). Or, if you're short of time, you can simply have them read the culture note and think about it.

pp. 7–8, Ex. 1

Have students work individually to find the places on the map. They'll need to turn back and forth from the reading to the map and write letters (from the map) on the lines. This exercise is basically a comprehension check focusing on prepositions of place.

Answers: D = Indonesian family's house; E = Japanese restaurant; A = Chinese church; C = park; B = Colombian family's house

pp. 8-9, Ex. 2 and 3

Exercise 2 introduces students to some common written directions that they'll see later in this book and in others. Read through these directions with the students before having them do Exercise 3, in which they practice following these same kinds of directions. Students should do Exercise 3 individually before you go over their answers with them. To give students additional practice and to reinforce reading with listening, you might give them some similar oral directions to follow.

Answers: 1. Circle Tokyo.   2. Copy Etsuko. 3. Underline restaurant.   4. Circle Mexican.   5. Answers will vary. 6. Capitalize the word Colombia.

p. 9, Ex. 4

In a simple way, Exercise 4 introduces the concept of categorizing. Following the examples, students find words (in the first box) that belong in each category or group in the second box. Have them put a check mark by each word in the first box after they've copied it.

Answers: Countries: Indonesia, Colombia, Japan; Trees: sycamore, elm, olive; Person (or Thing) from a Country: Italian, Mexican, Indonesian, American, Moroccan, Korean, Armenian, Japanese; Buildings: church, drugstore, apartment building, flower shop

p. 9, Ex. 5

Again, students should work individually to choose the correct word from the box for each blank.

Answers: 1. crowded   2. building   3. next 4. neighbors   5. front   6. different

p. 10, Ex. 6

In small groups, students answer the questions orally. Encourage them to "stretch," i.e., say as much as they possibly can instead of just giving short answers. You might have them choose a group secretary (a different person for each discussion) to make notes about their answers. If you have students of different nationalities in your class, make sure that there are at least two languages represented in each group, if possible. There is much more incentive for a student to practice speaking English if the other group members don't speak his or her own language; the discussion then becomes more natural, more "real."

Part Three

pp. 10–11, Scanning for Information
Students refer to the change of address form to complete the three sentences in the exercise. Have each student do this individually and then compare answers with another student before you go over the answers with them. For the culture note, follow the same suggestions for the culture note in Part Two. If you're teaching in the United States and this postal form is relevant to your class, you might bring in some change of address forms from your local post office for students to practice filling out.

Answers: 1. a. one person
2. c. Greenwich   3. a. December 4, 1992

Part Four

pp. 11–12, Getting Started
To prepare students to write one paragraph in Exercise 2 and another in Exercise 3, go over the boxed prepositions of place with the class. You might also put a small neighborhood map on the chalkboard with various buildings such as school, movie theater, bookstore, gas station, and video shop. Have students ask and answer questions about these buildings with a partner (e.g., Where's the movie theater?). Then, in Exercise 1, students should work individually and write answers to the questions on p. 12 by referring to the map and other information on p. 11. After you've gone over the answers with them, have each student use these answers to write a paragraph about Elena Paz in Exercise 2. Although the lines on the page are meant to guide students toward using paragraph form (indentations, margins), you should also tell them not to begin each new sentence on a new line but, instead, to continue on the same line. Make sure that they write in complete sentences. Exercise 3 is

also preparation for a paragraph, this time about themselves. The first three questions are self-explanatory. For the fourth question, have students write about four to five buildings in their neighborhood, beginning with their own house or apartment; remind them to use the prepositional phrases that they've already practiced in this chapter.

Answers: Ex. 1—1. Elena Paz /
Cuernavaca, Mexico   2. Chicago, Illinois
3. a student   4. on the corner of Clark and
North (or North and Clark)   5. a park
6. Bill's Bookstore

Ex. 2—Answers will vary somewhat but should be based on the information in Exercise 1.

p. 13, Writing Task
Using their notes from Exercise 3, students write a paragraph about themselves. As in Exercise 2, they should use paragraph form and complete sentences. When they finish, don't collect or correct students' writing. (They will edit it themselves in the next section.)

pp. 13-14, Editing Practice
Go through the boxed information on punctuation with students to make sure they understand everything. Then have them correct the mistakes in the paragraph in Exercise 4. They should look for and correct only mistakes in punctuation and capitalization.

Ex. 4, Corrected paragraph
My name is Nikos Samarakis. I'm from Athens, Greece. Now my home is in Dallas, Texas. My house is on Flower Street. It is across from a Chinese restaurant. I'm a student at the school on the corner. My classmates are from many countries. We're in an English class. English is necessary at school because nobody there speaks my language.

p. 14, Ex. 5

The students will now use the editing checklist to go back and correct their own paragraph from the Writing Task on p. 13. Although many students expect the teacher to correct everything they do in class, students need to begin, even at this early level, to understand the importance of self-correction. The better able they are to find and correct their own errors, the more independent they will be of their ESL books, classes, and teachers.

p. 14, Sharing Your Writing

In this section, students exchange and read each other's paragraphs. The point in this chapter is not to have students edit each other's work but instead to read for content and orally answer the few questions.

p. 14, Journal Writing

In each chapter of this book, there are journal writing assignments. Students should either keep a thin, separate notebook just for their journal entries or have a separate section in their three-ring binders for this same purpose. The choice of topic for each journal entry is related to the chapter theme. Students should write about their chosen topic without worrying about mechanics or grammar; in this way, journal writing is different from other writing assignments in the book. You can decide whether to have students (1) correct their own journal entries, as a review, at a later date, when they have some distance from them; (2) exchange and read each other's journal entries; (3) show their journals to you periodically; or (4) simply keep them as their own personal writing. If you decide to have students share their journal entries with you, it's important to make clear the fact that this is not for a grade. Students need to feel free to express themselves in their journals. You can grade them on other writing.

Chapter Two: Shopping—A National Pastime?

Part One

pp. 16–17, Getting Started

As in Chapter One, ask for student volunteers to answer the two questions. A number of answers are acceptable. For Item 1, students might tell you: The woman is at home / at her desk / in her office. She's on the phone / talking on the phone / having coffee / shopping from home. For Item 2, students will probably say that the people are at the market / at the supermarket / at (in) a store / at (in) a grocery store. The young man is saying, "Paper or plastic?" The man is answering, "No! Please use this." You can add any questions you want.

pp. 17-18, Reading

Have students read the three paragraphs silently as you either read aloud or play the cassette. Don't stop to explain anything or answer questions at this point.

p. 18, Ex. 1

In Exercise 1, students check to see if they've understood the main topic of the reading. Distinct from a main idea, the main topic (or subject) of a reading passage is simply a noun or noun phrase—not a sentence. It's probably too early to explain the difference to your students, however. In Exercise 1, after students have circled the letter of the answer (B), ask them why the other answers are incorrect. They should tell you that A and C are not important. (At this point you might teach the word *details*.) Answer D is not correct because this topic (subject) is not even in the reading passage.

Answer: b

pp. 18-19, New Words

As in Chapter One, the boxed explanation of another way to guess meaning from context will seem obvious to teachers; what could be more clear than a definition of a word in parentheses immediately after the new word? However, to students still clinging to their bilingual dictionaries, it's an important step toward trusting their own judgment. In

Exercise 2, have students work alone to write the answers. Check these answers with them before having them do Exercise 3—again, on their own. Exercise 3 (Details) checks both vocabulary and comprehension. Students identify items good or bad for the environment.

> Answers: Ex. 2—1. things in a supermarket
> 2. the air, land, and water around us
> 3. use them again and again for years
> 4. wash them   5. things in a store
> 6. babies
> Ex. 3—G (good): 2, 4, 6; B (bad): 1, 3, 5

p. 19, Ex. 4

If students can correctly circle the letter of the phrase to complete the sentence (C), they are demonstrating both that they are able to make an inference and have understood the main idea of the reading.

p. 19, Ex. 5

In this very short discussion, students just turn to the person next to them and answer the questions. You can walk around to be available in case students have a question.

p. 20, Writing Activity

Have students begin their one-paragraph letter with "Dear _____," (your name). For guidelines on doing this exercise, see Teaching Tips for Chapter One, p. 5.

p. 20, Culture Note

Follow the suggestions for doing culture note sections (Teaching Tips, Chapter One, p. 7).

Part Two

p. 20, Making Predictions

Either have students read the cartoon silently or read the dialog aloud as students read silently. Students should tell you that the woman has a problem with shopping / buys things that she doesn't need, etc. Ask the students if they sometimes buy "stupid" things on sale. You might teach some language for bargains: "It's usually_____, but it's on sale for only _____."

p. 21, Reading

Students read silently as you either read aloud or play the tape. As with previous readings, don't stop to explain or answer questions.

p. 21, Culture Note

To do the culture note, follow the guidelines for culture notes for Chapter One (Teaching Tips, Chapter One, p. 7).

pp. 22-23, Following Directions

As in Chapter One, students first see examples of common directions (Exercise 1) and then practice these directions in Exercise 2. After you read through the directions with students (Exercise 1), have students do Exercise 2 alone. You'll notice that Item 1 is a simple categorizing task.

> Answers: 1. Check: groceries, shirt, pants, products, clothing   2. Cross out: plastic
> 3. b. groceries;   a. again and again;
> c. mail order catalog   4. Draw lines from: diapers to things for babies to wear; environment to the air, land, and water around us; products to things in stores

p. 24, Ex. 3

Have students work alone to find and circle the six words. You might do this as a game; the student who correctly finds and circles all six wins the game. If students ask you what they'll win, tell them "love, happiness, peace," and so on, using any very positive nouns that they already know. They'll grin, and you won't have to bring candy to class.

Answers: Circle these words:
1. wearable, 2. understandable, 3. likeable, 4. liveable, 5. loveable

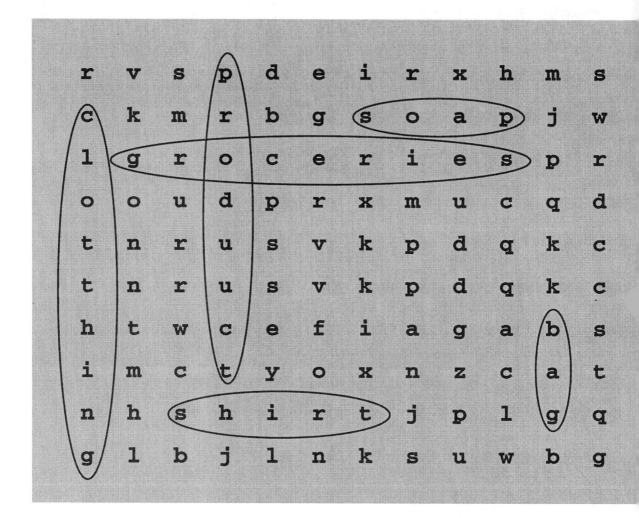

pp. 24-25, Understanding New Words

The boxed explanation introduces the concept of stems and affixes (without using those words). Exercise 4, to be done by students on their own, extends vocabulary without tedious memorization.

Answers: 1. wearable   2. understandable
3. likable   4. livable   5. lovable

p. 25, Ex. 5

Follow the suggestions for previous discussion tasks. When students finish answering these questions with a partner, bring the class back together and have students share their answers with the whole class. In a very small class, everyone can have a chance to speak (in which case the discussion with the partner was practice). In a large class, ask for a few volunteers to tell the class the same thing they told their partners.

Part Three

p. 25, Mail Order Catalogs

This would be a good time to bring in outside materials. You could bring in any mail-order catalogs that you think would be of high interest to your students. Have them work in groups with them and each select one thing they would like to order.

If you can, make an overhead transparency of the catalog page from p. 25 so that you can point at the pictures and make sure everyone understands the vocabulary (spray, chemicals, cleaner, shopping bag).

p. 26, Ex. 1

Have students work alone or in groups and decide what the words mean.

Answers: 1. c   2. e   3. b   4. a   5. d

p. 26, Ex. 2

This is a beginning-level sentence combining exercise that practices connecting two independent clauses with *because*.

Answers: 2. You're not going to need five or six chemical cleaners because Dr. Clean cleans everything in your house.
3. Insects are going to run away because they don't like chili-garlic spray.   4. You're going to say, "No paper or plastic" because you have a canvas shopping bag.

pp. 26–27, Using Order Forms

Once again, using a transparency is helpful—you can point to the picture of "Joe" and show that is he ordering from a catalog, and thinking about a variety of items. You can ask the class to describe (orally) what the items are and how many he wants.

p. 26, Ex. 3

Students fill out the order form for "Joe."

Answers: insect spray—quantity 2, total $5.00; canvas bag —quantity 2, total $8.00; hand soap—quantity 4, total $4.00; home cleaner—quantity 3, total $6.75; Total Amount $32.75

p. 27, Ex. 4

Students complete the personal information. If your class is not in the U.S., you may want to change this to reflect local postal address forms. The total amount is $32.75.

p. 27, Culture Note

If your class is not in the U.S., you might want to take this opportunity to discuss U.S. money a little. Compare the value of dollars and some of the simple forms of U.S. money (nickels, dimes, quarters, etc.) with your local currency. Likewise, you can ask students in the U.S. to compare U.S. currency with the currency in their native countries.

Part Four

p. 27, Getting Started

To focus on the use of the future form with *be going to*, the students should begin by underlining the six examples from the reading. This is to focus their attention on the form and also to give multiple examples in a real context.

p. 28, Ex. 1

You can introduce the pictures by asking for several student volunteers to form sentences orally, first. In this way, the exercise will be easier when they actually write. Again, a transparency is useful here.

Answers: 2. On Tuesday, she's going to mail her order to Sunshine Company. 3. On Wednesday, she's going to spray the garden with chili-garlic spray. 4. On Thursday, she's going to wash the clothes. 5. On Friday, she's going to go to the movies. 6. On Saturday, she's going to visit Mom and Dad.

pp. 28-29, Ex. 2

Students should write down phrases with a simple form of the verb. This is so that they can easily connect it with *be going to* in Exercise 3. Note that answers will vary.

p. 29, Ex. 3

Students use the phrases from Exercise 2 to make sentences in the future using *I'm going to . . .* Note that answers will vary, but all should include correct forms of *be going to.*

p. 29, Ex. 4

Students write down, almost like a dictation, three of the sentences their partner has written.

p. 29, Writing Task

Students write about their vacation plans—they should use at least some sentences using *be going to* for the future. Note that answers will vary.

p. 30, Editing Practice

Common problems with *be going to* include leaving out the verb *be* completely and not having subject / verb agreement.

p. 30, Ex. 5

Answers: I'm going to have a busy weekend. On Saturday, I'm going to meet my friend. My friend and I are going to go shopping. He's going to buy a new TV. I'm going to buy a new stereo system. Saturday night we're going to go out to eat at a restaurant.

p. 30, Ex. 6

Have students correct their own writing using the checklist. If you have time, you might want to have them write the finished work on a separate piece of paper and hand it in to you. Then you can correct it and give it back.

p. 30, Sharing Your Writing

Students don't correct this—they just read and talk about it.

p. 31, Journal Writing

Remember, if you correct this, you should only comment, not correct all the spelling and grammar mistakes. We're trying to encourage fluency and communication.

Chapter Three: Friends and Family

Part One

pp. 34–35, Getting Started

With the whole class, have students volunteer to answer the questions about the pictures. The picture of the extended family will give you an opportunity to review (or teach) vocabulary for family members; you can extend their vocabulary by adding terms such as great aunt, great uncle, and so on. Be sure not to explain the terms *nuclear family, single-parent family*, and *extended family*. These will be taught in the New Words section.

pp. 34-35, Reading

Follow the same suggestions for doing this reading as for readings in Chapters One and Two.

p. 36, Ex. 1

After students circle the letters of the correct answers for Items 1 and 2, you might have volunteers explain why the other answers are not correct in Item 1; students should tell you that A is a detail, not the main idea, and C is not in the reading at all.

Answers: 1. b 2. a

p. 37, New Words

Again, students learn a specific technique to guess meaning from context—in this case, using pictures with captions. Students will turn back to the pictures on pp. 34-35 to choose the correct answers in Exercise 2.

Answers: Ex. 2—1. b   2. a   3. c

p. 37, Ex. 3

This is the first reference exercise in the book. Before having students do Exercise 3, put a few easy examples on the board; underline the pronoun (or possessive adjective as in Item 3) and circle the noun or noun phrase to which it refers. Possible examples for you to put on the board are: There is my father. He is standing next to my brother. My sisters are sitting at the table in this picture. They look happy. Have students work alone to complete Exercise 3 as in the example(s).

Answers: 1. fifty to a hundred people
2. most men   3. many married women
4. some people   5. the new families

pp. 37–38, Ex. 4

Follow the same guidelines as for Chapter One, Discussing the Reading (Ex. 6), p. 10.

p. 38, Writing Activity and Culture Note

Follow the same suggestions as in Chapter Two.

Part Two

pp. 38–39, Making Predictions

Have students make predictions about the reading passage that follows by answering questions about the three pictures. They should answer these questions with the class as a whole. First, have students give you as many words for family members as they can (e.g., grandparents, aunts, uncles, nieces, nephews, grandchildren), and put these words on the board. Then have students tell you what the people are doing. To do this, they should use the present continuous tense. (For example: Some people are sitting at a table. One guy is wearing sunglasses. A young woman is barbecuing / is cooking. A girl is holding a baby.)

pp. 39-40, Reading

Follow the same guidelines for this reading passage as you did for previous readings. As usual, don't answer students' questions about vocabulary (such as the word *reunion* in the title) at this point.

p. 40, Culture Note

To this you might add another, optional, piece of cultural information: Every five, ten, twenty, and thirty years many people go to a high school or college reunion. This usually lasts for one evening. At this reunion, there is dinner, music, and dancing, but the main purpose of a high school or college reunion is simply to see old friends and acquaintances and to catch up on the news. Ask students if this happens in their country.

pp. 40, Ex. 1

Exercise 1 is a reading comprehension task. Students should do this on their own. When they're finished, go over their answers with them.

Because there is no New Words section in Part Two, you might give students a chance to ask about vocabulary at this point, after the reading and the comprehension exercise. However, instead of answering students' questions directly, try to ask them a short series of questions to guide them to guess the meaning of a new word themselves, if it is at all possible to guess from the context. For example, if a students ask about the word reunion, have them look at the first paragraph. Then ask them, "What do people (in this family) do every summer? Where do they come from? What do they do at the reunion? Why do they come together?" You might then extend this and ask, "Do all families have reunions? Why not? Why are reunions important for some families?" etc.

Answers: 1. b   2. a   3. b   4. c

pp. 41-42, Dictionary Use—Alphabetizing

In order to use a dictionary, students need to (1) know the order of letters in the alphabet and (2) be able to alphabetize. Even at intermediate levels, some students have difficulty with this because they never mastered it in a beginning-level class. These are the students who lean over to another student and ask "What page?" instead of looking up a word themselves whenever the class is working in a dictionary. This practice should lead them to depend on themselves instead of another student.

Read through the boxed explanation and examples with students. Add more examples if your students need them. Then give them about 30 seconds to do Exercise 2. Watch them very carefully as they do this. If you notice a few students having trouble writing out the alphabet, talk with them at break time or after class (not in front of other students) and tell them to practice writing out the alphabet for homework as many times as necessary until they can do it correctly in about 30 seconds. Exercise 3 has been carefully sequenced and must be done in order. Have students work on this alone. If you want, you can predict how much time it should take your students to do each box and time them with a stopwatch. Alternatively, you can make this into a game; the person who finishes all boxes first—and correctly—is the winner. Speed is essential if students are to use a dictionary efficiently.

Answers: Ex. 2—a b c d e f g h i j k l m n o p q r s t u v w x y z

Ex. 3—1. 3 2 4 1
2. 3 2 1 4
3. 2 1 4 3
4. 4 full; 5 marriage; 6 world; 2 environment; 1 change; 3 fire
5. 4 together; 8 visit; 6 trees; 5 traditional; 2 group; 9 volleyball; 3 guy; 7 very; 1 groceries
6. 12 special; 1 almost; 5 cry; 8 husband; 6 cultural; 9 reunion; 3 aunt; 10 safe; 7 hotel; 2 alone; 4 come; 11 shirt

pp. 42-43, Ex. 4
You may find that many students have never worked a crossword puzzle before, certainly not one in English. If this is the case, make sure they understand across and down; then show them how to follow the clues on p. 43, find a word to match the clue (in the box on p. 42), and put the word into the squares in the puzzle. Do one or two clues from each column with the class. Then have students work on their own to fill in the rest of the squares of the crossword puzzle.

Answers: Across—2. team   5. relatives
7. aunt   8. picnic   10. fire   11. night
14. parent
Down—1. lake   3. eat   4. divorce
5. reunion   6. lot   9. cousin   12. to
13. far

p. 44, Ex. 5
Although the directions for Exercise 5 tell students to work in a small group, you might, instead, have them all pick up their books and a pencil and walk around the room to find five students to interview. There is something wonderfully energizing to students about physically moving around a classroom and gathering information. Make sure that as students do this, they ask and answer the questions in English. They'll fill in answers on the chart in note form, not complete sentences.

Part Three

pp. 45, Scanning for Information
Use the pictures to introduce this section and to discuss all the vocabulary that will be necessary here—*furnished* and *unfurnished*, *bedrooms*, *building*, *pets*, *refrigerator*, *stove*, *yard*. You could also talk about other vocabulary items that appear in the picture. Again, it's very useful to have the pictures on an overhead projector.

p. 46, Ex. 1
To introduce the ads, you might want to bring in a classified section of a newspaper, either in the student's language or in English. Then look at the sample ads on p. 46. Discuss the abbreviations and make sure students can understand them. Now have them work alone or in groups and put the telephone number in the ad next to the description that would best suit the person described.

Answers: 1. 555-4826   2. 555-3211
3. 555-9277   4. 555-6138   5. 555-6292

p. 47, Ex. 2
If your students don't live in the U.S., you may want to skip over this part. If you can put this up on an overhead, you can call attention to the various parts. Then have students answer the questions below.

Part Four

p. 48, Getting Started

Again, the first step here is to have students look back at the reading on pp. 39-40 and find the 24 verbs that are in the simple present tense. Call attention to the ones that have the third person singular marker (*s* or *es*).

p. 48, Ex. 1 and Ex. 2

Students fill in the information about themselves, then circulate around the room and interview a classmate and fill in the information about that person.

p. 49, Ex. 3

This is an authentic piece of writing from an ESL student in Los Angeles. It is here to serve as a model for the student writing that follows.

p. 49, Ex. 4

Students pick out three things from the reading that they think are interesting. These will vary.

Possible answers: She lives in Los Angeles.
She works in a factory decorating clothes.
She likes to read books.

p. 49, Ex. 5

Here the students should pick four things about themselves that they would want to tell someone—this is building to a pen-pal letter on the next page, so it is really a "brainstorming" or pre-writing activity.

p. 50, Writing Task

This can be done simply as an exercise, but it would be far more interesting to actually have students find pen-pals (this can be done either with regular mail or e-mail). The continuing communication could be a source of language development throughout the semester.

p. 50, Editing Practice

This is a focus on using details to make writing more interesting and vivid. When you help your students, try to stress that they should include as many details as possible—that rather than saying "He was nice," it is far more interesting to say, "He said 'hello' to me every day with a big smile."

pp. 50-51, Ex. 6

Students rewrite these sentences and add details to make the sentences more interesting. You can have them use their own information, or make up imaginary information (e.g., I like classical music, especially the music of Handel. I like string quartets.)

p. 51, Ex. 7

The students go back to their writing from Ex. 1, p. 48 and try to add details and interest to their sentences there.

p. 51, Ex. 8

Students go back to their pen-pal letter (p. 50) and use their new information to rewrite it. Use the editing check list.

p. 52, Sharing Your Writing

Students read each other's work for communication, not to correct or criticize.

p. 52, Journal Writing

See previous chapters for details.

Chapter Four: Health Care

Part One

pp. 54–55

As in Chapters One–Three, have students volunteer to answer the questions about the pictures. For Question 3, students will tell you that the woman is running, which is correct, but you can add a vocabulary word for them to use, instead—jogging. To answer Question 4 in complete sentences, students will need to use verbs. *Exercise* and *study* are used as nouns in the pictures but are also verbs; *exercise* and *study* are sufficient. But for the other two pictures, students need to add verbs—*eat* and *meditate*: eat good food and meditate.

pp. 55–56, Reading

Follow the same suggestions for doing this reading as for readings in previous chapters.

p. 56, Culture Note

As in previous chapters, the questions that follow this culture point can be answered orally or in writing. You can extend the culture point by telling students that elderly Americans and Canadians sometimes don't begin jogging until they are well over sixty, but most who do jog report that they feel healthier and younger than they did twenty or thirty years earlier.

pp. 56-57

By circling the letter of the correct answer in Ex. 1 (d), students demonstrate that they understand the main idea of the reading passage. In Ex. 2, students work alone to identify the main idea of each paragraph in the passage. To do this, they'll need to turn back to the reading.

Answer: Ex. 1—d

Answers: Ex. 2— C; A; B; D

pp. 57–58, New Words

Again, the context clues to help students guess the meaning of a new word will seem obvious to the teacher, but students need constant encouragement if they are to be pried loose from their grip on the dictionary. Go through the boxed explanation with the students, and then give them a few minutes to write the answers to Ex. 3 on their own. Go through the second boxed explanation with them. You might add a few more sample sentences on the board; to truly focus on the task of figuring out a new word from the examples of it, use nonsense words. (Example: They have a lot of geblits—for example, dogs and cats. / We traveled to several emplubs such as Tokyo, Seoul, and Bangkok.) Give students a minute to write the answers to Ex. 4.

Answers: Ex. 3—1. too old 2. doctors for older people 3. think 4. a boxer

Answers: Ex. 4—1. swimmers, baseball players, and jockeys 2. swim, walk, play tennis, dance, or play a team sport

p. 58, Ex. 5

If necessary, students can turn back to the reading to find the answers to Ex. 5, but it shouldn't really be necessary. If students can correctly choose the activities of healthy people, they've demonstrated that they understand the important details in the reading.

Answers: Put check marks by: 3, 4, 6, 7

p. 58, Ex. 6

As the directions indicate, students should work in small groups to answer these questions. (Add any questions that you feel are relevant to your class.) At this point—if not before—you need to encourage students to make sure that every person in the group both speaks and listens to others when they speak. Aim for balance.

Note: Tell students to be sure to bring their dictionaries to class on the day you plan to do Part Two of this chapter.

Part Two

p. 59, Making Predictions

Before taking the health test, students simply write the one-word answer (good, average, or bad) to the prediction question, either in their books or on a piece of paper.

pp. 59–60, Reading

The reading in Part Two is actually a short self-test on health. This is not, of course, a test for a grade but is, instead, the kind of test we might find in a magazine. Students usually like this sort of test, and because it's "real" to them (they can find out the general state of their health), there is an incentive to doing the reading; this is not just English for the sake of English. Give students sufficient time to work alone and circle the letters of their answers. The only new word in the test might be *overweight*, but students should be able to guess the meaning from the picture. At the end of the test, students add up their scores, which are not meant to be "announced" to the class (but there are usually some students who volunteer—loudly—to do so!).

p. 60, Writing Activity

For this activity, follow the same guidelines as in previous chapters. To write this short letter, students should use their answers on the test as a basis. Before they write, put the phrases *too much, too many*, and *not enough* on the board.

p. 61, Ex. 1

This discussion with a partner allows students to practice reading (their partner's answers), speaking, and listening.

p. 61, Culture Note

Follow the same guidelines as in previous chapters. If students say that more people are beginning to smoke in their countries, ask them why.

pp. 61-62, Dictionary Use—Guide Words

Before doing this section, tell students about the steps to go through whenever they encounter a new word: (1) Try to guess the meaning from the context. (2) If you can guess, don't use a dictionary. (3) If you can't guess anything, you need to decide how important the word is. If it's not very important (to your understanding of the paragraph), don't worry about it. Just keep reading. (4) If you can't understand the paragraph without the new word, use a dictionary.

Even at this level, you can encourage students to use a monolingual dictionary. Recommend a simple learner's dictionary produced by an ESL / EFL publisher. At the very least, have several copies of such a dictionary available in the classroom, for students to use. Exercises 2-4 will give students practice in using guide words to find a new word quickly. Important: If students are using a dictionary that has no guide words, have them look at the first word and last word on the dictionary page, instead. Each student should work alone to complete Exercises 2-4. Ideally, in Ex. 4 all students should have a copy of the same dictionary, but this may not be possible. If they are working in the same dictionary, it's important that students not peer at another student's dictionary to find the right page; this would defeat the purpose of the exercise.

Answers: Ex. 3—1. no 2. yes 3. yes
4. no 5. yes 6. yes 7. yes 8. no

p. 62, Ex. 5

This is another sort of task in categorizing. Have students work on their own to cross out the word that doesn't belong in each group. When everyone is finished, go over their answers with them. In each case, after everyone has agreed on the word to cross out, ask them "why?" In other words, have students tell you why the other three words in each group belong together.

Answers: 1. friend 2. glass 3. dance
4. candy 5. overweight 6. walk 7. fish
8. begin

Part Three

Note: If your students don't live in the U.S., you might want to skip this section.

p. 63

This is a place to explain about the use of the emergency 911 numbers. You might also want to give your students the number of the local police station for non-emergency calls.

pp. 64–65, Ex. 1

You could use the pictures and vocabulary to discuss these emergencies in more depth, and ask students to share personal stories about having noisy neighbors, having someone break into their house, etc.

Answers : 3. It's an emergency. 4. Yes, she should. 5. It's a non-emergency. OR It isn't an emergency. 6. No, he shouldn't. 7. It's an emergency. 8. Yes, she should.

p. 65, Ex. 2

This is a chance to do some oral reinforcement of the writing. More advanced students should be encouraged to make up as many new situations as they can.

p. 65, Reading Get-Well Cards

This is a good chance to bring "realia" or real items into the classroom. You could bring in an assortment of typical cards, including the silly sort. Pass them around or make a transparency of them and show the class on the overhead projector. You could discuss the different ways of acknowledging or celebrating special events like birthdays in various cultures.

p. 66, Ex. 4
Answers 2. c   3. a   4. e   5. d

p. 66, Ex. 5
Answers: 2. a   3. d   4. c

p. 66, Ex. 6:
Answers: 2. George must take one capsule after every meal.   3. George must take one teaspoonful before bed.   4. George must take two tablespoonfuls four times a day. He must not take them with food.

Part Four

p. 67, Getting Started
The modal auxiliaries add information about the speaker's state of mind or beliefs—that is the difference between using the modals and other forms. The future with *be going to*, for example, adds no "opinion" of the speaker, but only states a fact: *I'm going to be there.* Using the modal *will*, however, adds an element that the speaker is sure of this, that the person believes this will definitely happen in the future, and therefore is often used in promises: *I will be there.*

p. 67, Ex. 1
Answers: 2. People should exercise their minds (or study, read and talk with people).   3. People should eat a lot of vegetables and fruits and not much meat or sugar.   4. People should relax.

pp. 67-68, Ex. 2
There are no correct answers. The verb, however, should be in the simple form (To have money you should <u>work</u> hard).

p. 68, Ex. 3
This can be done in groups—students tell each other their advice and the others copy it down. Or, you could have students walk around the room and collect various pieces of advice.

p. 68, Ex. 4
People often write New Year's resolutions just before the end of a year on December 31. They are a list of things a person wants to do better in their life the coming year. They are promises to yourself. This would be a good place to have students discuss various different New Year's customs. Then, make corrections in the exercise.

Corrected paragraph:
<u>This</u> year I will be healthier. I won't <u>eat</u> donuts every morning. <u>I</u> won't drink six cups of coffee a day—<u>I'll drink</u> only one. I <u>won't</u> smoke. I <u>will sleep</u> eight hours every night. I <u>will walk</u> two miles every day. And most of all, <u>I</u> won't worry about anything.

p. 69, Writing Task
If you want to stress correctness, you should have the students write a rough draft of this on a piece of paper. Then you can go over it with the student and make corrections and they can rewrite it into the book.

p. 69, Ex. 5
Students edit using the checklist before they complete their final draft.

Chapter Five: Men and Women

Part One

pp. 72-73, Getting Started
Do as in previous chapters. Additionally, you can ask students if the situations in the two cartoons (pictures) sometimes happen with their family or friends.

pp. 73-74, Reading
Do as in previous chapters. You'll notice that students have a chance to review the various techniques for guessing meaning from context that they've already studied, in addition to learning a new technique.

p. 75, Ex. 1

Have students do Ex. 1 on their own. Their answers should be based on information they learned in the reading, not on what they believe about communication styles in their own culture.

Answers: 1. M   2. W   3. W   4. M   5. W
6. M

pp. 75-76, New Words

Ex. 2 is a review of previously learned techniques—using examples and words in parentheses to guess a new word. Have students do this exercise on their own. Read through the boxed explanation with students; then have them do Ex. 3 on their own.

Answers: Ex. 2—1. b   2. c   3. e   4. a
5. d

Answers: Ex. 3—1. different   2. good things about themselves   3. do things

p. 76, Culture Note

At this point, students should simply think about the answer to the question, in preparation for the discussion that follows. (They'll answer this in Question 4 below.)

p. 76, Ex. 4

If possible, have an equal number of male and female students in each small discussion group. Questions 1 and 2 can be answered quickly, but students will need more time for Question 3 and especially 4. At the end of the discussion, have the secretary or recorder from each group report to the class as a whole on the group's answers to Questions 3 and 4.

Part Two

p. 77, Making Predictions

The concept of "talk therapy" or marriage counseling might be quite alien to your students. They might recognize the stereotypical Freudian psychologist in the picture but not know the word. You can give them the terms psychologist, psychiatrist, marriage counselor, and therapist. If anyone asks, you can tell them that a psychiatrist is the same as a psychologist but has a medical degree and can prescribe drugs, which a psychologist can't.

People in many countries don't frequent therapists as much as Americans seem to. You may need to explain that therapists are not just for "crazy people" but instead often help people (for just a few weeks or months) who are going through an especially difficult time—a crisis.

p. 77, Reading

Do as in previous chapters.

p. 78, Culture Note

Students can either discuss this or write about it. Or, if you're short of time, they can simply think about it at this point and add it to their discussion at the end of Part Two.

p. 78, About the Reading

Students can turn back to the reading in order to do Exercises 1 and 2, if necessary.

Answers: Ex. 1—Put check marks by 2, 3, 4

Answers: Ex. 2—Put check marks by 2, 3, 4

pp. 78-79, Reading Speed

Go through the explanation with students. They should read the examples silently, however, because it isn't possible to read aloud the second example (of words in phrases). After doing Ex. 3, if you want to give your students additional practice, have them go back to any previous reading, pencil in hand, and read it silently (and quickly), putting little slash marks between logical phrases. Point out that there may be several different places to break phrases.

p. 79, Building Vocabulary

Have students work on their own to do Ex. 4 and 5. You'll notice that Ex. 4 is as much a part-of-speech and grammar exercise as it is vocabulary. Check and discuss (if necessary) their answers before going on to Ex. 6.

Answers: Ex. 4—1. b   2. a   3. d   4. b
Answers: Ex. 5—1. S   2. D   3. S   4. S
5. D   6. D

p. 80, Ex. 6

Do as in previous chapters. This discussion should provide ideas for the writing assignment (the letter) that follows.

p. 80, Writing Activity

Students can write this one-paragraph letter either in class or for homework. Encourage them, as always, to use as much of their new vocabulary as possible.

Part Three

p. 80, Scanning for Information

This is a chance to discuss wedding ceremonies in various cultures. You might want to focus on the recent wedding of a celebrity—perhaps you could even bring some TV footage to class.

p. 81, Ex. 1

Answers: 2. c   3. b   4. b   5. c

p. 81, Culture Note

Americans do not give gifts as often as many cultures. When visiting for dinner, we often bring a bottle of wine or dessert. However, when we receive a gift it is very nice to write a note of thank you. The general rule of thumb is to say thank you and then to say something about the gift—some special feature it has, or how we will use it.

pp. 81–82, Ex. 2

Answers: 1. a blanket   2. a toaster
3. a teapot   4. a microwave   5. a flower vase   6. a coffee maker

p. 82, Ex. 3

Answers: 2. a   3. e   4. c   5. d

pp. 82–83, Ex. 5

Students pull the information from the exercises above. More advanced students can improvise and write more extensive notes.

Possible answers: 1. to make toast every morning; (student's name)   2. beautiful / wonderful / etc.; will; to serve tea to our special guests; again; (student's name)
3. beautiful / etc.; will use it to show our flowers; again; (student's name)   4. Dear;

Thank you for the wonderful / beautiful / etc.; We will use it to make coffee every morning. Thanks again, Sincerely, (student's name)

Part Four

p. 84, Getting Started

This focuses on the use of prepositions following a verb (before an object). No one expects students at this level to master this, but the idea is to focus attention on the structure so they will notice and pick them up. You could discuss the differences between using various prepositions after talk—*talk to, talk about, talk around, talk over (one's head), talk down to, talk with.* If you can draw simple illustrations of these (similar to the ones in the chapter) on the board it will help.

p. 84, Ex. 1

Answers: He doesn't talk <u>with</u> me. He talks <u>at</u> me.

p. 84, Ex. 2

Answers: 1. with   2. about   3. about
4. with   5. X

p. 85, Ex. 3

Answers: 1. They met.   2. They were in love.   3. He asked her to marry him.
4. They got married.   5. He never wanted to talk to her about work.   6. They were angry at each other.

p. 86, Ex. 4

This is a pre-writing activity. The students can fill in the names of people they know, or they can make up an imaginary story. They are getting ready for the writing activity to follow.

p. 86, Writing Task

Using the ideas from Ex. 4, students write a story about any two people—real or imagined—who are mad at each other, telling what happened and why.

p. 87, Editing Practice

The important message here is that it is absolutely necessary to rewrite many times. The physical use of space between the lines will help a lot. In the exercise we focus on capitalization and preposition use, but the important message is that the students get accustomed to editing and rewriting their work.

p. 87, Ex. 5

Corrections: <u>Henry's</u> wife is very angry <u>at</u> him. She thinks he doesn't understand her. <u>He</u> never talks <u>with</u> her.

Last night he came home from work and read the newspaper. He didn't talk <u>with</u> his wife at all. Then he washed the car. <u>After</u> that, <u>he</u> watched a baseball game on TV. His wife wanted to talk, but Henry just watched the TV all night.

His wife was angry <u>at</u> Henry. Henry didn't know his wife was angry. He watched the baseball game. He was happy. He was surprised when his wife said, "Henry, <u>I'm</u> really angry."

p. 88, Ex. 6

Students go back and edit their work, using the checklist.

Chapter Six: Native Americans and Immigrants

Part One

pp. 90–91, Getting Started

Do as in previous chapters. In addition to the questions in the book, you can ask students what words they know for the various things coming out of the cornucopia. They might tell you: corn, squash, tomatoes, potatoes, peanuts, chilies, and cotton. If they don't know these words, don't teach them at this point.

pp. 91-92, Reading

Do as in previous chapters.

p. 92, Main Ideas

Ex. 1 checks to see if students understood the main idea of the reading, and Ex. 2 checks for the main idea of each paragraph; students will need to turn back to look at the reading for this task. Have students do these two exercises on their own.

Answers: Ex. 1—2
Answers: Ex. 2—D, A, B, E, C

pp. 92-93, New Words

Go through the two boxed explanations with the class. The phrase *and other* will help students guess words much in the same way that such as *or for example* does. Ex. 3 is very simple. You might just do it orally in a few seconds with the class as a whole.

Answers: 1. Spain, England, and France
2. vegetables

p. 93, Quotation Marks

Students from most countries often misunderstand the use of quotation marks in English. They may know the use of quote marks for a direct quotation, but many students think that quote marks around a single word indicate emphasis, which isn't the case. Go through the boxed explanation with the class, focusing on the second explanation (quote marks around a word used incorrectly). Give students a little time to do Ex. 4 individually; they'll need to turn back to the reading, find words in quote marks, and decide the reason for the quote marks. After they write their answers, discuss these with the class.

Answers:
Words in Quotation Marks
1. "found"
2. "This is silk!"
3. "new"

Reasons for Quotation Marks
1. incorrect word
2. people's words (in their thoughts)
3. incorrect word

p. 94, Culture Note

Do as in previous chapters.

p. 94, Ex. 5

Do as in previous chapters. If you have the time, the equipment, and access to videos, you might bring in a video of a movie about Native Americans such as *Dances With Wolves*. This could be the basis of a series of lessons with much discussion.

p. 94, Writing Activity

If you have brought in a movie, you should have students write their impression of it (or what they learned from it) instead of the topic given in the book.

Part Two

p. 95, Making Predictions

Most students will probably not be able to answer the two questions because they truly don't know anything about Native American life these days. If they do know something, it might be a stereotyped idea, but at this point, that's not a problem. There are no "right" or "wrong" answers before they read. In the reading, they'll acquire more accurate information.

pp. 95–96, Reading

Do as in previous chapters.

p. 98, Ex. 1

Emphasize that Ex. 1 is not a true / false exercise but instead one in which students identify problems. (For this reason, students shouldn't put a check mark by Item 4; it's true but not a problem.)

Answers: Put check marks by: 1, 3, 5, 6

p. 98, Ex. 2

Ex. 2 provides students more practice with reference. It is similar to an exercise in Chapter Three. As in Chapter Three, you may want to put an example or two on the board before students actually do the exercise. Sample sentences might be: The woman visits the reservation several times every year to see her family. / When we eat, we don't realize that many of our foods came from Native American farmers.

Answers: Circle and draw an arrow to:
1. children 2. Earl Dean Sisto 3. The children 4. The Europeans

p. 98, Ex. 3

Ex. 3 is a short vocabulary check. Give students a few minutes to work alone and match the words with their meanings. Make sure students don't use a dictionary.

Answers: 1. c 2. a 3. e 4. b 5. d

p. 99, Ex. 4

This is a vocabulary review of Chapters Five and Six. Since this is the second crossword puzzle in the book, students should already understand how to do it, but just to make sure, you might do Item 1 Across and Item 2 Down with the class. Then give students some time to work alone and figure out the rest of the puzzle.

Answers: Across: 3. clan 5. reservations 7. easy 8. cloth 10. die 12. similar 14. equal

Down: 2. corn 3. cotton 4. friendship 6. Spain 9. million 11. tribe 13. kill 15. up

p. 100, Ex. 5

Do as in previous chapters.

p. 100, Culture Note

Because this immediately follows "Discussing the Reading," you may choose simply to add these questions to the discussion. In addition, this would be a good point to mention to students the importance (in the United States) of 12-step programs such as Alcoholics Anonymous, in which people who have a problem with alcoholism come together voluntarily several times each week, drink a lot of coffee, and talk about their problems. They help each other to stay away from alcohol or drugs, and no other program has been as successful.

Part Three

p. 101, Scanning for Information

You could use various maps of the U.S.—especially any that show geographical features—to tell a little about the geography of the U.S. (for example, that the Southwest is hot and dry and that the East is forested, that the middle of the country is the area of the Great Plains.) The pictures on the map are to aid in explaining the vocabulary (teepee, pottery, etc.).

p. 102, Ex. 1
Answers: 2. No, they didn't. 3. Yes, they are. 4. Yes, they did. 5. Yes, they did. 6. No, they didn't. 7. No, they weren't. 8. Yes, they did.

p. 102, Ex. 2
Answers: 2. They hunted buffalo. 3. They lived in the Southwest. 4. They made beautiful pottery and jewelry. 5. Yes, they did. 6. No, they didn't. 7. They made beautiful pottery and jewelry. 8. They grew corn and other crops.

p. 103, Ex. 3
Answers: 1. a. false b. true c. false d. false 2. a. false b. true c. true d. false 3. a. false b. false c. false d. true

Part Four

p. 104, Getting Started
This focuses on using the forms of the verb to orient yourself in time when reading (and writing). Knowing that the -ed regular past ending on a verb is always past will help. The irregular verbs of course must be memorized, but working on them will help students to recognize them, even if they may not be able to produce them yet.

p. 104, Ex. 1
Answers: 1. present 2. past 3. present 4. past 5. past 6. present 7. present 8. past

p. 105, Ex. 2
Answers: 1. He lived in a cabin. 2. He grew corn and other crops (or any close answer). 3. He hunted. 4. He rode horses. 5. He fished.

p. 106, Ex. 3
Answers: 1. He lives in an apartment building. 2. He buys his food in a supermarket (or anything close). 3. He works in an office (or anything close). 4. He thinks about the reservation (or anything close).

pp. 107-108, Writing Task
Part 1—Students should try to find an old person in their neighborhood (or they could call their grandparents). Obviously, they would be asking the questions in their native language and then translating the answers. If this is impossible, you could have the whole class work together and interview you, or better still, an older colleague who would remember more of the "old days." An advanced class could make up more questions to ask. Note that Part 1 is for "rough notes" about the answers. The following writing (Part 2) can be more polished.

Part 2—Students could write this rough draft on a separate piece of paper and use the space in the book for their final draft. You may also want to collect and "publish" these reports so the entire class can read them.

p. 109, Ex. 4
Corrections: Bobby Eagle <u>lived</u> on a reservation for many years. <u>He</u> lived in a cabin. He grew vegetables, and he <u>hunted</u> and <u>fished</u> for food. <u>Last</u> year, he <u>moved</u> to a big city. <u>Now Bobby lives</u> in an apartment. He buys food at a supermarket. He goes to college at night. He <u>studies</u> computer science.

p. 110, Ex. 5
Note that students should edit their work from the previous exercises.

Chapter Seven: Work and Lifestyles

Part One

pp. 113-114, Reading
Do as in previous chapters. There will probably be a few words that students can't guess from the context—or about which they can guess something but not everything. It's important for students to know that it's okay not to understand everything.

p. 114, Culture Note

Do as in previous chapters. (Note that in many countries there might not be a beach cleanup day, but there is a neighborhood cleanup day or something similar.)

p. 114, Ex. 1

Answers: D, A, B, F, C, E

p. 115, New Words

Go through the boxed explanation with the class. Emphasize (as is emphasized in the box by the use of italics) the importance of not having to understand every word exactly. Then give students a few minutes to do Ex. 2 on their own.

Answers: 1. sickness, loneliness, and homelessness   2. trees   3. ocean mammals

p. 115, Ex. 3

If students are able to choose the correct answer (c), they are demonstrating both that they have understood the main idea and are able to make an inference, to read between the lines.

Answer: c

p. 116, Ex. 4

If such a thing is available in your area, you can bring to class a pamphlet or list of volunteer opportunities in your city. If you're teaching in the United States or another English-speaking country, you can encourage students to volunteer somewhere as an opportunity to meet people, practice English, and make a contribution to their community. After discussing / brainstorming places to volunteer in the local community, have students break into small groups to answer the discussion questions, as in previous chapters.

Part Two

p. 117, Making Predictions

Do as in previous chapters. In addition, you can ask students for their perceptions of homeless people. These will differ, depending on the country in which you teach, but many students in the United States have a stereotyped view of the homeless; these students will probably tell the teacher that "all" homeless people are lazy or are alcoholics or drug addicts. This is certainly true of some, but one aim of the reading passage is to dispel this over-generalization.

p. 118, Ex. 1

Ex. 1 allows students to check their understanding of details in the reading passage. They work alone to cross out the incorrect word and replace it with the correct one.

Answers:

Cross out:	Write:
1. winter	summer
2. lunch	dinner
3. a few of	a lot of
4. all	some
5. ten	twenty

pp. 118-119, Building Vocabulary

Go through the boxed explanation with students and give them a few minutes to write words ending in -less in Ex. 2. In a small way, this exercise should help students gain confidence in their knowledge of English, as they realize that they're able to "create" actual words that they've never, perhaps, seen before, simply by adding a suffix to a word they already know.

Answers: 1. homeless   2. jobless
3. hopeless   4. friendless   5. sleepless
6. heartless   7. motherless

p. 119, Ex. 3

Ex. 3 is another categorization task. Give students time to work on their own and cross out the word that doesn't belong in each group. When they finish, go over their answers with them and then ask for volunteers to explain why the other words belong in the same group.

Answers: Cross out these words: 1. place
2. drugs   3. furniture   4. happy   5. North American   6. fruit   7. meal

p. 119, Ex. 4

The questions in Ex. 4 were intended for students living in the United States, but if you are teaching in another country, you can change them slightly to make them more appropriate for your students. You can keep Question 2 as it is but combine Questions 1 and 3 and ask: Are there homeless people in your country? In your neighborhood? If so, are there shelters for them? Who helps these people?

p. 119, Culture Note

You might choose to add these two questions to the discussion in Ex. 4. The second question (If there are more homeless people now than in the past, why?) aims at encouraging students to delve beneath the surface and think critically about this problem facing so many countries. Have them brainstorm reasons for increasing homelessness and list these reasons on the board.

Part Three

p. 120, Ex. 1

Remember that the skill being practiced here is scanning, so students should be encouraged to plunge in without having read and understood everything on the list first.

Answers: 2. Los Angeles Elder Care Corps
3. Homes For The Needy   4. East L.A. Summer Camp for Kids

p. 121, Ex. 2
Answers: 2. c   3. a   4. e   5. f   6. b

p. 122, Ex. 3
Answers:

6/95 to 9/95	Ace Construction Co. construction worker
6/94 to 9/94	Homes For The Needy painter (volunteer)
6/92 to 9/92	East L.A. Camp teacher's helper
1/92 to 6/92	Mike's Market supermarket clerk

Part Four

p. 123, Getting Started

This focuses on using the past continuous. The best advice at this level is to tell students to avoid using it unless they are sure they need to. Because it is regular, and thus much easier to use than the many irregular simple past verbs, students may have a tendency to over-use this form.

p. 123, Ex. 1
Answers: 8 verbs are in simple past; 2 verbs are in the past continuous.

p. 123, Ex. 2
Answers: Underline—was going; circle—worked, enjoyed, learned, helped, learned

p. 123, Ex. 3
Answers: 1. He worked at East L.A. Summer Camp.   2. b. He helped the teacher.   c. He learned about teaching children.

p. 124, Writing Task

Students can write about any work experience—they may want to talk about jobs they have done at home. This is a place to teach about how to put a "best face" on things, without stretching the truth. Encourage them to go into detail about their responsibilities and what they learned from the job.

p. 125, Editing Practice

This is a beginning exercise on complete sentences.

p. 125, Ex. 6
Possible answers: 1. My father and I worked (played) at the park.   2. I helped the teacher with the children.

p. 125, Ex. 7

Students go back to their writing and check it and edit it using the list.

Chapter Eight: Food and Nutrition

Part One

p. 130, Main Ideas

In Ex. 1, if students choose (2), they have identified the main idea of the selection. If they incorrectly choose (4), have them reread Paragraph D. In Ex. 2, have students turn back to the selection; matching these sentences to the paragraphs demonstrates that students recognize the main idea of each paragraph.

> Answers: Ex. 1—2
> Answers: Ex. 2—E, A, D, B, C

p. 130, Culture Note

Do as in previous chapters. If you choose to have students discuss this culture point, you'll need to add some questions: How is the way of eating changing in your country? Why?

p. 131, New Words

Give students a short time to do Ex. 3 on their own; they should be able to do this without looking back at the reading. Then, go through the boxed explanation with the class; if students need one, you can put another example on the board: My brother's cooking is usually too greasy, but sometimes it doesn't have a lot of oil, so then I like it. (Have students guess the opposite of "greasy"; they should tell you it's "without a lot of oil.") Give students a few minutes to do Ex. 4 on their own.

> Answers: Ex. 3—1. f 2. e 3. a 4. c
> 5. b 6. d
> Answers: Ex. 4—1. ugly 2. cooked 3. fat
> 4. lose

p. 132, Ex. 5

If students identify (A), they have shown that they correctly made an inference from Paragraph E.

p. 132, Ex. 6

Make sure that students work with a partner from a different country, if possible. Point out that the three meals on the chart listed under the United States are certainly not the only possible meals but are fairly typical. After filling in the chart, students should share their answers with their partner. If you have students from many countries, they can share their answers with the whole class to compare diets from different parts of the world.

Part Two

p. 133, Making Predictions

Do as in previous chapters. Note that there are no "right" or "wrong" answers to the third question, "Why don't the two women look happy?" Students will find the answer in the reading.

p. 134, Ex. 1

Students will probably need to look back at the reading to do Ex. 1.

> Answers: 1. writer 2. Harriet 3. Harriet
> 4. writer 5. writer 6. Harriet 7. writer

pp. 134-135, Understanding Organization

The concept in the boxed explanation is central to all academic writing in English: one main idea is supported by specific details. Being able to identify this structure within readings will help students prepare for their own academic writing. To complete Ex. 2, students need to turn back and find the main idea and details in Paragraph B; you can have them do this either alone or with a partner. (The spaces are small in Ex. 2, so tell the class to use short phrases only—not sentences—and to write small!) To give your students additional practice in recognizing this pattern of organization, you can have them do a similar chart for other paragraphs—perhaps B and C in "New Foods, New Diets" on p. 129.

> Answers: Main Idea: I'm overweight, so I want to lost weight.
>
> Details:
>
> | | | |
> |---|---|---|
> | love | went to | lost 10 lbs., |
> | went to a | lost 20 lbs., | nothing |
> | food | summer | gained 15 |
> | diet center | gained 24 | works |
> | camp | | |

pp. 135-136, Building Vocabulary

As in an earlier chapter, Ex. 3 has students check not only their vocabulary but also their understanding of grammar (especially parts of speech). Have students do this on their own before you go over their answers with them. Ex. 4 is a simple word-recognition game that each student does on his / her own, as fast as possible. Tell the class that the person who finishes first, with all ten words correctly circled, is the winner.

Answers: Ex. 3—1. a 2. b 3. b 4. c
Answers: Ex. 4

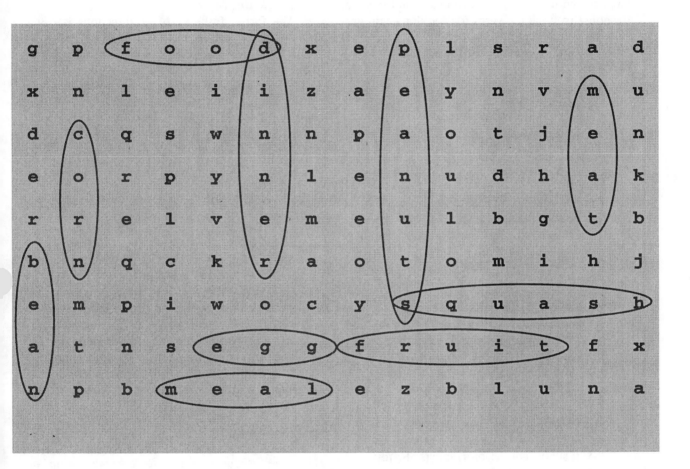

Part Three

p. 137, Scanning for Information

An adventurous teacher might want to bring in the ingredients for a salad—some teachers have even brought in a hot plate and prepared and cooked entire meals. It's an excellent opportunity to provide language with meaning. You can use Total Physical Response to teach the verbs for cooking—you give students commands like *cut up, pour, tear, mix, toss and serve* and the students do the actions with their hands and bodies.

pp. 137-138, Ex. 1

Answers: 2. a   3. c   4. a   5. b

p. 138, Ex. 2

Answers: 1. b   2. b   3. a   4. c

pp. 138–140

You could begin this section by discussing the pictures of "Bill's dinner" and "Maria's dinner." Discuss concepts like "fat" and "calories" and have students make guesses about how many calories and how much each meal or item has. Then have students use the chart to complete the exercises.

> Answers: Ex. 4—2. It has 14.7 grams.
> 3. They have 200 calories.   4. They have
> 10 grams of fat.   5. It has 819 calories.
> 6. It has 46 grams of fat.   7. It has more
> than 500 calories.

> Answers: Ex. 5—1. It has 130 calories.
> 2. It has 4.7 grams of fat.   3. They have
> 51 calories.   4. They have .1 grams.   5. It
> has 247 calories.   6. It has 5.1 grams.
> 7. You should eat Maria's dinner.   8. You
> should eat Maria's dinner.

p. 141, Ex. 6

Have the students answer the questions using the weight chart. You could survey the class before and find out how many people believe they are underweight (they weigh less than is considered good), average weight, or overweight (they weigh more than they should).

Answers: 2. She should weigh 126 pounds.
3. She should weigh 128 pounds.   4. He's overweight.   5. She's just right.
6. Answers will vary.

Part Four

p. 142, Getting Started

The form of the verb for directions is often called the "imperative," but it can be easier to understand as the simple present with no subject. This section focuses on using imperatives. Having drummed into students that there is always a subject in English (unlike many other languages), you now must tell them that there is no subject when giving directions. Students will want to write (or speak) forms like *You cut up* or *You can cut up.*

p. 142, Ex. 1

Answers: 2. put   3. tear   4. mix   5. add
6. pour   7. toss   8. serve

Note: You can ask students to volunteer more good "recipe verbs" and make a list on the board. Some possibilities are slice, chop, stir, combine, cook, fry, *etc.*

---

pp. 142-143, Ex. 2

Answers: Note that some have more than one possible answer. 1. cut; some (or a few or a lot of); put; bowl   2. up; an; some (or a little; a lot of)   3. a little (possible—some)

p. 143, Writing Task

This is open-ended and can be kept very simple (a recipe for eggs or salad) for a slower group, or expanded for a quicker one to included complicated ingredients and procedures.

p. 144, Culture Note

This is especially fun if you have a multi-ethnic class (it is obviously not so interesting if everyone comes from the same place). You could assemble descriptions and recipes for famous dishes of various countries and then "publish" the results in a class cookbook.

p. 144, Editing Practice

This focuses on looking for the simple form of the verb in instructions.

p. 144, Ex. 3

Answers: 1. First, <u>cut up</u> three tomatoes. 2. Next, <u>slice</u> an onion. 3. <u>Cook</u> the onion with the tomatoes in a frying pan. 4. After that, <u>add</u> the cilantro and <u>cook</u> for 30 minutes.

p. 145, Ex. 4

Students go back to their writing and check it and edit it using the list.

Chapter Nine: Travel and Leisure

Part One

pp. 149-150, Reading

If you have some students who lack in confidence, give them a quick "pep talk" before having them do this reading, which may seem a little daunting to them. Tell them that many of the words in this reading are a review of words they've already learned, and the few new words can be guessed from the context. After explaining this, do the reading as usual.

pp. 151-152, Main Ideas

Ex. 1 is a simple "identify-the-main-idea" task. Do this as in previous chapters. However, Ex. 2 will look new to the students. It is an extension of the paragraph-organization explanation in Chapter Eight. The main idea for each paragraph is already given; students need to identify the details that support that main idea. This will probably take them more time than many of the other exercises they've done. Allow them to work alone on this, turning back and forth from the exercise to the reading. You can have them either complete the exercise (Paragraphs A-D) before you go over the answers with them, or do just one paragraph at a time and then check before they do the next.

Answer: Ex. 1—1
Answers: Ex. 2—Put checks next to these sentences:

Paragraph A:
Some people swim, fish, cook over a fire, and sleep outside.
Some people stay at a hotel in a city.
Some people go shopping and dancing.
Some people go to special places such as Disneyland.

Paragraph B:
They want to learn something and maybe help people, too.
Some groups plan special adventures.
Earthwatch sends volunteers to different places in the world.
Earthwatch volunteers study the environment, work with animals, and learn about people of the past.

Paragraph C:
The professor is worried about chemicals.
People on this trip will ski sixteen kilometers every day.

Paragraph D:
Dolphins can follow orders.
Dolphins understand opposites.
Dolphins are intelligent.
Orcas travel in family groups.
Pollution is changing the lives of orcas.

p. 152, Ex. 3

Answers: 1. c   2. g   3. e   4. f   5. a   6. d   7. b

p. 152, Ex. 4

If students correctly answer (B), they have shown that they can "read between the lines" to make an inference.

Part Two

pp. 153-154, Making Predictions

Students look at the travel posters and predict what type of person might enjoy each vacation. Possible answers include: a person who likes cities / shopping / dancing / museums / discos / nightclubs, etc. (for Item 1); a person who likes the mountains / cool weather / adventure / hiking / camping / skiing / fishing / swimming, etc. (for Item 2); and a person who likes the ocean / warm weather / adventure / swimming / diving / sailing / water sports, etc. (for Item 3).

pp. 154-155, Ex. 1

This exercise / reading is actually another short self-test, but it is also a game, so students should enjoy it. On a separate piece of paper, students put down the number and location of the vacation that they would like (of the three vacations on pp. 153-154). They don't show this to anyone. Then they take the test in the book, circling one letter for each item.

p. 156, Ex. 2

In this exercise in making inferences, students take their partner's book, look over the answers, and guess which of the three vacations the person chose. (Note: It is hoped that you don't have to point this out to students, but if their partner has mostly (c) answers, that person probably chose the vacation in New York City. If the person has mostly (b) answers, that person probably chose the trip to the Caribbean Sea. If the person has mostly (a) answers, he or she probably chose the trip to the mountains.)

p. 156, Ex. 3

In this section students find out if their guess was correct. Then they give suggestions of other places to go that might be of interest to their partner, based on the preferences shown by the partner. Students should mostly use the modal *should* (or *shouldn't*). Often (for some reason that has always been a mystery to this writer), many students tend to use the modal *must* when giving advice, which makes them sound vaguely like a military drill sergeant. Don't mention this unless it occurs, but discourage the use of *must*.

p. 156, Ex. 4 and Ex. 5

Do Ex. 4 as in previous chapters. Before doing Ex. 5, explain the difference between opposite and different.

Answers: Ex. 4—Cross out 1. overweight
2. dairy   3. exciting   4. professor
5. vitamin

Answers: Ex. 5—1. O   2. S   3. D   4. D
5. O   6. O

p. 157, Ex. 6

Do as in previous chapters.

Answers: Across: 1. adventure   5. vacation
7. mountains   10. trees   11. orcas
12. trip
Down: 2. volcano   3. pollution   4. tourist
6. travel   8. ocean   9. stars

p. 158, Writing Activity

Do as before. Encourage students to use new vocabulary.

Part Three

p. 158, Scanning for Information

Encourage students not to read everything first—instead, as this is "scanning," they should look at the question and then look for the answer quickly, searching for only that information.

p. 158, Ex. 1

Answers: 2. Tour 3 is the longest.   3. Tour 4 is the most dangerous.

p. 160, Ex. 3

Answers: 2. Tour 2   3. Tour 4   4. Tour 1
5. Tour 4   6. Tour 3   7. Tour 2

pp. 161-162, Ex. 4

Answers: 2. It's on the green line.   3. It's on the green line.   4. It's on the green line.   5. No, it isn't. It's on the red line.
6. Yes, it is.

Part Four

p. 162, Using Notes

You can practice this by looking at any paragraph of any of the writing in this book and have students imagine what the initial notes of the writer might have been.

pp. 162-163, Ex. 1 and 2

These are pre-writing activities. These are chances to make notes and get a few ideas down on paper. This should not be corrected for accuracy.

Encourage students—you may want to have them close their eyes—to use their imagination.

p. 163, Ex. 3

Students can write down the name of any place in the world here.

pp. 163-164, Ex. 4

This is a model for the student writing that will follow.

Possible answers: 1. reading, swimming, relaxing, go or went fishing, catch or caught a sand shark   2. the ocean, islands, rocks and pine trees

p. 164, Writing Task

You could have students actually make "post-cards" from cardboard—they cut out or draw pictures for the front and write on the back. Then they could circulate them around the room. Encourage students to write as much as they can here.

p. 164, Editing Practice

Now students have a complete framework (which is only one of many) for the writing process—*make notes, write out ideas, edit and rewrite.*

Chapter Ten: Our Planet

Part One

pp. 168-169, Getting Started

Do as in previous chapters. For Item 1, have students brainstorm all of the reasons they can think of for cutting down trees. Put these on the board.

pp. 169-170, Reading

The fact that this is longer and appears more difficult than previous readings shouldn't be an obstacle; instead, it should make students feel good about how far they have come. Most of the words are review words; the few new words can be guessed from the context. Before doing this reading—or perhaps immediately after it—have students turn back and look briefly at the very first reading in Chapter One. Seeing where they started and where they now are should be an encouragement!

p. 171, Ex. 1 and 2

Do Ex. 1 as in previous chapters. Ex. 2 is an extension of an earlier concept in which students found supporting details for the main idea in individual paragraphs. Here, they look, instead, for details that support the main idea of the entire reading. If students write small, they'll be able to fit one short sentence into each of the three boxes.

Answer: Ex. 1— 4
Answers: Ex. 2—1. Trees give people both wood and fruit.   2. Trees absorb carbon dioxide.   3. Trees are good for the soil.

pp. 171-172, Ex. 3

Students will need to turn back to the reading to do this. Have them work on their own or with a partner.

Answers: 2. X   3. For example, they plant many fruit trees.   4. X   5. Other trees are good for firewood.   6. Third, all these trees are good for the soil.

p. 172, Ex. 4 and 5

Do as in previous chapters. (You'll notice this is a review of five ways to guess meaning from context.)

Answers: Ex. 4—1. CO_2 2. the air around the earth   3. drink in   4. the sun, wind, and heat from volcanoes   5. The world gets warmer because there is too much CO_2 and not enough trees.

Answer: Ex. 5—a

p. 173, Ex. 6

Do as in previous chapters. However, for the question about environmental problems in the students' countries, you might do this with the class as a whole. Have students brainstorm the answers and put them on the board.

Part Two

pp. 175-176, Reading

Before doing the reading as usual, you can tell students that Lourdes Oliveira is a real person, and this is her true story. At the time of this writing, she is in college in California and also working part-time.

p. 176, Ex. 1

This is the only exercise in the book in sequencing. Students work alone and look back at the reading to figure out the correct chronological order.

Answers: Ex. 1—2 3 1 6 5 4

p. 177, Ex. 2

This sort of idea map/outline guides students toward seeing graphically the relative importance of ideas on four levels in a reading: the single main idea, four "smaller" main ideas, details about these main ideas, and (in some cases) "smaller" details about the details. Doing this exercise should be one step in preparing students for more formal outlining in books at the next level (such as Interactions I and II). Students can work on their own, with a partner, or in a small group. They'll need to turn back to the reading to find details for the circles. Tell them to write small!

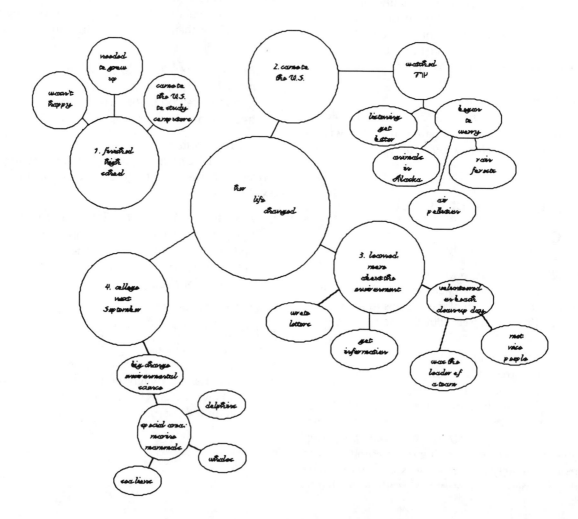

The Interactions Access Program, 2/e

p. 178, Ex. 3

Do this as in previous chapters.

Answers: 1. d 2. a 3. d 4. a 5. c

p. 179, Ex. 4

Do as in previous chapters, but for Item 3, you might, instead, have students in the class as a whole brainstorm many ways (not just two) to meet new people—especially people with whom they can practice English. Put these ways on the board.

p. 179, Culture Note

An extension of this is to ask why students choose to go to certain countries instead of others.

Part Three

p. 180, Scanning for Information

You can begin by discussing "garbage." Students could estimate how much garbage their household produces each day—also what kind and where it ends up.

p. 181, Ex. 1

Answers: 2. A person in Los Angeles makes more garbage every day. 3. A person in Paris, France, makes more garbage.
4. one person in Chicago 5. one person in Philadelphia

pp. 181-182, Ex. 2

Answers: 1. He threw out one pound of garbage. 2. Kano, Nigeria 3. Answers will vary.

p. 182, Ex. 3

Answers: 1. He threw out five pounds of garbage. 2. He lives in Chicago.

p. 183, Ex. 4

Answers: 2. Yard waste is a larger percentage of our garbage. 3. Glass is a larger percentage of our garbage. 4. 8.7
5. 17.9 6. 7.9

Part Four

p. 184, Writing

This is the last chapter, so send students on their way with this advice. All good writers—whether they write fiction, non-fiction or essays—would readily agree to this, we think. Probably the best thing students can do to improve their writing is to read (in English) good writers. Writing and rewriting as much as they can are the other important things. The advice seems simple, but it really is important.

p. 184, Ex. 1

Students don't need to write down anything here. You are imagining what notes for the story looked like. You could do this as a class—have students reconstruct the notes from the story (this could be done on the board, collectively). Then they could look at the outline and see if their notes look different or the same.

pp. 184-185, Ex. 2 and Ex. 3

Answers will vary. As in the last chapter, they are just brainstorming by writing down words and phrases.

p. 185, Ex. 4

This is to prepare students to use the correct tenses in their writing to follow. You might want to review past and future tenses. Then correct the verb forms.

Answers: 1. came 2. will finish 3. didn't speak 4. I will work (or I'm going to work or I'll work)

p. 186, Writing Task

Students use their notes to write an essay based on the model of the one in the chapter.

p. 186, Editing Practice

This is to encourage students to create their own "checklist." No two students will have the same problems with sentence construction, so they will need to identify their own specific problems and start to work on them individually. Here are some other things to check:

Is the verb in the correct form?

If there are prepositions, are they the correct ones?

Do your sentences begin with capital letters?

Do other words in the writing need capital letters?

Do your sentences end with periods?

Interactions Access, Reading/Writing
Chapters 1–2: Progress Test

Name_____   Date _____

Part 1: (10 points)

Put the correct words from this list in the blanks below.

population   crowded   diapers   monster
groceries   products   megacity   environment
mail-order   density   reusable   sycamore

1. We need some milk, fruit, and other _____.

2. Tokyo-Yokohama is an example of a _____.

3. Sometimes I buy things from a _____ catalog.

4. Cloth bags are _____.

5. I don't like a _____ city. I like small towns.

6. There is a big _____ tree in front of my house.

7. The population _____ of Hong Kong is 247,004 per square mile.

8. They buy cloth _____ for their baby to wear.

9. This soap is safe for the _____. It doesn't have any bad chemicals in it.

10. Many _____ are on sale at that store.

Part 2: Reading (10 points)

Read this selection. Then answer the questions.

Los Angeles is a strange city, in several ways. Its population is huge (very big), but the density is small. There are many square miles, so it isn't very crowded. In the downtown area, there are high-rise buildings (very tall office buildings), and there is often gridlock. (Gridlock is terrible traffic. Cars can't move.) But not far from the center of Los Angeles, there are also ranches (places for horses and cows)!

Los Angeles is between the mountains and the ocean. In the winter, some people have an interesting weekend. On Saturday, they go up to the mountains. They go skiing on beautiful, white snow. On Sunday they go to the beach. They go sailing (on boats) on a windy day and swimming on a warm day.

1. What is the main idea? Circle the letter. (1 point)

    a. Los Angeles is a big city, but the density is small.

    b. Los Angeles is strange.

    c. In Los Angeles, people can go skiing and swimming on the same weekend.

    d. Downtown Los Angeles is crowded.

2. Write a word for each meaning. (5 points)

    a. too many cars; bad traffic: _____

    b. very big: _____

    c. a sport on a boat: _____

    d. places for horses and cows: _____

    e. very tall office buildings: _____

3. Cross out the word that doesn't belong. (4 points)

    | a. boats | cars | ranches |
    | b. swimming | interesting | skiing |
    | c. beach | weekend | mountains |
    | d. windy | warm | winter |

Part 3: Editing (5 points)

There are five mistakes in the text below. Circle the mistakes and write the correction below each.

Example   I study⊙nglish.

                   ___English___

I live in paris, France. next year I'm going study in los Angeles, california.

_____

I'm going to go to the University of California.

_____

Interactions Access, Reading/Writing
Chapters 3–4: Progress Test

Name_____   Date _____

Part 1: (10 points)

Put the correct words from this list in the blanks below.

extended	picnics	athletes	nuclear
fire	marriage	single-parent	middle-aged
meditate	reunion	overweight	exercise

1. On a summer night, we sit around a _____ and tell stories.

2. There is a lot of divorce in the United States, so there are many _____ families.

3. In the summer, we have a lot of _____ on the beach. Each person brings a different kind of food.

4. People sometimes go to a _____ to see their old friends from high school.

5. One good way to relax is to _____.

6. Back home in Sri Lanka, I have a big _____ family: my parents, grandparents, brothers, sisters, aunts, uncles, and cousins-all live in one big house.

7. Swimmers, boxers, and other _____ are in the Olympics.

8./9. I'm a little _____, so I need to _____ and lose five pounds.

10. Some _____ people are afraid of old age.

Part 2: Reading (10 points)

Read this selection. Then answer the questions.

My grandmother is seventy-five years old, but sometimes I think she's younger than I am! She cleans her house so that it's always spotless—very, very clean. She works in the garden almost every day. She exercises every day. She doesn't play easy sports such as shuffleboard. Instead, she jogs and swims. Every year she runs in the Boston Marathon (a 26-mile race). Her diet is good. She eats a lot of vegetables and fruit because they have vitamins. She never eats junk food—for example, donuts, candy, or potato chips.

As you can see, my grandmother is very healthy. But she also keeps her mind active. She reads the newspaper every morning. She writes letters to friends abroad-in Japan, Mexico, and England. And she spends time with many other friends. She doesn't go to senior citizens' centers-centers for elderly people-because they are full of "old people." Her friends are of all ages-some young, some middle-aged, some elderly. They talk, laugh, and tell stories. They have a good time together.

There is just one small problem. My grandmother never seems to relax. She says, "I'll relax later, when I'm old. I don't have time to relax now."

1. What is the main idea? Circle the letter. (1 point)

    a. The writer's grandmother is seventy-five years old.

    b. The writer's grandmother exercises a lot; for example, she runs, swims, cleans her house, and works in the garden.

    c. The writer's grandmother has a problem with relaxation.

    d. The writer's grandmother is probably healthy because she exercises, eats well, has an active mind, and has friends.

2. Write a word for each meaning. (6 points)

    a. an easy sport: _____

    b. centers for elderly people: _____

    c. very, very clean: _____

    d. foods such as donuts, candy, and potato chips: _____

    e. in other countries: _____

    f. a 26-mile race: _____

3. What do these words mean? Write the meaning of each underlined word. (2 points)

    a. My grandmother is seventy-five years old, but sometimes I think she is younger than I am!

        she = _____

    b. Her diet is good. She eats a lot of vegetables and fruit because they have vitamins.

        they = _____

4. Put these words in alphabetical order. Number the words. (1 point)

_____ spotless

_____ shuffleboard

_____ sport

_____ senior

_____ sometimes

Part 3: Editing (5 points)

There are five mistakes in the text below. Circle the mistakes and write the correction below each.

Example   I study⊙nglish.

               ____English____

My name is james Lee I live in Korea, but my brother living in canada. Next year I will to go

_____

to visit him.

_____

Interactions Access, Reading/Writing
Chapters 5–6: Progress Test

Name_____   Date _____

Part 1: (10 points)

Put the correct words from this list in the blanks below.

apologize	activities	brag	tribe
active	equal	exist	reservations
similar	argue	squash	unemployment

1. Sometimes we get angry and _____ with each other.

2. The _____ rate is high in this city. Many people don't have jobs.

3. Very small boys and girls are _____ to each other, but soon there is a change. They become different from each other.

4. Let's have some _____ with the chicken for dinner tonight.

5. My little boy is very _____. He's always doing things—running, jumping, and playing games.

6. I said something terrible to her, and now I feel bad about it. I need to _____ to her.

7. She's a member of the Apache _____. She and other Native Americans are working to keep their traditions.

8./9. Many problems _____ on Indian _____.

10. Little girls usually want everyone in their group to have a(n) _____ position.

Part 2: Reading (10 points)

Read this selection. Then answer the questions.

Think of this situation. A husband and wife are on a car trip. After a few hours of driving, the wife asks her husband, "Are you getting hungry?" He says "no," and it's the end of the conversation. But there is one problem. The woman doesn't say anything, but she is fuming—in other words, getting more and more angry. And her husband is confused. He doesn't understand her anger. What's happening here?

Linguists—people who study language—can explain. Men talk to give or get information. In our example, the husband gives his wife information; he isn't hungry. But women talk for intimacy-in other words, a feeling of friendliness and closeness to people in their lives. In our example, the woman is opening a conversation.

Here is a conversation between two women:

A: Are you getting hungry?

B: Well, maybe a little. Would you like to stop and eat?

A: Maybe not right now, but soon. What kind of restaurant should we look for?

B: Italian is nice.

A: Yes. Italian sounds good. Or fish. There are some good fish restaurants in this area.

You can see something interesting in this conversation. The women are communicating more than information. They are showing intimacy and equality.

1. What is the main idea? Circle the letter. (1 point)

    a. Men and women—especially husbands and wives—often argue.

    b. The woman is angry because her husband doesn't talk with her.

    c. Men talk for information, and women talk for intimacy.

    d. The man is confused because his wife is angry.

2. Write a word for each meaning. (3 points)

    a. people who study language: _____

    b. getting more and more angry: _____

    c. a feeling of friendliness and closeness: _____

3. What do these words mean? Write the meaning of each underlined word. (3 points)

    a. The woman is fuming, and <u>her</u> husband is confused.

        her = _____

    b. In our example, the husband gives <u>his</u> wife information.

        his = _____

    c. Women talk for intimacy-in other words, a feeling of friendliness and closeness to people in <u>their</u> lives.

        their = _____

4. Are the meanings of these words similar or different? Write S (similar) or D (different) on the lines. (3 points)

    a. _____ talk-conversation

    b. _____ hungry-angry

    c. _____ friendliness-equality

Part 3: Editing (5 points)

There are five mistakes in the text below. Circle the mistakes and write the correction below each.

Example   I study(e)nglish.

            _____English____

Yesterday I comes home I reading the paper the same as always. My wife is angry to me and I

_____

don't know why.

_____

Interactions Access, Reading/Writing
Chapters 7–8: Progress Test

Name_____   Date _____

Part 1: (10 points)

Put the correct words from this list in the blanks below.

volunteers	heartless	raw	gain
dairy	attractive	hardships	slender
calories	shelter	vitamins	diseases

1./2.   I can't eat this cake because it has too many _____, and I'm on a diet. I don't want to _____ weight.

3.   For a few months, he lived in a _____ for homeless people.

4./5.   Cooking vegetables takes away some _____ (such as A and C), so a lot of people eat _____ vegetables.

6.   I try to eat nonfat _____ products—milk, yogurt, and cheese.

7.   _____ give their time to help other people.

8.   She's _____! She doesn't care about anyone!

9.   Homeless people have many _____ such as loneliness and sickness.

10.   There are _____ —for example, cancer and AIDS.

Part 2: Reading (10 points)

Read this selection. Then answer the questions.

Everyone seems to be so busy these days! Many Americans don't have time for hobbies. They don't have time to relax. They don't have time to cook. But everyone has to eat, and this is causing several new food trends-new directions-in the United States.

In the past, people could go to a Chinese restaurant and buy take-out food-food to take home. They could go to an Italian restaurant and buy a pizza to take home. But nothing else. These days, in most cities, many different kinds of restaurants are selling take-out food. Busy people can stop at a restaurant on their way home from work. They can buy salads, hot soup, casseroles, stews, and desserts. They can even take home gourmet food (very special, expensive food).

Most people don't have time for hobbies, but they want to spend time with friends and family. And they like to eat well. Maybe this explains the sudden appearance of many new restaurants in big cities. Eating is becoming a new "hobby." People especially like to try different ethnic foods: Thai, Spanish, Moroccan, Peruvian, Greek, even Ethiopian! For a few hours, they can relax in an attractive restaurant. They visit with friends. And they don't have to cook.

1. What is the main idea? Circle the letter. (1 point)

    a. People don't have free time these days.

    b. People in the United States don't cook these days.

    c. In U.S. cities, people enjoy food from many countries

    d. For busy people in the United States, it's possible to eat well and not spend time in the kitchen.

2. Write a word for each meaning. (4 points)

    a. very special, expensive food: _____

    b. new directions: _____

    c. from many countries: _____

    d. food to take home: _____

3. What do these words mean? Write the meaning of each underlined word. (2 points)

    a. Many Americans don't have time for hobbies. <u>They</u> don't have time to relax.

        they = _____

    b. Busy people can stop at a restaurant on <u>their</u> way home from work.

        their = _____

4. Cross out the word that doesn't belong. (3 points)

    a. trends   directions   foods

    b. Spanish   United States   Moroccan

    c. ethnic   relax   eat

Part 3: Editing (5 points)

There are five mistakes in the text below. Circle the mistakes and write the correction below each.

Example   I study ⑭nglish.

               ____English____

In 1996 I volunteered for an environmental organization named trees for Peace we planting trees

_____

and also talk to children about the problems of pollution.

_____

Name_____   Date _____

Part 1: (10 points)

Put the correct words from this list in the blanks below.

sightseeing	dolphins	absorb	volcanoes
atmosphere	team	pollution	campfire
explosion	energy	adventure	greenhouse effect

1. On our camping trip, we cooked over a _____.

2. _____ look like fish but are really ocean mammals.

3. A _____ of volunteers is working to study marine mammals near Alaska.

4./5. We usually go _____ on our vacations, to places such as Disneyland, but next year we're going to have a real _____! We're planning to go rafting down the Colorado River.

6./7. Some factories send gases such as CO_2 into the _____. Other factories cause water _____ when they pour chemicals into rivers and lakes.

8. It's dangerous to cut down trees because they _____ CO_2.

9./10. We should stop using oil and coal. We should begin to use other kinds of _____ such as wind, the sun, and heat from _____.

Part 2: Reading (10 points)

Read this selection. Then answer the questions.

Think about your family's weekly trash. How many bags of garbage do you throw away every week? What is in each bag? Kitchen garbage (chicken bones, apple cores, banana peels)? Paper? Plastic? And what happens after the garbage truck takes your trash away? Where does your trash go?

In many cities of the world, the trash goes to a dump-in other words, a huge place for garbage just outside the city. In some areas of the United States, the trash goes to a landfill. A landfill is similar to a dump, but it is in a narrow valley—a low place between mountains. After many years, the landfill is full of garbage. Then workers put soil on top of it. They cover it completely. They plant trees and make a park. Good idea?

Garbage such as chicken bones, apple cores, and banana peels is organic (from something that was living). In usual conditions, organic garbage is biodegradable. In other words, it becomes part of the soil after several months or years. Plastic is not organic, so it is not biodegradable. It will never become part of the soil. It will be here on earth for hundreds—no, thousands—of years. And in a land-fill, organic garbage is not biodegradable, either. Landfills are airless, sunless dumps. In landfills, garbage will remain for our grandchildren and their grandchildren and their grandchildren and their grandchildren and their grandchildren. Maybe landfills aren't such a good idea.

1. What does the writer think? What can you guess from the reading? Circle the letter. (1 point)

   a. We are throwing away too much garbage.

   b. People enjoy the parks on landfills.

   c. Landfills are better than dumps.

   d. There are more landfills than dumps in the United States.

2. Write a word for each meaning. (6 points)

   a. garbage: _____

   b. the outside (yellow) part of a banana: _____

   c. a big place for garbage: _____

   d. the "inside" part of an apple: _____

   e. something that is (or was) living: _____

   f. something that can become part of the soil after a long time: _____

3. Cross out the word that doesn't belong. (3 points)

   a. dump   truck   landfill

   b. garbage   trash   organic

   c. plastic   organic   biodegradable

Part 3: Editing (5 points)

There are five mistakes in the text below. Circle the mistakes and write the correction below each.

Example   I study(E)nglish.

                   _____English_____

I studying English in my country last year i will to go to the us next year.

_____

Answer Key: Progress Tests, Interactions Access, Reading/Writing

Chapters 1-2

Part 1:

1. groceries   2. megacity   3. mail-order   4. reusable   5. crowded   6. sycamore   7. density
8. diapers   9. environment   10. products

Part 2:

1. b   2. a. gridlock   b. huge   c. sailing   d. ranches   e. high-rise buildings   3. a. ranches
b. interesting   c. weekend   d. winter

Part 3:

I live in Paris, France. Next year I'm going study in Los Angeles, California.

I'm going to go to the University of California.

Chapters 3-4

Part 1:

1. fire   2. single-parent   3. picnics   4. reunion   5. meditate   6. extended   7. athletes
8. overweight   9. exercise   10. middle-aged

Part 2:

1. d   2. a. shuffleboard   b. senior citizens' centers   c. spotless   d. junk food   e. abroad   f. (Boston)
marathon   3. a. My grandmother   b. vegetables and fruit   4. 5—spotless 2—shuffleboard 4—sport
1—senior 3—sometimes

Part 3:

My name is James Lee I live in Korea, but my brother is living in Canada. Next year I will go to visit
him.

Chapters 5-6

Part 1:

1. argue   2. unemployment   3. similar   4. squash   5. active   6. apologize   7. tribe   8. exist
9. reservations   10. equal

Part 2:

1. c   2. a. linguists   b. fuming   c. intimacy   3. a. the woman   b. the husband   c. women   4. a. S
b. D   c. D

Part 3:

Yesterday I came home. I read the paper, the same as always. My wife was angry wtih me and I don't know why.

Chapters 7-8

Part 1:

1. calories 2. gain 3. shelter 4. vitamins 5. raw 6. dairy 7. Volunteers 8. heartless
9. hardships 10. diseases

Part 2:

1. d 2. a. gourmet food b. trends c. ethnic d. take-out food 3. a. Many Americans b. Busy people 4. a. foods b. United States c. ethnic

Part 3:

In 1996 I volunteered for an environmental organization named Trees for Peace. We planted trees and also talked to children about the problems of pollution.

Chapters 9-10

Part 1:

1. campfire 2. Dolphins 3. team 4. sightseeing 5. adventure 6. atmosphere 7. pollution
8. absorb 9. energy 10. volcanoes

Part 2:

1. a 2. a. trash b. peel c. dump d. core e. organic f. biodegradable 3. a. truck b. organic
c. plastic

Part 3:

I studied English in my country last year I will go to the U.S. next year.

Interactions Access: Listening/Speaking

Philosophy

This text is designed to give students the opportunity to practice speaking and listening skills and develop fluency in English. Although some activities encourage the use of specific grammar structures, in general the activities are intended to promote fluency and improve communication skills. All activities are task-oriented; that is, students focus on a task rather than on language. The language is the means, rather than the end. This allows for more natural, less self-conscious communication and keeps motivation and interest high. Motivation and interest are also fostered by a variety of visual input, ranging from photographs to realia such as maps, menus, and charts.

Sequencing and Pace of the Course

The text has been designed to progress in difficulty, so we suggest that you follow the sequence of the book. You may want to omit parts or whole chapters, however, given the schedule of your particular course. The text offers enough material for at least sixty contact hours in an ESL setting, depending on your students and the nature of your course. Each chapter has a wide variety of activities that may take fifteen to twenty minutes of class time each. There are both longer and shorter activities in each chapter, so you can choose those that best fit your lesson plans.

Chapter Organization and General Teaching Suggestions

The text has ten chapters, each of which has a central theme. All chapters are divided into four parts. Here are descriptions of the four parts, along with general tips for using each. The following section of this manual, "Teaching Tips and Answer Key," has many specific teaching tips for exercises and activities in each chapter.

Part One: Listening to Conversations

Getting the Main Idea: In Part One, students listen to a conversation among a group of characters that appear throughout the text. The conversation relates to the theme of the chapter and introduces some of the language that students will practice in later sections.

The first exercise introduces vocabulary that students need to understand the audio tape. Model the pronunciation of these words and discuss their meanings with the students. Encourage students to listen for the meaning of these words in the context of the conversation rather than looking them up in the dictionary. Then, the students practice with the vocabulary words by using them to complete sentences.

Before listening to the taped conversation, students see general questions about the conversation. Encourage students to read these questions before listening to the tape so that they know what they are listening for. Reassure students that they do not need to understand every word of the conversation the first time they hear it. The questions in Ex. 3 are to encourage global listening—listening for general understanding—to show students how much meaning they can get from listening to natural, spoken English. Finally, a second exercise may ask students to listen to the tape again to answer more specific questions.

Stress: The students listen to the first part of the conversation again. They have in their texts a transcript of the conversation with some words left out. They also have a list of the words they need to complete the transcript, so they do not need to be concerned about spelling at this point. They should focus on listening to discern the missing words so that they can write them in the spaces in their texts. Then the students listen to the second part of the conversation again. This time, they look at the transcript in their texts and mark the stressed words they hear. Emphasize that in English the important, information words in a sentence are stressed. Unstressed words tend to be shortened—sometimes almost disappearing entirely. This means that different words might be stressed in the same sentence if the speaker is emphasizing different information. Words that are often very short may be given more time, which can change the pronunciation of the vowels in the word. Point this out to students when it occurs in the conversation.

Contractions: This exercise introduces students to the way native speakers of American English pronounce words in natural speech. The students look at the complete, written sentence, and a rough approximation of how it sounds in natural, spoken English while they listen to the tape.

Then the students listen to sentences in either reduced, natural speech, or formal speech and circle the sentence they hear. The students are not asked to reproduce the reduced forms since they can always be understood when producing the full, formal form. The purpose of these exercises is to help them understand native speakers of American English in informal settings.

Speaking Activity: Part One of each chapter ends with a speaking activity that encourages students to use the vocabulary and forms they have heard in the taped conversation in a communicative activity.

Part Two: Expressing Yourself

This section emphasizes oral production of some particular type of expression that students will find useful in academic work, their careers, or their everyday lives. The type of expression in each chapter is introduced through the audio tape, with vocabulary and comprehension exercises. Then students participate in an interactive, communicative activity, often in small groups or pairs, that allows them to practice what they've learned.

Part Three: Listening Tasks

Guessing Information: The purpose of this section is to help students develop inferencing skills. Students hear the first part of a brief conversation. Then they answer a question that requires them to draw a conclusion from the information they heard. If students have not done this type of exercise before, they may need help figuring out how to approach this task. Stop the tape and elicit from the students the pieces of information they need to draw the correct conclusion. This section should become easier for them as they progress through the text.

The other exercises in this part of each chapter ask students to listen to conversations, and then use information from the tape to complete a task.

As with all the taped exercises, you can play the taped segments as many times as the students need so that they can answer the questions or complete the task. You can also stop the tape at any point to give the students a chance to write or to elicit from them what they have heard.

Part Four: Speaking Up

In this part, students learn more vocabulary and use it to discuss practical, everyday topics and situations, such as the weather and clothing. Many of the interactive, communicative activities in this part draw on the situations and language that the students have heard in previous sections.

Part Four is especially important in developing fluency. Students should be encouraged to focus on communicating information in these exercises even though they may not be ready to use the structures of English with consistent accuracy at this point.

Teaching Tips and Answer Key
Chapter One: Neighborhoods, Cities, and Towns

This chapter focuses on life in various kinds of communities, from large cities to small towns. In this chapter, students will learn some informal greetings, how to give personal information such as their addresses and phone numbers, how to get information about taking a bus and renting an apartment, and how to give dates in American English.

Part One

pp. 2–3, Getting the Main Idea

Explain to students that they are going to meet some characters on the first tape who they will follow through the book. Rob and Lee are students at Faber College, a small college in the U.S. Beth is Rob's cousin. Draw the students' attention to the picture.

p. 2, Ex. 1:

Ask students to look at the list of words in Ex. 1 and circle any they don't know. Discuss the words with them if necessary. They can look the words up in a bilingual or English-English dictionary, but point out that many words in English have more than one meaning. They will need to listen carefully to the conversation to decide which meaning is being used.

p. 3, Ex. 2

Students complete the sentences with the words from Ex. 1. There are several ways to conduct this exercise. You might try varying the technique from one chapter to another.

- Give students a few minutes to do the exercise individually. Then go over the exercise, eliciting answers from the students as a class or by calling on specific students.

- Put students in pairs or small groups. Let them complete the exercise together. Then call on groups to give answers. This is particularly good if the students vary in skill level. Weaker students can learn from the stronger ones without being embarrassed.

- Ask students to complete the exercise individually, and then compare their answers with those of another student. If they agree, the answer is probably correct. If they disagree, they can decide on the correct answer by discussing or by checking with two more students. This helps them recognize that they can rely on resources other than the teacher.

> Answers: 2. transportation   3. population
> 4. hometown   5. international   6. cousin

p. 3, Ex. 3

Tell students that they are going to listen to a conversation. Ask them to look at the four questions in their texts. Read through the questions with them to make sure they understand the questions. If necessary, practice with the class by asking various students where they are from and if they are from a small town. Explain to students that they do not have to understand every word when they listen to the conversation. They should only listen for the answers to the four questions.

Play the tape. If the students seem to have gotten the answers to the questions, elicit the answers from them. If they have not been able to answer most of the questions, play the tape again, stopping it if necessary to point out where the necessary information was contained in the conversation.

> Answers: 1. Seoul, Korea (just Korea is OK)
> 2. no   3. Charlottesville, Virginia (just
> Virginia is OK)   4. yes

p. 3, Ex. 4

Direct the students to look through the three questions and answers to Ex. 4. Read through the questions and answers. Point out that, this time, they are listening for greetings and introductions. Point out that this conversation is among three students, and that the language used here is informal. All the possible answers are common, informal usages in American English. Now play the tape, and then go over the answers.

> Answers: 1. b and c   2. a   3. b

p. 3, Ex. 5

An exercise in each chapter asks students to listen for stressed words. This is important because English is a stress-timed language. That is, stressed words get more time. Other words become shorter. Often, the vowels in unstressed words and syllables change and become "shwas" (like the "a" at the end of sofa). It's important for students to hear this rhythm of English and to understand how stressing different words changes the sound of the sentence.

In Chapter One, students are only asked to listen and read the script in their books, which is marked to show which words are stressed. Point out the difference between Lee's statement, "Nice to meet you" and Beth's, "Nice to meet you."

p. 4, Ex. 6

Contractions are commonly used by native speakers of English. Speech without contracted forms sounds stilted and unnatural. In each chapter, an exercise on contractions helps students practice natural, fluent speech.

In this chapter, the focus is on contractions with the verb "to be." You might write the contracted forms *I'm, you're, he's, she's, it's, we're, they're* on the board. Then discuss with students how the same contractions occur with other subjects—*who's, where's, what's, how's, there's, who're, where're, what're, how're, there're.* This is a result of the shortening of unstressed words, discussed in Ex. 5.

p. 4, Ex. 7

Now students listen to a speaker say either the full, uncontracted form of the sentence or the contracted form, and they identify which they hear. Developing the ability to hear stressed and unstressed forms, contracted and uncontracted forms is important for them to be able to process the natural language they hear and to learn from native speaker models.

Answers: 1. b   2. a   3. b   4. b   5. b

p. 5, Speaking Activity

This activity gives students a chance to practice some of the forms they have heard on the tapes with content that is meaningful to them. Arrange students in groups of four. Have them write each other's name in the spaces on the chart on p. 5. Go over the questions they will need to ask each other to complete the chart. Write the questions on the board if needed. Ask the students to look at the answers given by "Sally." Ask them where she is from, what the capital of her country is, and so on. Then model the activity by having a student ask you "Where are you from?" Give an answer and show students how to write the answer in the space under Teacher. Then have the students ask you the rest of the questions, either in unison or by calling on individuals. Now give students 15 minutes to interview each other in their groups to complete the chart. They should take turns asking each other the questions. Circulate among the groups, listening to be sure they are using full question forms and making sure they are doing the activity correctly. When they are finished, call on groups to tell something about their members.

Note: If all your students are from the same city or town, change this activity to make it more interesting. Ask the students to take on an imaginary identity. They should think of a name and hometown for their person they are pretending to be. Then they can answer the questions for their made-up identity.

Part Two

p. 6, Ex. 1

Being able to give and understand addresses, phone numbers and names is important whether students are living in an English-speaking country or may be communicating socially or at work with people from other countries. If necessary, go over the numbers between 1 and 10 in English and how to say the names of the letters of the alphabet. Then go around the classroom and have each student give his or her name, spelling the name, address, and phone number. You might have other students write down this information when they hear it. This is good practice for them, and they will have each other's numbers if they need to call about an assignment.

p. 6, Ex. 2

Now students will listen to native speakers of English give personal information. Tell them to listen to the tape and fill in the blanks in their books. Go over the answers with them. Point out that in the first two examples, the speakers do not give the city and state because they live in the same city as the questioner. In the last example, the speaker lives in a different city and gives the city, state and zip (postal) code.

> *Note: All the phone numbers on the tape start with 555. That number is never actually used in American phone numbers. It is used in movies, TV shows, and other published materials to avoid using someone's real phone number.*

Answers: 1. Gordon McKey, 1223 East Park Avenue, Apartment 2B, 555-7950. 2. Alicia Morales, 456 Southern Avenue, 555-2486. 3. Frank Cane, 196 Anderson Place, Seattle, Washington, 90324, 901 555-4987

Part Three

p. 7, Ex. 1

In this exercise in each chapter, students listen to the first part of a conversation. Then they answer a question in their books, and listen to the end of the conversation, which gives the correct answer. To do this exercise, students must make inferences from the conversations they hear. You might start by asking students to look at the first question and the three possible answers. Tell them to listen to the first conversation to find out whether the speakers say that Mexico City is a town, a city, or a very large city. Play the tape up to the point where the Narrator asks the question. Stop the tape. Ask students to tell you the answer. Since the tape says that there are around 20 million people in Mexico City, students should be able to choose the correct answer, C. Then play the rest of the conversation. Point out that Frank says, "That's a really large city!"—which agrees with the answer they determined from the clues in the first part.

Answers: 1. c   2. c   3. b   4. b   5. a

p. 7, Ex. 2

Discuss the questions with the students. They may live in places where there are many forms of public transportation, including subways, buses, trams, etc. Explain that in the U.S., only a few big cities have subways. Other cities and towns usually have buses.

p. 8, Ex. 3

Go over the vocabulary with the students. You might have them use each word or phrase in a sentence.

p. 8, Ex. 4

Have students look at the series of pictures in their books. Ask them to tell you what they think is happening in each picture. You might need to tell them that on American buses, people usually have to have the exact amount of the fare. They put it into a glass box near the driver when they get on. Play the first part of the tape, and then stop the tape. Ask the students who is speaking to Rob on the tape. If needed, play each part of the conversation again, showing students how the conversation relates to the first two pictures. In the first picture, Rob is asking the driver how much the bus fare is; then he puts the fare (sixty-five cents) in the box. In the second picture, Rob is asking if Park Place Shopping Center is near, and the driver says it's about two miles away. The third picture shows Rob's destination.

p. 8, Ex. 5

Look at the two pictures and discuss them with the students. Picture A shows Rob about to get on a bus to Park Place. Picture B shows Rob waiting for a bus to Brentwood Center. Now play the last part of the conversation. Ask the students which picture shows the information Rob received from the driver at the end.

> Answer: B—Rob found out that he needs to wait for the bus back to school at the stop across the street from Park Place.

p. 9, Ex. 6

Play the whole conversation. When students have circled the answers to the questions, they can check their answers by comparing with another student or by listening to the tape again.

Answers: 1. b 2. c. 3. a.

pp. 9-10, Finding a Place to Live

In this section, students practice skills they will need if they are going to look for and rent a place to live in an environment where they will be communicating in English. Even if your students never expect to be in that situation, this exercise is good practice in the names of rooms and other vocabulary used to talk about houses and apartments.

p. 9, Ex. 7

Have the students look at the pictures of the apartments. Go over the names of different rooms: living room, dining room, kitchen, bedroom, and bathroom. You might also introduce vocabulary for furniture here: tables, chairs, sofa or couch, bed, chest of drawers. Ask students to make short sentences describing the pictures, following the models in their books. Or if your students are ready, they might write a few sentences about the pictures and then read the sentences to the class.

p. 10, Ex. 8

Go over the vocabulary before playing the tape for Ex. 9.

p. 10, Ex. 9

Play the first conversation on the tape. Direct students to look at the pictures in Ex. 7 while they listen. Stop the tape. Ask students to identify the picture that matches what they heard on the tape. If necessary, play the tape again, stopping to point out the important clues: three bedrooms, two bathrooms. Play the rest of the conversations and discuss the answers.

Answers: 1. a 2. b 3. c

Part Four

p. 10, Ex. 1

Go over the names of the months. Point out that in the U.S., January, February, and March are the coldest months, with snow in all but the southern-most states. In April, May, and June, the weather gets warmer and flowers bloom. July, August, and September are very warm, and in October, November, and December, the leaves on most of the trees turn red, yellow and orange, and then turn brown and fall off the trees.

p. 10, Ex. 2

In the U.S., dates are usually written Month, Day, Year. In Great Britain, they are written Day, Month, Year. This can be confusing if only numbers are used, but there is no problem if the abbreviation for the months are used. Have students read the dates, using the ordinal numbers first, second, third and so on.

Answers: 1. January second 2. December third 3. February first 4. August twenty-fifth 5. November fifteenth 6. September thirtieth

p. 10, Ex. 3

The preposition "in" is used with a period / length of time such as a month or year. The preposition "on" is used for a specific date. Ask students to fill in the blanks with either "in" or "on," and then go over the answers.

Answers: 1. in 2. on 3. on 4. in 5. in 6. on

pp. 11-12, Ex. 4

This is an Information Gap activity. Students must ask each other questions and listen for the answers in order to complete the information on their charts. Go over the directions for the activity in the students' text. You may need to model the exercise by asking the first question, "When is Sally's birthday party?" When the student with Calendar A gives you the answer, show the student with Calendar B where to write in the information. Show the class the student's book with the new information written in. You may need to model the pronunciation of the items in the lists under the two calendars.

Give students a time limit for completing the activity—15 minutes should be enough. Circulate among the pairs to make sure they understand how to do the activity and to answer questions.

Answers, Calendar A:
1. Mother's Day is on May 14.
2. Memorial Day is on May 29.
3. The doctor's appointment is on May 26.
4. The grammar test is on May 12.
5. The baseball game is on May 20.

Answers, Calendar B:
1. Sally's birthday party is on May 15.
2. The final exam is on May 31.
3. The concert is on May 6.
4. The school picnic is on May 7.
5. The dentist appointment is on May 10.

p. 12, Ex. 5

In this exercise, students get to make up their own conversations based on the ones they have heard on the tape. Put the students in pairs. You may need to model the first sentence. Ask the class to supply some words that might go in the first blank. If the students cannot think of any, ask what they would say to get someone's attention. They should be able to come up with "excuse" or "pardon." Then give them 10-15 minutes to complete the dialogue. You might have a few pairs read their completed dialogues to the class. Note that answers will vary.

Sample answers:
Passenger: Excuse me, is this the bus to Union Square?
Driver: Yes, it is.
Passenger: Great! How much is it?
Driver: Eighty-five cents.
Passenger: Will you take a dollar bill?
Driver: No, you need exact change.
Passenger: Here you go.
Driver: Thank you. Please move back.

p. 13, Ex. 6

Now the students write dialogues similar to the one in Ex. 5, but they are free to write any questions and answers they want. Give a time limit (15-20 min.) and circulate to answer questions and prompt them to use correct verb forms, etc. If time allows, have them perform their dialogues for the class.

p.13, Ex. 7

Model the questions for the students. Discuss possible answers.

pp. 13-14, Ex. 8

This is another Information Gap activity. Set it up as you did in Ex. 4. Model the first question and answer with one of the students if necessary. Give students 10 minutes. Circulate while they complete the task. Have them check their answers by looking at the other page in their texts.

Sample answers for Apartment 1:
Q: What is the rent?
A: It's $650 a month.
Q: How many bedrooms does it have?
A: It has two bedrooms./Two.
Q: How many bathrooms does it have?
A: It has one and a half bathrooms./One and a half.
Q: How far is it from the college?
A: It's a half a mile from the college.
Q: Is it still available?/When is it available?
A: It's available now.

Sample answers for Apartment 2:
Q: What is the rent?
A: It's $865 a month.
Q: How many bedrooms does it have?
A: It has three bedrooms./Three.
Q: How many bathrooms does it have?
A: It has two bathrooms./Two.

Q: How far is it from the college?

A: It's two blocks from the college.

Q: Is it still available?/When is it available?

A: It's available in two weeks.

Follow-up

If you are in an English speaking environment, you might send students out to pick up brochures from apartments in the area, or you might bring a selection of brochures to the class. Discuss the different apartment complexes convenient to the school. What do the brochures feature besides the number of bedrooms and bathrooms?

In a non-English speaking environment, students could look at newspaper ads or brochures in the local language and translate parts of them into English—the number of rooms, etc. Then they could choose which they would like to rent or buy.

Chapter Two: Shopping—A National Pastime?

Chapter Two focuses on shopping and money. In this chapter, students will practice talking about budgets and practice language related to shopping, such as giving reasons for a return, comparing prices, and describing clothing.

Part One

pp. 16-18, Getting the Main Idea

Tell students that they will again encounter Rob, Lee and Beth. In this chapter, they will meet two new characters, Alicia and Ali, who are also students at Faber College. Discuss the chapter opening picture.

p. 16, Ex. 1

Ask students to look at the list of words in Ex. 1 and circle any they don't know. Discuss the words with them if necessary. They can look the words up in a bilingual or English-English dictionary, if they want. Then play the conversation.

p. 17, Ex. 2

Students complete the sentences with the words from Ex. 1. There are several ways to conduct this exercise. See Teaching Tips for Chapter One, p. 3, for a list of suggestions.

Answers: 1. allowance   2. credit card
3. shopping   4. window-shopping
5. mall/shopping center   6. shopping center   7. dorm/dormitory; work on
8. spend

p. 17, Ex. 3

Tell students that they are going to listen to a conversation and answer some questions about it. Read the three questions with them before they listen and make sure they understand them. Remind students that they do not have to understand every word when they listen to the conversation. They should only listen for the answers to the questions.

Play the tape as many times as necessary for students to get all of the answers. If students are having problems with a particular question, stop the tape at the point where the necessary information is located.

Answers: 1. Her budget   2. Because she's spending too much money   3. Yes

pp. 17-18, Ex. 4

This exercise requires students to listen for and fill in the stressed words in a conversation for the first time. To prepare students, first have them repeat the words in the list that precedes the dialogue. Then have them listen at least once to the conversation without writing. Ask them to focus on the stressed words in each sentence. Tell them to listen for the words that sound longer—these are most likely the stressed words. If necessary, have them listen a second time before they write.

Now have students listen for and write down the missing stressed words in the blanks in the conversation. Repeat the tape as many times as necessary for everyone to get the words.

Answers: 1. in   2. Beth   3. How   4. doing
5. good   6. Ali   7. Egypt   8. Ali   9. Nice
10. meet   11. you   12. why   13. studying   14. Saturday   15. shopping
16. come   17. sorry   18. can't   19. not
20. working   21. budget

p. 18, Ex. 5

This exercise is similar to Ex. 4, except students see the entire dialogue, a continuation of the previous one. This time, though, they listen for and underline the stressed words. Have them listen at least once to the conversation before they write. Then have them listen and underline the stressed words. Play the tape again, if necessary.

See Tapescript, Chapter Two, p. 164, of the text for the answers.

p. 18, Ex. 6, Reductions

Like contractions, reductions are common in spoken English. Students need to be able to understand reduced forms when they hear them. This exercise, and others like it in the text, give students practice with these forms. This chapter focuses primarily on the reductions native speakers often produce when they run two words together (for example, how + are). Have students listen to the examples. You might want to provide additional examples contextualized in sentences, either on the board or orally (for example, hafta for have to, why're for why are, etc.), and have students try to guess the long forms.

p. 19, Ex. 7

In this exercise, students listen to sentences with either a reduction or the long form and identify the version they hear. Repeat the exercise, if necessary.

Answers: 1. b 2. a 3. a 4. a 5. a

p. 19, Speaking Activity

This activity gives students a chance to practice asking questions inspired by the conversation from Part One. Get them into groups of four. First, go over the questions and make sure they understand each one. Have them look at Sally's answers and turn them into complete answers. Then have them practice the questions by asking you first. Make sure each group member asks a question. Now have them write their group members' names in the blanks on the chart and take turns asking each other each of the questions. At this point, walk around the room and give help where needed. When all the groups have finished, call on students to report on their answers.

Part Two

pp. 20-21, Ex. 1

In this exercise, students listen to a short conversation for global understanding—they only have to determine where the speakers are. First have them look at and discuss the two pictures. Then tell them to listen to the conversation and decide where the speakers are; in other words, which picture goes with the conversation. Remind them that they only have to listen for this one bit of information. Most likely, they will only have to listen one time, but repeat the tape if necessary.

Note: It is common in the United States and Canada to return an item to a store. The process is very simple, and while it is polite and helpful to give the store a reason for the return, it is not required in most cases. A common expression in American business is: "The customer is always right."

Answer: B

p. 21, Culture Note

Notice the Culture Note that follows this exercise. Have students look at the picture and read the note. Then have them talk about the differences, if any, between the way people give money to clerks in the United States and the way it is done in their country.

p. 21, Ex. 2

Now students listen to the same conversation they heard in Ex.1, but this time, for more specific information. Have them read the questions first, and then listen to the conversation. This helps them focus on and listen for only the information they need to answer the questions. Repeat the tape if necessary.

Note: This type of listening task appears on the TOEFL exam.

Answers: 1. b 2. c 3. c

p. 22, Ex. 3

Ex. 3 extends the material on returns in the previous conversation and prepares students for the speaking activity in the following exercise. First, read the lists of items and reasons aloud with the students, and make sure they understand them. Then have them work in pairs to match them.

Sample answers: 1. d; f   2. b; d; f; g
3. a; b; d   4. a; b; d; e   5. d; f; g
6. a; b; d   7. c

p. 23, Ex. 4

Model the conversation for the students. Then have them practice it with the partner they worked with in Ex. 3. Walk around and offer help, if necessary. Select pairs (or have them volunteer) to perform the conversation for the class.

p. 23, Ex. 5

Have students prepare the role-play in pairs. Go over the form and make sure students understand it. Tell them to use the items and reasons from Ex. 3, or think of their own. Walk around and give help if necessary, and make sure they switch roles.

Part Three

p. 24, Ex. 1

As in Chapter One, students listen to the first part of a conversation. Then they answer a question in their books, and listen to the end of the conversation, which gives the correct answer. To do this exercise, students must make inferences from the conversations they hear. There are five conversations in this exercise.

To prepare students, discuss the picture. Point out that ATMs are common sights in American shopping malls, and ask them what other things they might see in a mall. Then have them read the answer choices along with you, making sure they understand each one.

Now students are ready to listen to the conversations. You might want to stop after the first one and have students give you the answer. Then when you are sure they understand how to do this type of

listening exercise, play the rest of the tape. Go over students' answers when they are finished. Replay the tape if necessary to clarify correct answer choices.

Answers: Part 1—a bank ATM;
Part 2—a sports supply shop;
Part 3—a bakery;
Part 4—a bookstore;
Part 5—a clothing store

p. 25, Ex. 2

Discuss the questions and Ali's budget with the students. Even students who live with their families may have budgets. If not, have them imagine the kind of budget they would need if they lived on their own.

p. 25, Ex. 3

This is another global listening task. Go over the question, and remind students that they only have to listen for this information. Then play the tape and elicit students' answers.

Answer: Ali spends the most money on rent.

p. 25, Ex. 4

For this exercise, students will listen to the conversation again, focusing only on the amounts of money Ali needs for each expense. Play the tape. Repeat, if necessary. If students have difficulty hearing the amounts, stop the tape after each one—many students have trouble distinguishing *fifty* (50) from *fifteen* (15).

Answers:
Rent: $435
Food: $240
Electricity: $50
Telephone: $24
Transportation: $25
Entertainment: $150

p. 25, Ex. 5

Ex. 5 again requires students to listen for specific information in the conversation. Have them read the questions first, and then listen to the conversation and mark their answers. Repeat the tape, if necessary.

Answers: 1. b 2. a 3. c

p. 25, Ex. 6

Discuss the questions with the students as a class, or have them work in pairs.

p. 26, Ex. 7

Go over the vocabulary with the students. You might have them use each word or phrase in a sentence.

p. 26, Ex. 8

For this exercise, students only have to match each ad they hear with the product it represents. Read the product names first, so they won't sound strange when the students hear them in context. For the first playing, stop the tape after each ad and ask students to name the product. Then play the tape through without stopping.

Answer: Wild West

p. 26, Ex. 9

Have students look at and discuss the three ads. This time, they will hear the same ads, but will be listening for information that ties the recorded ad to the print ad—in this case, the store name. Say each store name before you play the tape . Then play the tape. Stop after each ad if students are having difficulty. Otherwise, play the tape through, and repeat, if necessary.

Answers: Ad 1—CostClub; Ad 2—Lowe's; Ad 3—Morton's

p. 26, Ex. 10

This exercise is like Ex. 9, only the students will be listening for the price of the jeans in each ad. Say the amounts before you play the tape. Then play the tape through, and repeat, if necessary.

Answers: $21.99—Lowe's; $25.99—Morton's; $19.99—CostClub

p. 27, Ex. 11

Have students read the two questions, and then listen to the conversation again. Then have them discuss their answers in pairs.

Answers: 1. Morton's 2. CostClub (The lowest price for the same item)

Part Four: Speaking Up

p. 27, Ex. 1

Review the items in Ali's budget. Then have students work in pairs, helping each other make their own budgets. Again, if students do not live on their own, have them make up a budget for personal or day-to-day items and for entertainment, for example.

pp. 27-28, Ex. 2

Go over the clothing names in the list. Have students work in pairs to match the names with the pictures. Extend their vocabulary by eliciting the names of every visible item of clothing in the room. You can help students extend their vocabularies by putting categories on the board and listing (or having them list) types of items for each, such as *Shoes: running shoes, tennis shoes, flats, pumps, loafers,* etc.

Answers: 1. pants 2. shirt 3. blouse
4. dress 5. jacket 6. shoes 7. shorts
8. jeans 9. sweatshirt (or sweater)
10. baseball cap 11. boots 12. T-shirt

p. 29, Ex. 3

This is a guessing game. Suggest that students make the game more challenging by going beyond the clothing names in this section and using ones from the extended lists you generated in Ex. 2.

p. 29, Culture Note

Discuss the Culture Note. Many clothing "rules" in the United States reflect the informality of American culture; for example, many corporations now have "dress down" Fridays, when employees are allowed to wear casual outfits to the office.

p. 29, Ex. 4

This is an Information Gap activity. Students must ask each other questions and listen for the answers in order to answer the questions. Go over the store names and model the first question in each set. Remind students not to look at each other's ads. As they work, go around and offer help if necessary.

Answers: 1. Morton's—$25.99; Lowe's—
$21.99; CostClub—$19.99;
2. Morton's—$29.99; Lowe's—$21.99;
CostClub—$24.99;   3. Morton's—$39.99;
Lowe's—$49.99; CostClub—$35.00

p. 31, Ex. 5

In the same groups, have students discuss their answers to these questions. Circulate and give help, if necessary.

Answers: 1. CostClub   2. Lowe's
3. CostClub

Follow-Up

If you are in an English speaking environment, you might ask students to bring clothing ads into class to discuss. Have them talk about and compare stores, products, prices, and any other information in the ads that makes them interested or disinterested in buying the product. You can also have them compare clothing ads in their native countries to those in English-speaking countries.

If you are not in an English speaking environment, you might want to purchase an English, American, Australian, or Canadian fashion magazine and photocopy a selection of ads to discuss. If they exist, have students discuss American clothing companies with outlets in your area (such as The Gap). Do students have the impression that there are differences between products, prices, and advertising here and in the United States? Why or why not?

Chapter Three: Friends and Family

Chapter Three is all about friends and family. Students talk about friends, family, and homesickness, practice listening to and leaving phone messages, and learn ways of describing people.

Part One

pp. 34-37, Getting the Main Idea

Students meet Rob, Beth, and Lee again. To begin, have students look at and discuss the opening photo. Encourage them to talk about their families. If they are away from home, discuss homesickness. If they are in their home environment, ask them to think of a time when they were far from their families, and to describe how they felt.

p. 34, Ex. 1

Ask students to look at the list of words in Ex. 1 and circle any they don't know. Discuss the words with them if necessary. They can look the words up in a bilingual or English-English dictionary, if they want. Then play the conversation.

p. 34, Ex. 2

Students complete the sentences with the words from Ex. 1. There are several ways to conduct this exercise. See Teaching Tips, Chapter One, for a list of suggestions.

Answers: 2. to miss   3. to be homesick
4. to guess

p. 35, Ex. 3

Tell students that they are going to listen to a conversation and answer some questions about it. Read the three questions with them before they listen and make sure they understand them. Remind students that they do not have to understand every word when they listen to the conversation. They should only listen for the answers to the questions.

Play the tape as many times as necessary for students to get all of the answers. If students are having problems with a particular question, stop the tape at the point where the necessary information is located.

Answers: 1. He misses his family.
2. By phone   3. Call his family

p. 35–36, Ex. 4

As in Chapter Two, this exercise requires students to listen for and fill in the stressed words in a conversation. To prepare students, first have them repeat the words in the list that precedes the dialogue. Then have them listen at least once to the conversation without writing. Ask them to focus on the stressed words in each sentence. Tell them to listen for the words that sound longer—these are most likely the stressed words. If necessary, have them listen a second time before they write.

Then have students listen for and write down the missing stressed words in the blanks in the conversation. Repeat the tape as many times as necessary for everyone to get the words.

Answers: 1. Lee 2. Beth 3. I 4. movie
5. with 6. OK 7. minute 8. What
9. reading 10. letter 11. family
12. why 13. sad 14. miss 15. homesick
16. I 17. homesick 18. family 19. too
20. really 21. family 22. friends
23. Charlottesville

p. 36, Ex. 5

This exercise is similar to Ex. 4, except students see the dialogue, which is a continuation of the previous one. This time, though, they listen for and underline the stressed words. Have them listen at least once to the conversation before they write. Then have them listen and underline the stressed words. Play the tape again, if necessary.

See Tapescript, Chapter Three, p. 170, of the text for the answers.

p. 37, Speaking Activity

This activity gives students a chance to practice asking questions inspired by the conversation from Part One. Start off by asking the class as a whole how they keep in touch with friends and family who are far away. Then get students into groups of four. First, go over the questions and make sure they understand each one. Have them look at Sally's answers and turn them into complete answers. Then have them practice the questions by asking you first. Make sure each group member asks a question. Then have them write their group members' names in the blanks on the chart and take turns asking each other each of the questions. At this point, walk around the room and give help where needed. When all the groups have finished, call on them to report on their answers.

Part Two

p. 38, Ex. 1

As in Chapter Two, this exercise requires students to listen to a short conversation for global understanding only. First have them look at and discuss the two pictures. Then tell them to listen to the conversation and decide where the speakers are—in other words, which picture goes with the conversation. Remind them that they only have to listen for this one bit of information. Most likely, they will only have to listen one time, but repeat the tape if necessary.

Note: Americans often begin conversations with new people at parties by asking them where they are from or what they do (what their profession is). Also, it is perfectly acceptable for women to start conversations with men they don't know, and vice versa.

Answer: A

p. 39, Ex. 2

Now students listen to the same conversation they heard in Ex. 1, but this time, for more specific information. Have them read the questions first, and then listen to the conversation. This helps them focus on and listen for only the information they need to answer the questions. Repeat the tape if necessary.

Answers: 1. c 2. c 3. b

p. 39, Ex. 3

Ex. 3 extends the material from the previous conversation. First, read the expressions and make sure students understand them. Then have them repeat the expressions. Explain the chart and the difference between "formal" and "informal" by giving a few examples, if necessary. Elicit further examples from the students. Then have them work in small groups to complete the chart. Encourage them to add their own expressions. Go around and offer help, if necessary. When they are finished, have them report on their results.

Possible answers:

Formal/People You Know: Hello. How are you? It's nice to see you again.

Formal/People You Don't Know: Hello. My name is . . . ; Excuse me. Do you know when the next bus is coming?; Excuse me. May I ask you a few questions about . . . ?

Informal/People You Know: Hello. How are you? It's nice to see you again; Hi. How's it going?

Informal/People You Don't Know: Hi. How's it going?; Excuse me. Do you know when the next bus is coming?; Excuse me. May I ask you a few questions about . . . ?

p. 40, Ex. 4

This exercise is similar to the preceding one. Follow the procedure for Ex. 3.

Possible answers:

Formal/People You Know: Would you excuse me please? I'm late for a meeting.; Thank you for your help. Good-bye.

Formal/People You Don't Know: Would you excuse me please? I'm late for a meeting.; It was nice to meet you; I've enjoyed talking to you. Thank you for your help. Good-bye.; Maybe we could get together sometime?

Informal/People You Know: I've got to go now. I'll talk to you later.; Let's get together some time. Call me when you get a chance.

Informal/People You Don't Know: I've got to go now. I'll talk to you later. It was nice to meet you. Let's get together sometime. Call me when you get a chance.; I'd better get going. Nice talking to you.

p. 41, Ex. 5

Go over the idea that people can discuss some subjects with some people, and others with other people. Give examples, and have the students offer their own. Then go over the items in the two lists, "Who" and "When," as well as the topics in the

chart. Have students get into small groups to discuss and complete the chart. Go around and offer help, if necessary. Have the groups report on their results when they are finished. Note that answers will vary.

p. 42, Culture Note

Discuss the Culture Note. It is considered impolite in American culture to ask people how much money they make. It's impolite to ask someone how much he or she paid for something (e.g., a item of clothing, an appliance, etc.) unless the person is a very good friend. Americans, especially in social situations, also tend not to ask each other what religion they belong to or which political party they support.

p. 42, Ex. 6

Explain to students that Americans vary the way they greet each other, depending on the situation. Go over the situations in the chart and give further examples. Act out the greetings, if necessary. Then have students get into pairs to complete the chart. Have them take as much time as they need to think of examples from their own culture. If you are in a homogeneous situation, this task will be fairly easy. When they are finished, have students share their examples with the class. Note that answers will vary.

Note: This exercise prepares students for the role-play in Ex. 7.

---

p. 42, Ex. 7

Note that for this role-play, students are asked to role-play the U.S. or Canadian behavior. A variation, which works well in a non-homogeneous situation, is to have students act out the behavior in their native cultures, as well.

Part Three

p. 43, Ex. 1

As in the previous chapters, students listen to the first part of a conversation. Then they answer a question in their books, and listen to the end of the conversation, which gives the correct answer. To do this exercise, students must make inferences from the conversations they hear. There are five conversations in this exercise.

To prepare students, discuss the picture. Point out that ATMs are common sights in American shopping malls, and ask them who they see. Then have them read the questions and answers choices along with you, making sure they understand each one.

Now students are ready to listen to the conversations. You might want to stop after the first one and have students give you the answer. Then when you are sure they understand how to do this type of listening exercise, play the rest of the tape. Go over students' answers when they are finished. Replay the tape if necessary to clarify correct answer choices.

Answers: 1. b 2. b 3. c 4. c 5. a

p. 44, Ex. 2

Discuss the questions with the students. Then discuss the expressions in the list. Have students listen to them on the tape. Discuss any additional expressions and phone services students might be familiar with, such as "voice mail."

p. 44, Ex. 3

Have students read the list of expressions and circle any they don't know. Then have them listen to the tape. Discuss them with the students.

p. 44, Ex. 4

This is another global listening task. Go over the question, and remind students that they only have to listen for the number of people who left a message for Danny. In other words, they will have to count the messages they hear.

Answer: 5

p. 45, Ex. 5

For this exercise, students will listen to the conversation again, this time focusing on the content of each message. It might help to have them look at and describe each picture before you play the tape again. Play the tape again, if necessary, and go over students' answers.

Answers: Picture 1—Message 1;
Picture 2—Message 4;
Picture 3—Message 2;
Picture 4—Message 3;
Picture 5—Message 5

p. 45, Ex. 6

Have students read the list of words and expressions and circle any they don't know. Then have them listen to the tape. Discuss them with the students.

p. 45, Ex. 7

Have students look at and discuss the two pictures on p. 46. Ask them to describe the two women. Tell them that they will hear Beth describing her friend Sue. Play the tape and have students identify the woman Beth is talking about.

Answer: B

p. 46, Ex. 8

For this exercise, students will listen to Beth's description again. This time, students will listen for specific information about Sue's appearance. Have students read the questions first. Then play the tape. Play it again, if necessary, and then check answers.

Answers: 1. b 2. a 3. b

Part Four

p. 47, Ex. 1

First discuss students' experiences with and feelings about telephone answering machines. They are so common nowadays that most people are quite used to them. However, leaving a message on an answering machine in a foreign language can be quite daunting. This exercise provides students with a repertory of appropriate answering machine expressions, which will give them confidence when they are confronted with this task in real life.

First, have students repeat the expressions in the chart. Answer any questions they may have about the vocabulary and expressions. Then get them into small groups. Explain that in their groups, they will take turns picking a situation, recording a message, and then guessing which situation each message refers to.

p. 48, Ex. 2

Review the words and expressions for describing people. A good way to do this is to bring in magazine pictures that illustrate each one. Make sure students understand them.

p. 48, Ex. 3

Have students work on this role-play in pairs. Walk around and offer help, if needed. You may want to supply them with the language they will need to play their roles fully, i.e., for the police officer: "Can you describe the robber?" For the witness: "Yes, sir/ma'am. S/he . . ." etc.

p. 49, Ex. 4

You may need to supply the pictures for this activity. Your students might enjoy using photos of favorite movie starts, TV personalities, fashion models, and pop stars.

Follow-Up

Have students combine phone messages with describing people. Using the tape recorders from Ex. 1, and the magazine photos from this exercise, have them pretend they are setting up a blind date between a classmate and a "friend" of theirs—one of the people in the photos. Have them call the classmate, get the answering machine, and record a description of the blind date. Prepare them with any extra words and expressions they might need to do this activity, such as:

Student 1: "Clara is really looking forward to meeting you. She'll meet you at (a place in the neighborhood or at school) at 7 P.M. She's tall and has long black hair . . ." etc.

Then, have students listen to the message and try to pick the person being described from the photos.

p. 49, Culture Note

Discuss these ideas with your class. North Americans are particularly sensitive about things they cannot change, such as their size or weight. For example, you never ask a North American how much he or she weighs. Ask students to think of

similar issues that people in their culture(s) are sensitive about, and if there are any rules for discussing or not discussing these issues, such as using euphemisms.

Chapter Four: Health Care

In Chapter Four, students talk about illnesses and problems and giving and getting advice. They also learn how to make appointments and requests and practice following instructions.

Part One

p. 51, Opening

Have students look at and discuss the opening photo. Encourage them to talk about illnesses and different ways of dealing with them. If students are unfamiliar with acupuncture, do a little research on it and share it with them. Acupuncture is becoming quite popular in the United States, along with other alternative approaches to healing such as herbal medicine and chiropractic medicine.

p. 52, Ex. 1

Ask students to look at the list of words in Ex. 1 and circle any they don't know. Discuss the words with them if necessary. They can look the words up in a bilingual or English-English dictionary, if they want. Then play the conversation.

p. 52, Ex. 2

Students complete the sentences with the words from Ex. 1. There are several ways to conduct this exercise. See Teaching Tips, Chapter One, for a list of suggestions.

Answers: 2. to make an appointment
3. ID card   4. health clinic   5. insurance card

p. 52, Ex. 3

Tell students that they are going to listen to a conversation and answer some questions about it. Read the questions with them before they listen and make sure they understand them. Remind students that they do not have to understand every word when they listen to the conversation. They should only listen for the answers to the questions.

Play the tape as many times as necessary for students to get all of the answers. If students are having problems with a particular question, stop the tape at the point where the necessary information is located.

Answers: 1. The health clinic.   2. He has the flu./He's sick.   3. Tomorrow at 1:00 P.M.   4. His health insurance card.   5. No.

pp. 52-53, Ex. 4

As in previous chapters, this exercise requires students to listen for and fill in the stressed words in a conversation. See Chapters 1–3 for details on how to proceed with this exercise.

Answers: 2. help   3. Yes   4. think   5. flu
6. like   7. appointment   8. doctor
9. right   10. you   11. tomorrow   2. afternoon   13. 1:00   14. I   15. then   16. Oh!
17. bring   18. money   19. No   20. ID
21. insurance   22. card

p. 53, Ex. 5

This exercise is similar to Ex. 4, except students see the dialogue, which is a continuation of the previous one. See previous chapters for details on how to proceed.

See Tapescript, Chapter Four, pp. 175-176, of the text for answers.

p. 54, Reductions

See Chapter Two for an explanation of reductions. Have students listen to the examples. You might want to provide additional examples contextualized in sentences, either on the board or orally (for example, *hafta* for *have to*, *why're* for *why are*, etc.), and have students try to guess the long forms.

p. 54, Ex. 7

As in Chapter Two, students listen to sentences with either a reduction or the long form and identify the version they hear. Repeat the exercise, if necessary.

Answers: 1. b   2. a   3. b   4. b

p. 55, Speaking Activity

This activity gives students a chance to practice asking questions inspired by the conversation from Part One. Start off by reviewing the problems and North American solutions. Make sure students understand each item. Then get them into small groups to complete the chart with solutions from their cultures for each problem. This works just as well with homogeneous groups, as students may have personal or regional variations in how to solve the problems.

After they finish, have students share their solutions with the rest of the class. You can extend the exercise by eliciting other services, either in the U.S. and Canada, or in the students' home countries, that don't appear in the chart.

Part Two

p. 56, Ex. 1

Ask students to look at the list of words and circle any they don't know. Discuss the words with them if necessary. They can look the words up in a bilingual or English-English dictionary, if they want.

p. 56, Ex. 2

As in previous chapters, this exercise requires students to listen to a short conversation for global understanding. However, this particular listening task is a little more difficult than those in previous chapters. Have them read the two questions, and then play the tape. You may have to play it more than once.

Answers: 1. Her friend is angry with her.
2. He tells her to write a letter, and then call about a week later.

p. 56, Ex. 3

Now students listen to the same conversation they heard in Ex. 1, but this time, for more specific information. Have them read the questions first, and then listen to the conversation. This helps them focus on and listen for only the information they need to answer the questions. Repeat the tape if necessary.

Answers: 1. a   2. c   3. b

p. 57, Ex. 4

Ex. 4 extends the material from the previous conversation. First, read the advice expressions and make sure students understand them. Then have them repeat the expressions. Have students read the problems, and make sure they understand them, as well.

After this, have students work in pairs to practice giving and getting advice. Walk around and offer help as needed. Encourage students to be creative and make up their own problems and advice.

p. 57, Ex. 5

This is a combination role-play and listening activity. Have students pick their best exchange from Ex. 4 and perform it for the class. While the class watches, the students must listen carefully to answer the questions in the chart. Go over the questions to make sure students understand them and know what they are going to be listening for.

p. 57, Culture Note

Discuss this note with the class. Radio talk shows are not only popular in the U.S. but they sometimes have a great influence on public opinion. Have students compare the role of radio talk shows in North America and their home cultures.

Part Three

p. 58, Ex. 1

Ask students to look at the list of words in Ex. 1 and circle any they don't know. Discuss the words with them if necessary. They can look the words up in a bilingual or English-English dictionary, if they want.

p. 58, Ex. 2

As in the previous chapters, students listen to the first part of a conversation. Then they answer a question in their books, and listen to the end of the conversation, which gives the correct answer. To do this exercise, students must make inferences from the conversations they hear. There are five conversations in this exercise.

To prepare students, discuss the picture and the eight services listed. Make sure students understand what each is, and the reasons for calling them. Students will hear conversations about five of these.

Now students are ready to listen to the conversations. You might want to stop after the first one and have students give you the answer. Then, when you are sure they understand how to do this type of listening exercise, play the rest of the tape. Go over the students' answers when they are finished. Replay the tape if necessary to clarify correct answer choices.

Answers: 1. health clinic   2. help line
3. police department   4. dental clinic
5. poison control

p. 59, Ex. 3

This exercise affords an opportunity to expand the discussion you had at the beginning of the chapter about acupuncture. Encourage students to discuss various ways of dealing with the same health problem, and to make culture comparisons, if possible.

p. 59, Ex. 4

Discuss the expressions in the list. Have students listen to them on the tape. Discuss any additional health-related expressions students might be familiar with, or that may have come up in the discussion in Ex. 3.

p. 59, Ex. 5

This is another global listening task. Go over the question, and remind students that they only have to listen for what is wrong with Ali.

Answer: He has the flu (influenza).

pp. 59-60, Ex. 6

For this exercise, students will listen to the conversation again, this time focusing on the doctor's advice. Before you play the tape, have students look at the pictures and read the advice in Items 1-5. Then play the tape. It may be necessary to play the tape more than once.

Answers: 1. You should stay in bed and rest as much as possible.   2. You can take two aspirin four times a day.   3. Be sure to drink plenty of fluids. Fruit juice and hot tea are the best.   4. Here's a prescription for some cough medicine. You can take it to any drug store.   5. Be sure to take your medicine with your meals because it might upset your stomach.

p. 60, Ex. 7

Have students read the list of words and expressions and circle any they don't know. Then have them listen to the tape. Discuss them with the students.

p. 60, Ex. 8

Have students read the three questions before they listen to the tape. Then play the tape. Go over their answers, and play the tape again if there is any confusion.

Answers: 1. 6   2. 3   3. 1. (1) headache; (4) toothache; (5) pain in ankle/sprained ankle

p. 61, Ex. 9

Students listen to the speakers again. This time, they match the advice with the speaker it best corresponds to. Play the tape a second time so students can check their answers.

Answers: Speaker 4: You should take two aspirin for the pain and see a dentist . . . ; Speaker 5: You should wrap a tight bandage . . . ;   Speaker 6: You can take some medicine . . . ;   Speaker 3: You must go to a doctor and get a cast . . . ;   Speaker 2: You shouldn't eat anything . . .

Part Four

p. 61, Ex. 1

This role-play gives students a chance to use some of the language they've heard in previous conversations. First review some of the vocabulary and expressions students have heard for describing the flu and for giving advice. Then have them work in pairs. Go around and offer help as needed. Encourage students to be creative and go beyond the language you've just reviewed, if possible. You can have particularly strong students perform their role-plays for the class.

p. 61, Ex. 2

Have students discuss these questions in small groups. If you have a heterogeneous group, mix cultures as much as possible. If you have a homogeneous group, mix ages, genders, etc., and encourage students to share personal and family remedies. They can also compare how colds and other illnesses were treated in the past with how they are treated today.

p. 62, Ex. 3

Explain what a survey is to the students. Tell students they are going to do a survey of class members to find out how healthy they are. Review the questions in the chart. Explain how to check answers "Yes" or "No." Point out that Question 6 is open-ended; that is, it requires a longer answer than just "Yes" or "No."

Get students into groups of 4–6 and have them begin the survey. Walk around and offer help as needed. When every group has finished, get the class back together to share the results. Help students summarize their group's results so that they can then synthesize all the groups' results and answer the final question: Is your class healthy?

p. 63, Ex. 4

In pairs, have students read the list of words and expressions and circle any they don't know. Walk around and offer help as needed. Students can use dictionaries, if necessary.

p. 63, Ex. 5

This is a fun game for practicing and reviewing body parts. However, depending on the make-up of your class and the cultures represented, it may not work to have students touching each other. Here's an alternate way to do this activity. Get a large sheet of heavy white paper at an art supply store. You'll need a piece that is longer than you are tall and about three feet wide. Put it on the floor. Lie down on it. Have a friend draw an outline of your body. Use this outline to create a person. Make all the body parts listed in Ex. 4 as visible as possible. You can make it male or female and give him or her a name. Then pin the outline on a wall in your classroom and have students use it to do the exercise.

p. 63, Ex. 6

Follow the directions for Ex. 5 for this exercise.

p. 64, Ex. 7

Make sure you think of an exercise that doesn't require uncomfortable or inappropriate movements for modest students. If you have the kind of students that will really enjoy this activity, get music to accompany the exercise lessons. You can even have students prepare their lessons and choose their own music as a homework assignment.

p. 64, Ex. 8

Talk about exercise with the class. Have them compare the role it plays in people's lives today with the past. If there have been changes, to what do students attribute these changes? Go over the questions in the chart, and have students complete it in small groups. Have them share their results with the class when they have finished.

As a follow-up, discuss the culture note. You might add that in North America, it is impolite to ask someone how much they weigh.

Chapter Five: Men and Women

This chapter focuses on social relationships, especially those between men and women. This chapter is especially important for students who expect to use English to communicate with people from other cultures because it includes discussion of some social customs and how they are different from culture to culture.

Part One

pp. 66-68, Getting the Main Idea

In this conversation, Beth, Alicia and Lee discuss different customs related to finding marriage partners.

p. 66, Ex. 1

Ask students to look at the list of words in Ex. 1 and circle any they don't know. Discuss the words with them if necessary.

Note: The expression "to make a date" with someone can be used for social situations other than dating. For example, a friend might say "Let's make a date to have dinner together soon" without implying any romantic relationship. However, "to make an appointment" is the more commonly used expression for business meetings, doctor's visits, job interviews, and other occasions that take place in an office.

p. 66, Ex. 2

Ask students to look at the three questions in their texts. Read through the questions with them to make sure they understand the questions.

Play the tape. If the students seem to have gotten the answers to the questions, elicit the answers from them. If they have not been able to answer most of the questions, play the tape again, stopping it if necessary to point out where the key information was contained in the conversation.

Answers: 1. a guy in her French class
2. a girlfriend from gym class   3. go out with Alicia's friend

pp. 66-67, Ex. 3

Play the first part of the conversation again. The students are to fill in the blanks in their textbook with words from the list. You may need to play the tape more than once. Go over the answers.

Answers: 1. tomorrow   2. seven   3. that
4. special   5. Jack   6. nice   7. French
8. asked   9. out   10. accepted   11. one
12. boyfriend   13. boyfriend   14. yet
15. happy   16. Mexico   17. parents'
18. date   19. boy   20. Korea   21. 10
22. 20   23. all   24. marriages   25. strict
26. arranged   27. dates   28. marriages
29. common

p. 67, Ex. 4

Remind students of the importance of stressed words in English. Play the second part of the conversation. Students underline the words they hear stressed. There aren't really right and wrong answers for this exercise, as stress is often complex and difficult to hear. However, students should be underlining content words, not articles or prepositions unless they are unusually stressed in a sentence for a reason.

See Tapescript, Chapter Five, p. 182, of the text for the answers.

p. 68, Ex. 5

Words that are written separately are often combined when spoken. When that happens, the same pronunciation rules that operate inside words also operate on the combined words. So the combination of *did* and you becomes *didja* just as the word *education* is often pronounced *edjucation*. Now, play the tape and direct students' attention to the reduced sound.

p. 68, Ex. 6

Answers: 1. a   2. b   3. b   4. a   5. b   6. a

p. 68, Speaking Activity

This activity gives students a chance to use some of the vocabulary about dating and marriage that they heard in the taped conversation, and to discuss changes in customs. Circulate while the students are working in groups to answer questions and supply any vocabulary they need. Have groups report some of their answers to the class.

Note: When we give examples about the United States, we are referring to the what is usually considered the mainstream culture. There are, of course, many groups in the U.S. with different customs. If students in your class belong to any of those groups, ask them to contrast their customs to those commonly portrayed on TV in the U.S.

Part Two

p. 69, Ex. 1

Encourage students to listen to the conversation for general understanding. Go over the two questions in their books. Check the answers; then play the tape one or two more times so students can listen for more specific details.

Answers: 1. yes   2. at a party or social gathering

p. 70, Ex. 2

Go over the parts of a small-talk conversation with the students. Then play the tape. You might want to stop the tape often and ask students to identify what they just heard as a greeting, a small-talk topic, or a leave-taking. Discuss how people perform greetings and leave-takings in the students' culture(s).

Answers: 2. small talk   3. more small talk
4. leave-taking

pp. 70-71, Ex. 3

Brainstorm some greeting and leave-taking expressions appropriate for each of the listed situations with the students before starting this activity.

Explain to the students that they are supposed to find people who are interested in sports, movies, and so on to fill in the chart in their books, but that they should do this in the context of mingling at a party. That is, they should not forget the greetings and leave-takings. Circulate while they do this activity to prompt them to practice "small talk."

Note: Making a chart or graph to display the information is an important part of this activity. The ability to use graphics with text is an important skill, especially for students studying—or planning to study—technical fields. The students should be able to write sentences that indicate the important points from their charts and graphs.

Part Three

p. 72, Ex. 1

Conduct this as you have in preceding chapters.

Answers: 1. c   2. b   3. c   4. b   5. a

p. 73, Ex. 2

Discuss the questions with the students. Ask them how they invite people for dinner. Do they entertain at home or at a restaurant? What kind of food do they serve? Do guests bring anything?

Discuss the vocabulary words and phrases. Point out that "We're having chicken for dinner" means they are eating chicken, while "We'd like to have you for dinner" is an invitation. Americans are more likely to add the word "over," as in "We're having the Johnson's over for dinner" to avoid confusion and unintended humor.

p. 73, Ex. 4

Encourage students to listen for general understanding.

Answers: 1. yes   2. 7:00 P.M. (1900 international time)

p. 74, Ex. 5

You may need to play the tape more than once for students to identify the words they hear. Note that this is a good opportunity to discuss the difference between "bring" and "take."

Answers: How; doing; calling; over; come; love; going; bring; have; see; about; then

p. 75, Ex. 7

Brainstorm possible answers with the students. Write their suggestions on the board. A few possible answers are given below, but many more expressions are acceptable.

Possible answers: 1. I'd love to. Yes, I'd be happy to.   2. I'd like to, but I'm afraid I can't make it. I'm sorry, but I won't be able to come. Could we do it another time? Perhaps we could get together next week.   3. The same as for number 2, but without the suggestion to get together at another time.

p. 75, Ex. 9

Play the whole conversation. When students have decided on the answers to the questions, they can check their answers by comparing with another student or by listening to the tape again.

Answers: 1. to a basketball game   2. Beth

Part Four

p. 75, Ex. 1

Concepts of time are very different from culture to culture. There are many stereotypes about cultures where people are "always late" or "always on time." In fact, in every culture, there are rules about time that members of the culture understand, but outsiders usually don't. This exercise is designed to help students explore these rules, first by looking outside their culture. The exercise will be most helpful to students living in the U.S. or Canada, but can lead to discussion that will help students interpret time rules whenever they encounter another culture. After discussing the answers to each question, ask students to reflect on the same situation in their own culture. Again, U.S. means mainstream, predominantly Anglo-Saxon culture.

Possible Answers: 1. People tend to eat dinner earlier in the U.S. than they do in many other cultures. When a host invites people to dinner at 7:00, it often means that dinner is timed for 7:30, after half an hour of conversation and perhaps drinks and snacks. In an informal survey, most people from the U.S. who were asked this question said that they would normally arrive no more than 5 to 10 minutes after the time stated for a dinner party. If they arrived at 7:15, they would casually say something about the traffic being bad. If they arrived at 7:30, they would feel the need to apologize and offer a good excuse.

2. Time rules for parties other than dinner are more relaxed. People can arrive at any time up to the expected ending time of the party. If, for example, you know that the party is likely to continue until 1:00 or 2:00 in the morning, you can arrive as late as 10:00. Many people, especially at holiday times, go to more than one party in an evening.

3. Many international students in the U.S. have reported confusion related to statements like this. People will often say "I'll call you" as a polite leave-taking, not because they really intend to call. Most

members of the culture know this and do not wait for a call or experience disappointment when it doesn't come.

p. 76, Culture Note

Students may be unfamiliar with this kind of party. In many cultures, the host or hostess is expected to provide all the food and drink for the guest. Students may receive invitations including the instruction B.Y.O.B. (Bring your own bottle—wine, beer, whatever you want to drink) or "potluck," which means that you are expected to bring some food. Discuss the pros and cons of this kind of entertainment with your class.

Pros: People without a lot of money can afford to entertain more often. Everyone brings a specialty so the food is often very interesting and good.

Cons: Guests have to do some of the work. You never know what kind of food you're going to have—it could be eight salads and no meat (although most hosts provide at least one main dish) or all desserts.

p. 76, Ex. 2

Have students match the pictures with the vocabulary. Then go over the words. Discuss what each weather condition is like. Ask if they have ever been in or seen snow or a tornado.

Answers: 1. a 2. f 3. e 4. g 5. c 6. d
7. b

p. 77, Ex. 3

Elicit as many weather words as possible. Write them on the board. Then, for Item 1, circulate while students are drawing to make sure they understand not to write the word on their pictures. Call on each student to hold up the picture while the class guesses the word.

For Item 2, have students discuss the weather sayings in pairs. Then ask them to report their answers to the class. Accept any reasonable interpretation of the sayings.

p. 77, Ex. 4

Write the students' predictions on the board or on a large sheet of paper and hang it on the wall, if possible. Then, the next day, students can read the predictions and decide if they were right.

Chapter Six: Native Americans and Immigrants

This chapter focuses on the American West, native Americans (formerly called "Indians"), and language related to traveling and giving directions. Parts of this chapter will be especially relevant to students whose families have moved to the United States from another country.

Part One

pp. 80-83, Getting the Main Idea

Rob, Beth, and Ali are looking at photographs taken on a trip to California.

p. 80, Ex. 1

Ask students to look at the list of words in Ex. 1 and circle any they don't know. Discuss the words with them if necessary.

Note: The terms "West Coast" and "East Coast" are commonly used designations for regions of the U.S. and for the lifestyles of those regions. East Coast generally refers to the cities of New York, Washington, Boston and the areas between them. West Coast often refers to the Hollywood-Los Angeles entertainment community and the outdoor life of California.

p. 80, Ex. 2

Students fill in the blanks in their textbooks with words from the list.

Answers: 1. coast 2. community
3. native 4. tribes 5. take; pictures
6. ethnic 7. immigrant

p. 81, Ex. 3

Ask students to look at the three questions in their texts. Read through the questions with them to make sure they understand the questions.

Note: The term "Indian" was used in the past for the people who lived in North and South America when the first Europeans arrived. Columbus and the other Europeans thought they had sailed to the shores of India. This term was the result of a mistake, so now we use the term "Native Americans" or the tribal names.

Answers: 1. pictures (photographs)
2. Los Angeles   3. The Southwest (Native American communities)

p. 81, Ex. 4

Play the first part of the conversation again. The students are to fill in the blanks in their textbook with words from the list. You may need to play the tape more than once. Go over the answers.

Answers: 1. pictures   2. took   3. Bridge
4. all   5. these   6. looking   7. West
8. Coast   9. this   10. did   11. That's
12. large

p. 82, Ex. 5

Remind students of the importance of stressed words in English. Play the second part of the conversation. Students underline the words they hear stressed. There aren't really right and wrong answers for this exercise, as stress is often complex and difficult to hear. However, students should be underlining content words, not articles or prepositions unless they are unusually stressed in a sentence for a reason.

See Tapescript, Chapter Six, p. 188, of the text for the answers.

p. 82, Ex. 6

Play the tape and direct students' attention to the reduced sound.

pp. 82-83, Ex. 7

Answers: 1. a   2. b   3. a   4. b   5. b

p. 83, Speaking Activity

This activity gives students a chance to use some of the vocabulary about travel that they heard in the taped conversation, and to discuss places they would like to visit. First, brainstorm with the class vocabulary for the categories. Then circulate while the students are working in groups to answer questions and supply any vocabulary they need. Here are some ideas for categories:

Natural scenery: mountains, rivers, lakes, valleys, trees, hills, plains, parks, snow, beaches, palm trees

Man-made sights: houses of famous people, historical buildings and monuments, names of museums

People: different clothing, ethnic groups such as Gypsies, Serbs, etc., cultural practices such as those of the Amish in Pennsylvania who still use horse-drawn carts

Other: famous stores, food, customs

Part Two

p. 84, Ex. 1

Begin this section by asking students if they have seen movies or TV shows about Native Americans (Indians). What do they know about these people? Then, discuss the vocabulary words with the class. Finally, have them complete the nine sentences.

Answers: 1. survived   2. smallpox
3. ancestors   4. buffalo   5. treaty
6. acres   7. settle   8. come close to
9. peaceful

p. 85, Ex. 2

Encourage students to listen for general meaning the first time they hear the tape. Go through the questions with them before they listen to the tape.

Answers: 1. happy   2. yes   3. the west (Montana and Wyoming)

p. 85, Ex. 3

Read the sentences with the students. Make sure they understand the meanings. You may need to play the tape more than once.

Answers: 5; 3; 1; 4; 2

p. 86, Ex. 4

Now the students need to listen for more specific details. Stop the tape after you hear the answer to each of the questions and check for comprehension.

Answers: 1. b 2. d 3. a 4. c 5. a 6. c

p. 86, Culture Note

Differences in body language often lead to misunderstandings between people from different cultures. Do you or your students know of any other differences in body language? Talk about hand gestures and ways of sitting and standing, in addition to eye contact.

pp. 87-88, Ex. 5

This exercise helps students from diverse populations learn about each other and helps students value their families' experiences. If your students are living near their parents or other family members, give them a chance to interview the family before completing this activity.

Part Three

p. 89, Ex. 1

Conduct this as you have in preceding chapters.

Answers: 1. c 2. b 3. a 4. b 5. c

p. 90, Ex. 2

Discuss the questions with the students. Ask if they've had any funny or interesting experiences trying to find their way around in a strange place.

p. 90, Ex. 3

Discuss the vocabulary words and phrases.

p. 90, Ex. 4

Encourage students to listen for general understanding.

Answers: 1. Chinatown 2. walk 3. half an hour

p. 90, Ex. 5

You may need to play the tape more than once for students to identify the correct map.

Answer: Picture B

p. 91, Ex. 6

Play the tape. Stop and play parts again if necessary so that students can hear the words that go in the blanks in their textbooks.

Answers: 1. on 2. get 3. right 4. down 5. left 6. along 7. on 8. come

p. 91, Ex. 7

Discuss Question 1. Accept any responses. If students have no background information about the American West, tell how Europeans landed first on the east coast (from around Boston to Virginia and North Carolina), then moved west to find better farmland. They didn't know how far the land went until it reached water or what mountains and other barriers were in the way.

p. 91, Ex. 8

Encourage students to listen for general understanding.

Answers: 1. to find a route to the Pacific
2. Sacagawea (an Indian woman)
3. 1 1/2 years

p. 92, Ex. 9

Make sure students have identified the starting point of Lewis and Clark's journey (St. Louis) before you start the tape. Stop the tape if necessary to give students time to find the places mentioned on the map.

Answer: The group traveled north on the Missouri River until they reached a Mandan village, where they built Fort Mandan near the border with Canada. They later continued west to Great Falls and then crossed the Rocky Mountains. They navigated the Clearwater River to the Columbia River and finally reached the West Coast.

Part Four

pp. 92-94, Ex. 1

This exercise gives students practice giving directions. You may have to demonstrate with two students how the exercise works. Read through the directions with the students. Practice the expressions for giving directions on p. 92 with them. Make sure that each student in each group is looking at a different map. Then show them how to take turns asking each other how to get to the different locations on their lists. Circulate to answer questions and make sure all students are taking part in the activity.

p. 94, Ex. 2

Ask students to report on the directions their partner gave.

p. 94, Ex. 3

Ask the students to turn back in their texts to the map of Lewis and Clark's journey. Have students work in pairs to answer the questions.

Answers: 1. about 1,500 miles 2. roughly nine or ten 3. It was easier than traveling over land through the trees and over hills. 4. Possible problems include encountering wild animals, finding food, experiencing extreme cold and hot weather, crossing water, and climbing mountains.

p. 95, Ex. 4

Encourage students to be imaginative in doing this exercise. If they want to visit Mars, that's OK. Circulate as the students work in groups. Help them to think of places to get resources about their trip, including pictures and maps.

Chapter 7: Work and Lifestyles

This chapter focuses on the students' job plans and on communicating on the job. Even if students have already chosen their professions, they will learn work-related language in this chapter that will be useful to them.

Part One

pp. 98-100, Getting the Main Idea

Ali and Alicia are talking about summer job plans and their careers.

p. 98, Ex. 1

Ask students to look at the list of words in Ex. 1 and circle any they don't know. Discuss the words with them if necessary.

p. 98, Ex. 2

Students fill in the blanks in their textbooks with words from the list.

Answers: 1. reporter   2. public health
3. part-time   4. experience   5. journalism

p. 98, Ex. 3

Ask students to look at the three questions in their texts. Read through the questions with them to make sure they understand the questions.

Answers: 1. find summer jobs   2. public health and journalism   3. Alicia worked for a newspaper and Ali worked in a lab.

p. 99, Ex. 4

Play the first part of the conversation again. The students are to fill in the blanks in their textbook with words from the list. You may need to play the tape more than once. Go over the answers.

Answers: 1. really   2. public   3. health
4. sure   5. experience   6. part-time
7. lab   8. great   9. writing   10. newspaper   11. reporter   12. journalism
13. great   14. Mexico   15. City

p. 99, Ex. 5

Remind students of the importance of stressed words in English. Play the second part of the conversation. Students underline the words they hear stressed. There aren't really right and wrong answers for this exercise, as stress is often complex and difficult to hear. However, students should be underlining content words, not articles or prepositions unless they are unusually stressed in a sentence for a reason.

See Tapescript, Chapter Seven, p. 196, of the text for answers.

pp. 99-100, Ex. 6

Play the tape and direct students' attention to the reduced sound. Point out that the vowel changes they will hear in these sentences happen because those words and syllables are unstressed.

p. 100, Ex. 7

Answers: 1. a   2. b   3. b   4. b   5. a

p. 100, Speaking Activity

This activity asks students to think about what training is needed for different professions. Even students who are currently engaged in study in a specific field or who are practicing a profession will learn some new vocabulary in this exercise.

Answers: medical researcher—Chemistry; marketing director—Marketing; newspaper reporter—Journalism; computer programmer—Computer Science; systems analyst—Computer Science; x-ray technician—Medical Technology; actuary—Mathematics

Part Two

p. 101, Ex. 1

Begin this section by asking students if they have ever had to complain about someone's performance on the job—perhaps an incompetent clerk in a store or a waiter in a restaurant. What would they do if they had a co-worker who was incompetent or lazy?

Then, play the conversation once. Encourage students to listen for general meaning the first time they hear the tape. Go through the questions with them before they listen to the tape.

Answers: 1. She's having a problem with another worker.   2. that they talk to the other worker together

p. 101, Ex. 2

Go through the questions and answers before playing the tape. Make sure students understand the possible answers.

Answers: 1. c   2. a   3. c

pp. 101–102, Ex. 3

Read the situations with the students. Make sure they understand the meanings. Point out that people in different cultures would handle these situations differently. For example, Americans frequently send food back in a restaurant if it isn't prepared properly (Situation 2) but rarely tell other people to be quiet in the movies (Situation 6) because they don't want to start a fight. Allow about 15–20 minutes for them to discuss the situations in pairs and decide if they would make a complaint. Count the responses for each situation. Is there agreement among the students? Discuss why they would or would not complain in each situation.

p. 102, Ex. 4

This will work best if each pair of students has a different situation to role-play. They have to decide first what their roles are—who is the appropriate person to complain to? Circulate while they write their dialogues and encourage them to follow the four suggestions in their texts (be specific, use positive statements, try not to get angry, and try to find a solution).

Part Three

p. 102, Ex. 1

Conduct this as you have in preceding chapters.

Answers: 1. c   2. a   3. b   4. a   5. b

p. 102, Ex. 2

Ask if anyone in the class has ever interviewed for a job. If none of your students has ever had a job interview, ask if anyone expects to interview for jobs in the not-too-distant future and what the person expects to be asked on a job interview.

p. 102, Ex. 3 and 4

Discuss the vocabulary words and then encourage students to listen to the interview for general understanding.

Answers: 1. He likes computers.
2. department manager

p. 102, Ex. 5

Answers: 1. a   2. c   3. b

Part Four

pp. 104–105, Ex. 1

The purpose of this exercise and the next one is to get students to think about what kind of job or working environment would be right for them. If your students are already employed in their professions, you can still have them do Ex. 1, and then discuss which of those statements describe the job they currently have. Students should do Ex. 1 individually. Don't ask them to reveal their answers to this exercise.

p. 105, Ex. 2

Ask students to match the statements in Ex. 1 with the professions listed in Ex. 2. For example, a computer programmer should enjoy sitting at a computer for a long time, so students should write a "1" by computer programmer. Note that answers will vary.

p. 105, Ex. 3

Students should choose a profession from Ex. 2 and tell their partner why they would be good at that job. They should use the statements from Ex. 1. Explain that it doesn't matter if they are already working at a profession that isn't listed or if they don't really want to work at any of the jobs listed.

p. 106, Ex. 4

Now the students should write the information they gave orally in Ex. 3. The first blank should be filled in with one of the professions from Ex. 2. The reasons should come from the list in Ex. 1. Circulate as the students work to help them decide which statements support their career choice.

The second part of this exercise is optional. If your students have enjoyed talking about the various professions, take up their papers and read the statements from Ex. 4. Ask the class to guess who wrote each statement. This works well with a class that has been together long enough that the students know their classmates fairly well.

p. 106, Ex. 5

An interview grid like this one gives students a task that requires genuine communication. First, go over the questions with them. Practice the question forms if needed. Then have a few students ask you the questions so you can model the activity for them. Give your answers and show them how to note your answers in the appropriate spaces in the interview grid. Then put students in groups and have them take turns asking each other questions and noting the answers in their grids. Circulate to make sure they understand the directions and that everybody gets a chance to ask the questions.

p. 107, Ex. 6

Discuss the results of Ex. 5. You might draw the interview grid on the chalkboard and compile the results for the class. For example, if 12 people in the class say they want to have children in the future, write the number 12 in the space for that question. After you have discussed all the questions, have students write a paragraph about the class. For example, one sentence might be "Twelve members of the class hope to have children in the future, but three people do not want any children."

Chapter Eight: Food and Nutrition

In this chapter, students will practice using English to understand and talk about activities related to food and eating. They will learn how to (1) order in restaurants, (2) shop for food, (3) understand and use recipes to prepare dishes, and (4) compare foods and dishes common in the West with those from their native country or countries.

Part One

pp. 110–114

Before listening to the conversations, have the students (in pairs, small groups, and/or as a whole class) discuss the pictures on pp. 109 and 110. For the picture on p. 109, ask the students where the man is (in a supermarket) and in what section (the produce section). Ask the students to make a list of different sections one would find in a large, modern supermarket and then to list five items one would find in each section (for example, produce section: apples, lettuce, bananas, carrots, melon). For p. 110, ask the students where they think the people are (a fast-food restaurant) and why (because they're standing in line to order their food). You can also have the students talk about their food shopping and eating habits by asking questions such as: How often do you go food shopping? What kinds of food and drinks do you usually buy? How often do you eat in restaurants? Do you like fast-food restaurants? If so, what kinds do you like? If not, why not? Then begin the exercises. Follow the same procedures as outlined in previous chapters for Exercises 1–7.

p. 111, Ex. 2

Answers: 2. worry about   3. an order of
4. bad for you   5. diet

p. 111, Ex. 3

Answers: 1. at a fast-food restaurant
2. a double cheeseburger and a large order of fries   3. they have a lot of fat   4. it's bad for your teeth   5. because there's no sugar in a diet cola

pp. 111–112, Ex. 4

Answers: 1. order   2. hungry   3. cheeseburger   4. order   5. fries   6. eat
7. picnic   8. what   9. like   10. worried
11. healthy   12. fat

p. 112, Ex. 7

Answers: 1. a   2. b   3. b   4. b   5. a

p. 114, Speaking Activity

The teacher should circulate among student pairs to monitor the students' spoken English; make sure students are using *is* for non-count nouns and *are* for count nouns. After the pairs have finished with the 12 items, review differing answers. For example, "eggs" can be bad for you because they have a lot of fat (cholesterol), but they're good once or twice a week because they are inexpensive and have protein.

Possible answers:
1. A: Is soda good for you?
   B: No, I don't think so.
   A: Why not?
   B: Because it has a lot of sugar.
2. A: Are cigarettes good for you?
   B: No, I don't think so.
   A: Why not?
   B: Because they can give you cancer and heart problems.
3. A: Is orange juice good for you?
   B: Yes, I think so.
   A: Why?
   B: Because it has a lot of vitamin C.
4. A: Are cheeseburgers good for you?
   B: No, I don't think so.
   A: Why not?
   B: Because they have a lot of fat.
5. A: Is beer good for you?
   B: No, I don't think so.
   A: Why not?
   B: Because it has alcohol (and can make you fat).
6. A: Is rice good for you?
   B: Yes, I think so.
   A: Why?
   B: Because it is a basic and inexpensive food.

7. salad dressing / bad / has a lot of fat
8. vegetables / good / have a lot of vitamins   9. beans / good / don't have fat
and have protein   10. ice cream / bad /
has a lot of fat   11. skim milk / good /
doesn't have fat and has protein
12. eggs / good / inexpensive / but / bad
/ have a lot of fat (cholesterol)

Part Two

pp. 114–116
Follow the same procedures as outlined in previous chapters for this part.

p. 114, Ex. 1
Answers: Picture B

p. 115, Ex. 2
Answers: 4; 5; 1; 3; 2

p. 115, Ex. 3
Answers: 1. We'd like to sit near the win-
dow, please. 2. I'll just have water.   3. I'll
have the lamb chops. 4. I'd like the
spaghetti.   5. Could I have some lemon
for my tea, please?   6. We'd just like the
check, please.

p. 116, Ex. 4
Before beginning this role-play exercise, the
teacher should review the items on the menu. First,
discuss with the class the meaning of the menu sections: "appetizers," "soups," "salads," etc. Then,
review the items in each section. Several of these
items are found only in certain parts of the U.S. (and
possibly Canada); these include:

"chicken fingers"—deep-fried strips of chicken
meat; "nachos"—Mexican-style corn chips topped
with melted cheese; "guacamole"—a Mexican-style
sauce made of avocados, tomatoes, and onions.

After reviewing the menu vocabulary, the
teacher might want to check the students' comprehension by asking questions such as "What are
foods you eat before the main meal to make you
hungry?" (appetizers); "What's a meat entree made
from ground beef and sometimes served with
cheese?" (a hamburger).

To prepare for the role-play, the teacher might
bring in "realia" such as tablecloths, napkins, sil-
verware, etc. During the role-play, the teacher
should circulate among the students to monitor
their English. Those playing "waiters" should write
down orders on a pad of paper and ask the "cus-
tomers" appropriate questions such as "What kind
of salad dressing would you like?" if a salad is
ordered, or "How would you like your hamburger
(cooked)?" if a hamburger is ordered.

Part Three

pp. 117-118
Follow the same procedures as outlined in previous chapters for this part.

p. 117, Ex. 1
Answers: 1. a   2. c   3. a   4. c   5. b

p. 118, Ex. 3
Answers: 1. c   2. d   3. a   4. g   5. e   6. b
7. f

p. 118, Ex. 4
Answer: chili con carne

p. 118, Ex. 5
Answers: 4; 2; 1; 3

Part Four

pp. 119-122
Procedures for Ex. 1 and Ex. 2 are given in the
book; answers will vary.

p. 121, Ex. 3
During this exercise, the teacher should strong-
ly encourage the students not to rely too much on
their dictionaries when trying to explain different
foods, ingredients, and cooking procedures. Instead,
encourage the students to circumlocute terms unfamiliar to them (for example, if a student doesn't
know the English word for "mince," ask him/her,
"What is the word similar to?" If the student says
"cut" or "chop," continue to narrow the possibilities by asking, "OK. Cut or chop into big, medium,
or small pieces?," and so on).

While the students are working in groups of four, the teacher should circulate to make sure the students who are listening are also taking notes on the dish the other student is describing. After all groups are finished, the teacher might want to have everyone decide which three dishes sound the most delicious and why.

p. 122, Culture Note

Possible answers: "An apple a day keeps the doctor away," means that if you eat good food such as fruit and vegetables, you won't get sick often. "A watched pot never boils," means that if you wait anxiously for something, it will take longer to get it. "Too many cooks spoil the soup," means that too many people working on the same job can make that job more difficult or impossible. "Variety is the spice of life," means that life is better when you do different (varied) things. "You are what you eat," means that the foods you eat will decide what kind of person you are physically (for example, if you eat fattening foods, you'll be fat).

Chapter Nine: Travel and Leisure

In this chapter, the students will have opportunities to improve their ability to use and understand English to (1) make travel plans, (2) listen to weather reports, (3) use a car and other forms of transportation, and (4) talk about sports. The students will be introduced to the technique of persuasion, especially as it relates to planning trips.

Part One

pp. 123-127

Prior to doing the listening exercises, have the students (in pairs, small groups, then as a whole class) discuss the pictures on pp. 123 and 124. If possible, discuss the parks and other attractions mentioned in this chapter using a world map placed in the front of the classroom.

Questions you can ask to generate discussion (for these and the other attractions mentioned in the chapter) include: (1) Where is this park (or attraction) located? (2) What animals can you see there? (3) What time of year is it in the picture? How do you know? (4) What is (or are) the best time (or times) of year to go to this place? Why? (5) What things can people do in this park?

The students might also spend some time discussing trips they remember taking; have them say (1) where they went; (2) when; (3) who they went with; (4) what they did; and (5) how they felt about the trip.

Then begin the exercises. Follow the same procedures as outlined in previous chapters for Exercises 1-7.

p. 125, Ex. 2

Answers: 1. scenic; scenery   2. spare tire
3. flat tire   4. pull over   5. change a tire

p. 125, Ex. 3

Answers: 1. They're in Zion National Park in Utah (U.S.A).   2. the scenery   3. The car had a flat tire.   4. Beth and Ali

p. 125, Ex. 4

Answers: 1. isn't   2. scenic   3. even
4. beautiful   5. Valley   6. Arizona
7. know   8. mean   9. I   10. more
11. Uh-oh   12. wrong   13. car   14. Why
15. slower

p. 126, Ex. 7

Answers: 1. b   2. b   3. b   4. b   5. a

p. 127, Speaking Activity

Possible Answers: 1. A: Are Rob, Beth, and Ali in the Northeast? B: No, they aren't. They're in the Southwest.   2. A: Are they in Monument Valley, Arizona? B: No, they aren't. They're in Zion National Park, Utah. 3. A: Does Ali like Monument Valley more than Zion National Park? B: No, he doesn't. He likes Zion National Park more. 4. A: Does Rob think Zion's scenery is better than Monument Valley's? B: No, he doesn't. He thinks Monument Valley's is better.   5. A: Does the car not have any problems? B: Yes, it does. It has a flat tire. 6. A: Does Rob pull over to a restaurant? B: No, he doesn't. He pulls over to the side of the road.   7. A: Are they going to buy a flat tire? B: No, they aren't. They're going to change a flat tire.

8. A: Are Ruth and Ali going to help Rob drive the car? B: No, they aren't. They're going to help Rob change the flat tire.

Part Two

p. 128, Ex. 1
Answers: Lee—spending a day at the beach; Ali—bike riding; Beth—walking in the mountains; Alicia—shopping

p. 128, Ex. 2
Answers: 1. think   2. I'd   3. I   4. rather

p. 128, Ex. 3
After having the students repeat the expressions (but before the group activity), the teacher might want to have the students do a chain drill alternating suggestions and opinions. This procedure can be followed: (1) put a list of 5-10 activities on the board, e.g., "go to the beach" "go fishing" "go to the mountains" etc.; (2) have the first student initiate the chain drill with "let's" or "would you like" (e.g., "Let's go to the beach!"); (3) a second student responds with "I don't like the beach" or "I'd rather" and another activity; (4) continue the chain until all the students have responded.

The teacher can also make some inappropriate suggestions and have the students respond accordingly. For example:

Teacher: Let's go hiking at the beach!

Student: I'd rather go sun bathing at the beach. Let's go hiking in the mountains!

Part Three

pp. 130-133
Follow the same procedures as outlined in previous chapters for this part.

p. 130, Ex. 1
Answers: 1. a   2. c   3. b   4. c   5. c

p. 131, Ex. 3
Answers: 1. b   2. d   3. f   4. a   5. e   6. c

p. 131, Ex. 4
Answers: 1. Atlanta   2. Georgia

pp. 131-132, Ex. 5
Answers: (numbers as they appear from left to right on the map on p. 132): 4; 1; 2; 3

p. 132, Ex. 6
Possible answers: 2. Martin Luther King, Jr. Historic Site: memorial to a great leader, grave   3. Stone Mountain: hill of stone, picture of three Civil War generals   4. Six Flags Amusement Park: large, many roller coasters

p. 133, Ex. 9
Answer: Picture B

p. 133, Ex. 10
Answers: 1. b   2. c   3. a

Part Four

pp. 134–135, Ex. 1
A variation on this activity is to have the students select one famous place from a list at the board or from a set of cards the teacher prepares. The teacher should encourage the students not to make their descriptions too easy (e.g., for "Paris," rather than saying "This is the capital of France," the student might say "This is a city famous for museums, restaurants, . . . ").

p. 135, Ex. 2
The teacher should circulate to monitor the students' English; correct any errors in (1) the pronunciation of -*s* endings for fare prices and advance purchase days and (2) use of prepositions (e.g., "It arrives at 12:47").

p. 136, Ex. 4
Answers: 1. f   2. i   3. b   4. j   5. e   6. h
7. a   8. d   9. g   10. c

p. 137

After completing Ex. 4, the teacher might also want to have students make oral statements that other students respond "true" or "false" to. For example: A: Baseball has five players. B: False! Baseball has nine players. (etc.)

Note that this can be conducted as a game by dividing the class into two teams and awarding points for correct answers.

During Ex. 5 and Ex. 6, the teacher should promote active listening by requiring students to take notes while their classmates are describing a sport or sport-related newspaper article.

Chapter Ten: Our Planet

In this chapter, students will practice understanding and using English to talk about local and global issues such as pollution and overpopulation. They will learn expressions of agreement and disagreement in order to have simple debates. They will also be introduced to vocabulary and concepts dealing with cause and effect as they relate to global problems such as acid rain and endangered species (plants and animals in danger of becoming extinct).

Part One

pp. 139–143

In preparation for the listening exercises, have the students (in pairs or small groups, then as a whole class) talk about the pictures on pages 139 and 140. For the earth photo on p. 139, the students can be divided into two "teams" and allowed five minutes to make a list of as many things they (1) can see in the picture and (2) know about planet earth, life on the planet, and global problems. For the picture on p. 140, students can be divided into pairs and allowed 5 minutes to create dialogs with the teacher cue, "What do you think Alicia and Lee are saying to each other?" As a whole class, the students might want to discuss the need to "Save the Earth," as the sign Alicia is carrying indicates. The problems students mention can be written on the blackboard along with possible solutions.

In going through the exercises, follow the same procedures as outlined in previous chapters for exercises 1-7.

p. 140, Ex. 2
Answers: 2. environment   3. to give a speech   4. to pollute

p. 140, Ex. 3
Answers: 1. She's making a sign for Earth Day.   2. They think about pollution and other problems with the environment. 3. Alicia   4. because he wants to help the environment

p. 141, Ex. 4
Answers: 1. in   2. Hi   3. doing   4. making   5. sign   6. Earth   7. Day   8. that 9. people   10. pollution   11. problems 12. environment   13. Really   14. is 15. Monday

pp. 141-142, Ex. 6
Suggested answers: 1. A: What is Lee interested in?   B: He's interested in going with Alicia on Earth Day and helping her.

2. A: What is Alicia planning?   B: She's planning to give a speech about pollution.

3. A: What is Lee looking forward to? B: He's looking forward to Earth Day.

4. A: What does Lee want?   B: He wants to help the environment.

5. A: What is Alicia excited about? B: She's excited about giving a speech and carrying a sign on Earth Day.

p. 142, Ex. 8
Answers: 1. b   2. b   3. a   4. a   5. b

p. 143, Speaking Activity
The teacher might want to conduct a chain drill prior to this activity to ensure that the students understand the meaning of the expressions they are to use in questions. For example, the teacher can have Student 1 ask Student 2 if s/he is looking forward to doing homework tonight (expected response: No!); then have Student 3 ask Student 4 if s/he hopes to get a good job someday (expected response: Yes).

Part Two

p. 144, Ex. 1
Answers: 1. air pollution   2. They disagree.

p. 144, Ex. 2
Answers: 1. have a point   2. don't agree
3. too   4. your point of

p. 146
Prior to beginning Ex. 4, the teacher should have the students practice using the expressions they repeated in Ex. 3 by applying them to the topics provided in Ex. 4. Explain to the students that all of the "debates" can begin with a student on either side (A or B) saying, "In my opinion," + one of the positions suggested in the book. After that, have the students repeat chorally some of the statements prefaced with, "In my opinion," followed by responses prefaced by "That may be true, but I think . . . ," or "You have a point, but I think . . . ," + the opposing statement.

Next, explain that opinions need to be supported by reasons expressed by "because." List some "because" clauses on the board and have the students (in pairs and/or small groups) match them with the appropriate topic and side provided in the book. For example: . . . because cars cause air pollution (SIDE A, 1) . . . because students need exercise for their physical health (SIDE B, 3), etc.

After that, have the students divide into two groups (SIDE A and SIDE B) of equal (or almost equal) size. If the students do not divide evenly by themselves, ask for volunteers to go to the smaller side.

Then, allow 5–7 minutes for each side to think of reasons for their position; circulate to check on their reasons; offer suggestions if needed (but be sure each side is helped equally!). At this level, the students can write down their reasons and use their notes during the "debate."

During the actual "debate," require that each student in the group give an opinion in order to receive a point. Make sure to keep a tally of the points at the blackboard. Give extra points to those students who respond directly to another student's opinion.

Note: The teacher should not expect the students to be able to carry out an actual debate—an extremely sophisticated task—at this level; satisfactory performance means that they are able to use the expressions in Ex. 3 in appropriate contexts at appropriate times.

Part Three

pp. 146–148
Follow the same procedures as outlined in previous chapters for this part.

p. 146, Ex. 1
Answers: Speaker 1. crime   2. air pollution
3. water pollution   4. overcrowding
5. the environment

p. 147, Ex. 4
Answer: the center of Europe

p. 147, Ex. 5
Answers: 1: the Netherlands, Belgium, Luxembourg, Germany, the Czech Republic, western Poland, and the southern part of Sweden   2: Great Britain, northern France, Switzerland, Austria, most of Slovakia, eastern Poland, most of Sweden, and southern Norway and Denmark   3: western Scotland, Spain, Portugal, Italy, Hungary, Russia, Estonia, Lithuania, Latvia, northeastern Norway and northwestern Denmark

p. 148, Ex. 6
Answers: 1. Western Europe   2. Spain, Portugal, Italy, Hungary, Russia   3. (possible answer) countries with more pollution use dirty sources of energy (for example, coal)

p. 148, Ex. 7
Answers: 2. Belgium 15-25%   3. Czech Republic 25%   4. Denmark 15%
5. France 15-25%   6. Germany 25%
7. Great Britain 25%   8. Hungary 15%
9. Italy 15%   10. Luxembourg 15-25%
11. Netherlands 25%   12. Norway 15%

13. Poland 15-25%   14. Portugal 15%
15. Russia 15%   16. Slovakia 25%
17. Spain 15%   18. Sweden 15-25%
19. Switzerland 25%

Part Four

pp. 149–151

Prior to doing Ex. 1, have the students (in pairs or small groups, then as a whole class) discuss what they know about extinct and/or endangered species; if possible, the students should mention any species they know about from their home countries. The teacher might also want to write on the board the following well-known animals and have the students tell as much as they know about them: the Dodo bird: a large, flightless bird that became extinct in the 16th Century; the Giant Panda: a large, bear-like animal that is endangered but now protected and living in western China; its only food is bamboo; the Buffalo: a large grazing animal that lives in the western U.S.; it almost became extinct in the late 1800s but is now protected and numbers in the tens of thousands.

p. 150, Ex. 2

Possible answers: Reason 1: bluefin tuna; Reason 2: Black Rhino; Asiatic Black Bear; Tiger; Reason 3: Grey Parrot; American Box Turtle; Egyptian Tortoise; Reason 4: Giant Panda; Tiger; Reason 5: Bluefin Tuna

p. 151, Ex. 3

Possible answers: 1. We are fishing and catching too many bluefin tuna. We should be fishing less and catching fewer tuna; we should be fishing for less time during the year. 2. We are catching and killing these animals for their fur, feathers, tusks, etc. We should not be catching and killing any more of these animals; they should (and must) be completely protected; hunters should be arrested if they try to hunt any of these animals. 3. These animals are being captured and sold as pets. We should not capture any more of these animals for pets; they should be completely protected. 4. We are continuing to cut down forests, so these animals have no place to live. We should stop cutting down the forests. 5. We are continuing to pollute the water and air. We should stop polluting the water and air.

p. 152, Ex. 4

After student pairs have interviewed each other about environmental problems in their countries, have them explain to each other why they believe these problems exist and what possible solutions might exist.

Interactions Placement Tests

Placement

Institutions using the *Interactions Access, Interactions, and Mosaic* programs utilize many different methods for evaluating and placing their students. Some use their own placement tests. Others use standardized tests such as those produced by the Educational Testing Service and the University of Michigan. Below is a guide for placement with those examinations for students in English-speaking countries.

For students in English speaking countries

	Michigan Placement	Michigan Proficiency	TOEFL
Interactions Access	below 35	below 25	n/a
Interactions One	35–50	25–35	n/a
Interactions Two	50–60	35–50	app. 425
Mosaic One	55–75	45–55	app. 450
Mosaic Two	75 or higher	56–70	app. 475–480

The Interactions Placement Tests

This manual contains placement tests for the *Interactions Access, Interactions I* and *Interactions 2* programs, only. Placement tests are also available for the *Mosaic I* an 2 programs. The tests consist of separate multiple-choice examinations for Grammar and Usage, Reading, and Listening. Individual tests can be given, or two or more components may be used together. In addition, this manual has suggestions for oral interviews and writing samples, along with guidelines for holistic scoring. Although the tests have been field-tested, they have not been validated against other standardized tests and are only meant for placement within the *Interactions Access, Interactions,* and *Mosaic* programs, we solicit comments and feedback that will enable us to increase their usefulness.

Please note that while the various tests have been included in this manual, some or all may be extremely difficult for students at the *Interactions Access* level. In fact, you may choose not to use any placement tool because the level of the students is obvious. Of course, the tests may be used as exit exams at the end of the course, instead of as placement tools.

Administering the Placement Tests

The following are some guidelines for test administration:

1. Tell the students to use a pencil rather than a pen.

2. Go over all directions at the beginning to make sure that students understand them.

3. Make sure that students have scrap paper if they need it.

4. Make sure that there is a clock so that students can keep track of time. If there is no clock available, announce when the test is half finished and when there is only two minutes left.

Test Descriptions and Scoring

You may choose to use any/all of these placement tools. However, if you feel that most of your students fall into a beginning level *(Interactions Access)*, you may prefer to use only one or two components of the test, or to use none at all. When students are at a very low level, such tests can be meaningless, and at the same time, demoralizing for the students. If, however, you feel that some students may place at a higher level *(Interactions I or II)* you will need to use one or more tools to place these students appropriately.

For *Interactions Access* students, these tests can also be used as "exit" exams, administered at the end of the course as opposed to at the beginning. In this way, *Interactions Access* students can have a relative register of their progress after completing this level.

Grammar and Usage

This test includes structures covered in *Interactions Access, Interactions I* and *Interactions II* grammars. Allow 15 minutes for the test. Below are guidelines for placement.

	Interactions Access	Interactions 1	Interactions 2
Grammar and Usage	0–7*	5–12	13–20**

*Students who score above 6 should be evaluated further.
**Students who score above 20 should be evaluated further.

Reading

This reading test has two passages. Students should be given 15 minutes to complete the test. Reading speed is an important variable of reading ability, so time should be kept very strictly.

	Interactions Access	Interactions 1	Interactions 2
Reading	0–4*	3–5	6–8**

*Students who score above 3 should be evaluated further.
**Students who score above 8 should be evaluated further.

Listening

The listening test consists of two short conversations. The test should last about ten minutes. Explain to students that they will hear the questions only once. Therefore, it will be helpful for them to read the answers before they hear the questions. Make sure that students have paper in order to take notes.

Guidelines for the Speakers

The short conversations require two speakers. It is not absolutely necessary that they be native speakers of American English. However, if the speakers do not have native or near-native pronunciation, the test will not be as accurate a predictor as it would be otherwise. If the students and the speakers have the same native language, the resulting scores are likely to be higher than they would be with a native speaker. This should be taken into account when making placements. If native or near-native speakers of English are not available to administer the test, an oral interview (see below) can be used, instead, to test listening ability on a somewhat more subjective basis. Please note:

- Before administering the test, speakers should read the conversations and questions aloud several times so that they can read it through without hesitations and false starts.
- During the test, the conversationss should be read in a normal speaking voice, at normal cadence. The speakers should take care to preserve natural rhythm and liaisons between words (e.g. ham n'eggs) and avoid unnatural emphasis or breaks.
- During the test, the conversations should be read only once. Each question should be followed by a ten-second pause.

	Interactions Access	Interactions 1	Interactions 2
Listening	0–4*	3–5	6–8**

*Students who score above 3 should be evaluated further.
**Students who score above 8 should be evaluated further.

Oral Interview

At the *Interactions Access* level, an oral interview may take only 2–4 minutes. There are ten suggested questions ranging from personal information to more sophisticated topics. At this level, interviewers should expect to ask only two or three questions. Begin with the first question, and then decide which other questions (if any) to ask. Continue with personal topics if the student is at all conversant in English.

Following are holistic guidelines for placement. Note that *Interactions Access* students will be at an even lower level than *Interactions One* students. *Interactions Access* students may not be able to sustain enough conversation to properly evaluate in this way.

Scoring and Placement

Students whose scores fall below these limits should be evaluated further. They may place in Interactions Access.

	Interactions One	Interactions Two	Mosaic One	Mosaic Two	Beyond Interactions/Mosaic Program
Overall Clarity	very difficult to understand	understandable for basic information	understandable with some problem areas	easy to understand	native-like communication
Fluency	very hesitant, numerous stops and starts	frequent hesitation	some hesitation	little hesitation	natural speech, with only normal stops and starts
Pronunciation	numerous problems with individual sounds and with intonation and stress	problem areas that sometimes interfere with intelligibility	some problems with discrete sounds or with stress and intonation, but overall intelligible	a few problem areas that don't interfere with intelligibility	clear, native-like pronunciation
Oral Grammar	many mistakes even with very basic structures	many mistakes, some interfere with meaning	some mistakes, but overall meaning is clear	some mistakes, but able to self-correct many, meaning is clear	few or no mistakes
Vocabulary	uses only very basic words and phrases	some command of basic, high-frequency vocabulary	good command of basic vocabulary, some command of more sophisticated language	uses a good blend of basic and sophisticated language	uses a full range of sophisticated vocabulary

If the oral interview is conducted for listening purposes. The following guidelines can be used.

Interactions One The student is able to understand only the most basic questions about his/her personal life. He/she shows almost no understanding of extraneous comments. and comprehends only basic vocabulary and few idioms.

Interactions Two The student is able to understand questions about his/her past and future. He/she demonstrates comprehension of some extraneous comments. Some fairly sophisticated vocabulary and idioms are understood.

Mosaic One The student is able to understand all the questions posed. He/she understands many extraneous comments and shows comprehension of a fairly wide range of vocabulary and many idioms.

Mosaic Two The student understands all the questions posed and virtually all of the extraneous comments as well. He/she has no problem understanding fairly sophisticated vocabulary and idioms.

Writing Sample

At the *Interactions Access* level, students may be able to write virtually no English, and you may choose not to get writing samples. In the event that you do, this manual includes five suggestions for topics ranging from personal information to more sophisticated topics. You may wish to create others. For this level, we recommend choosing personal topics and limiting the writing time to 1—15 minutes, at most.

Following are holistic guidelines for placement. Note that *Interactions Access* students will be at an even lower level than *Interactions One* students. *Interactions Access* students may not be able to write enough to properly evaluate in this way.

Scoring and Placement

Whenever possible, writing samples should be evaluated by more than one person. Having at least two readers for each paper will increase the accuracy of the holistic grading system. Students whose scores fall below these limits should be evaluated further. They may place in Interactions Access.

	Interactions One	Interactions Two	Mosaic One	Mosaic Two	Beyond Interactions/Mosaic Program
Overall Clarity	very difficult to understand	understandable for basic information	understandable with some problem areas	easy to understand	native-like communication
Content	very simple, basic ideas	good basic ideas but lacking any sophistication	ideas somewhat interesting, but lacking development, few examples or supporting details	good ideas, fairly well-developed, but could use more examples/ supporting details	very interesting well-developed ideas, very good examples and/or supporting details
Organization	disorganized, no coherency	some organization but difficult to follow at times	fairly coherent but with some problems in the flow of ideas	generally well-organized, some problems with coherency	Well-organized, coherent
Written Grammar	control of only very basic structures	some control of basic structures, numerous problems with complex structures	control of basic structures and some complex structures, most errors don't interfere with meaning	few errors, most with complex structures, generally not interfering with meaning	strong command of both basic and complex structures, few or no errors
Vocabulary	uses only very basic words and phrases	some command of basic, high-frequency vocabulary	good command of basic vocabulary, some command of more sophisticated language	uses a good blend of basic and sophisticated language	uses a full range of sophisticated vocabulary

Answer Keys

Grammar and Usage

Part 1

Answers:
1. b
2. b
3. a
4. d
5. a
6. c
7. d
8. d
9. b
10. d
11. b
12. c
13. d
14. b
15.c
16. a
17. c
18. c
19. a
20. a
21. b
22. c
23. d
24. b
25. c

Reading

Part 1.

Answers:
1
1. a
2. d
3. c
4. b
2
1. b
2. b
3. d
4. a
5. d
6. b

Listening

Part 1.

Answers:
1
1. b
2. c
3. c
4. d
5. c
2
1. d
2. c
3. d
4. c
5. b
6. a

Student Data Sheet

Student _____   Date _____

Native country and language _____   Age _____

Current Address _____

Time Studying English in US _____ abroad _____

Oral Interview: Name/s of interviewer/s _____

Overall Clarity	1	2	3	4	5	
Fluency	1	2	3	4	5	
Pronunciation	1	2	3	4	5	
Oral Grammar	1	2	3	4	5	
Vocabulary	1	2	3	4	5	**Total** _____

Writing sample: Name/s of reader/s _____

Overall Clarity	1	2	3	4	5	
Content	1	2	3	4	5	
Organization	1	2	3	4	5	
Written Grammar	1	2	3	4	5	
Vocabulary	1	2	3	4	5	**Total** _____

Grammar and Usage	Part 1 _____	Part 2 _____	**Total** _____
Reading	Part 1 _____	Part 2 _____	**Total** _____
Listening	Part 1 _____	Part 2 _____	**Total** _____

Placement Test for the Interactions Programs

Name _____ _Date: _____

Grammar and Usage: (15 minutes)

This test will help to determine your level of English for placement in the Interactions program. The test is multiple choice. It has 25 items. Choose the one answer that correctly completes the sentence in formal English.

Example: At the market, we bought ———-.

    a. several kind of fruit

    b. several kind of fruits

    (c.) several kinds of fruit

    d. several kinds of the fruits

1.   Would you mind ———- these bags?

    a. to help me to carry

    b. helping me to carry

    c. to help me carry

    d. helping me carrying

2.   The new student ———- in town since last Tuesday.

    a. is

    b. has been

    c. has being

    d. is being

3.   He was the ———-.

    a. fastest swimmer of the group

    b. most fast swimmer of the group

    c. fastest swimmer the group

    d. most fastest swimmer of the group

The Interactions Access Program, 2/e

4. Tonight we have ——-.

   a. a lot homework

   b. a lot homework

   c. a lot of homework

   d. a lot of homework

5. We gave ——-

   a. the present to her

   b. to her the present

   c. the present to herself

   d. herself the present

6. The Smiths called you about the party, ——-?

   a. didn't he

   b. he did

   c. didn't they

   d. they did

7. What ——- when the fire started?

   a. you were doing

   b. was you doing

   c. you did do

   d. were you doing

8. You don't look very well. You ——- rest for a while.

   a. would better

   b. had better to

   c. must to

   d. should

9.   It's important ——- all the assignments.
        a. for you do
        b. for you to do
        c. you to do
        d. your doing

10.   When we were children, we ——- in Boston.
        a. used to living
        b. were used to live
        c. would live
        d. used to live

11.   It's ——- outside for a long time.
        a. too cold enough to stay
        b. too cold to stay
        c. cold enough stay
        d. too cold stay

12.   In recent years, many new discoveries ——- about the solar system.
        a. has made
        b. has been made
        c. have been made
        d. have made

13.   I ——- go to the meeting if I don't want to.
        a. must
        b. must not to
        c. have to
        d. don't have to

14.   She's saving money ——- a computer.

    a. for to buy

    b. so that she can buy

    c. in order buy

    d. for buy

15.   John and his sister ——- there several times.

    a. have already went

    b. has already gone

    c. have already gone

    d. already goes

16.   Our professor ——- lunch right now.

    a. is eating

    b. eats

    c. eat

    d. is eaten

17.   We ——- the instructions.

    a. confused by

    b. were confused

    c. were confused about

    d. were confusing about

18.   Mary ——- upset.

    a. seem

    b. is seeming

    c. seems

    d. has been seeming

19. While ——- to create a light bulb, Edison experimented with hundreds of metals.

    a. he was trying

    b. to try

    c. he trying

    d. he was tried

20. We ——- several people from France.

    a. know

    b. are knowing

    c. has known

    d. have know

21. Major developments occurred in computer science during ——-.

    a. the 1980

    b. the 1980s

    c. 1980s

    d. the years of 1980s

22. They ——- .

    a. still haven't finish the project

    b. have finished the project yet

    c. have already finished the project

    d. have just finish the project

23. There ——- people in line.

    a. was only a few

    b. were only a little

    c. was only a little

    d. were only a few

24.   Bill ——- to invite us for dinner.

    a. call us up

    b. has called us up

    c. called up us

    d. is calling up us

25.   There was ——- that he arrived at work an hour late.

    a. so many traffic

    b. such a traffic

    c. so much traffic

    d. so traffic

Interactions Reading Placement Test

Name _____ Date: _____

(15 minutes)

1. Read the text and answer the questions. You have 15 minutes to finish this part of the test. Do not worry if you do not finish the test.

Baseball is a competitive game of skill. It is played with a hard ball and bat between two teams of nine players each. Baseball is one of the oldest and most popular spectator sports. The game as we know it today started during the early 1800s among children and amateur players.

The baseball season in the United States goes from April to October. There are adult professional leagues and many children play Little League baseball in the spring. Sometimes girls and boys play on the same teams, but usually girls and boys have different teams. While they are still young, winning games is not very important. "It's not whether you win or lose; but it's how you play the game that counts." as the saying goes. However, by the time they reach high school age, winning seems to become more important than having a good time.

Many adults also love to play baseball, but most prefer to be spectators. Professional baseball attracts millions of fans to ballparks each year. It also entertains millions more through radio and television. People in many different countries play baseball. However, because of its strong tradition and great popularity, most Americans consider it the national pastime of the United States.

1.   The article implies that

a.   baseball is more popular in the United States than in other parts of the world.

b.   children become less competitive when they get older.

c.   more adults watch baseball in ballparks than in stadiums.

d.   spectator sports are more popular than other kinds of sports.

2.   Which pair of words are opposites?

a. popularity/tradition   b. fan/spectator

c. ballpark/stadium   d. amateur/ professional

3.   To play baseball you need a ball, a bat and:

a.   nine players   b. ten players

c. eighteen players   d. two players

4.   A spectator sport is one that

      a. many people play and few watch   b. many people watch and few people play

      c. few people play or watch   d. everyone watches

2. Read the text and answer the questions.

Exciting discoveries in the past thirty years have led to great changes in the field of astronomy, producing what many people are calling a 'golden age of astronomy'. These new findings are coming fast—every month and sometimes even weekly. Each new discovery leads to more questions and often to differing interpretations of the discovery. Astronomers and physicists have made many recent advances but one fact is certain: the questions that are brought up by such advances sometimes make the universe seem more enigmatic and puzzling, not less. Most of the discoveries of the last three decades have to do with the surprising violence of the universe.

When many of us look into the night sky, it seems to us that the universe is very still and serene. However, scientists now tell us that just the opposite is true; the universe is neither unmoving nor calm. There is strong evidence that the universe has always been a very violent place. It even began violently. Recent observations provide evidence that the cosmos began with the Big Bang (an enormous explosion that occurred twenty billion years ago) and has been expanding ever since. One of the most significant of these observations was the discovery of radio waves left over from the Big Bang. Now there is a big question in the field of cosmology: Will this expansion of the universe continue forever? Some theorize that if the growth stops, the universe will completely collapse.

Another recent astronomical discovery has been black holes. These extraordinary and exciting objects allow scientists to learn more about the importance of gravity—the force that keeps people and things here on earth, for example, instead of floating away in space. A black hole is most likely the end of a star's life. When a star dies, gravity becomes so intense that the star cannot maintain its stability; however, what happens next is uncertain. It is quite possible that the end to a star's life is complete collapse; it loses strength and falls inward. All that is left is a black hole—an area into which everything near it is suddenly pulled. We can still feel the gravity from the hole, but we can't see it because even light itself is pulled into it.

Black holes contain the strongest gravity in the known universe, but other objects known as quasars are probably the most energetic. Discovered in 1963, quasars appear in photographs to be small dots; they look, at first, just like ordinary stars. However, closer study shows that the light from quasars is much redder when it reaches earth than it was when it left the quasar. Most scientists believe that this redshift means that the quasars are very far away, more distant than the most distant visible galaxies. This means that quasars must be exploding and sending off a huge amount of light. It's almost impossible to imagine how much energy is involved; some galaxies (enormous groups of stars) send off as much energy in one second as our sun releases in ten thousand years, and it seems conceivable that quasars discharge even more light than an average galaxy.

1.   The main idea of this reading is:

    a. The universe began violently with the Big Bang.

    b. Many recent discoveries show that the universe is violent.

    c. Black holes and quasars are mysteries.

    d. Scientists agree about the explanations of recent discoveries.

2.   The 'golden age of astronomy'
      a. has ended.   b. began 30 years ago.
      c. has just started.   d. will end in 30 years.

3.   *Enigmatic* probably means
      a. difficult   b. large
      c. violent   d. mysterious

4.   Which pair are opposites?
      a. serene/violent   b. expansion/growth
      c. intense/enormous   d. average/ordinary

5.   *Cosmology* is the study of
      a. galaxies   b. the Big Bang
      c. black holes   d. the universe

6.   In the last paragraph, the writer gives an example which shows that
      a. the light from quasars is redder when it is first released.
      b. our sun is relatively weak.
      c. average galaxies have more energy than quasars.
      d. quasars are almost as far as the most distant visible galaxies

Interactions Listening Placement Test

Name _____ Date: _____

1. Read the answers below. Then listen to the conversation and take notes. Finally, listen to the questions and answer them.

1.
   a. They work together
   b. They used to work together.
   c. They are neighbors.
   d. They are good friends.

2.
   a. Brian fired a lot of people.
   b. A few people were hired.
   c. Many people lost their jobs.
   d. Brian got fired.

3.
   a. Telephone sales.
   b. Brian.
   c. Her new job.
   d. ICD.

4.
   a. A promotion.
   b. A new boss.
   c. A vacation.
   d. A new job.

5.
   a. They've just hired ten new people.
   b. There's no work .
   c. She'll ask about jobs openings.
   d. She can't help him.

2. Read the answers below. Then listen to the conversation and take notes. Finally listen to the questions and answer them.

1.   a. They are friends.

        b. They are employer/employee

        c. They are teacher/student.

        d. They are interviewer/job applicant

2.   a. An electrician.

        b. A computer programmer.

        c. A systems analyst

        d. An electrical engineer.

3.   a. He got sick.

        b. He needed money.

        c. He found a job.

        d. He was bored.

4.   a. It was easier.

        b. It was more skilled.

        c. It was more practical.

        d. It was cheaper.

5.   a. A giant software company.

        b. A computer company.

        c. A technical school.

        d. An electronics firm.

6.   a. The man borrowed money to finish college.

        b. The man never finished college.

        c. The man didn't like studying about computers.

        d. The man doesn't want to work with computers anymore.

Listening Placement Test Script

1. Listen to the conversation and take notes.

A: Hi Brian!

B: Hi Tina. How've you been? I haven't seen you since you left ICD.

A: I'm just fine. My new job is working out great. My boss is really nice and I love the work.

B: Better than telephone sales, huh.

A: You bet! I'd rather starve than do that again. Oh, sorry Brian. Are you still working there or have they fired you too?

B: No, unfortunately, I'm one of the few people they haven't fired yet. But I'm going to spend my vacation looking for another job. I just can't stand it anymore. And with Peters as my boss, I'll never get a promotion. Oh well...Hey, do you know of any jobs at Basic Industries?

A: Well, there's a rumor that they're going to hire about ten new people but I'm not sure. I'll ask around. If I can help you, I will.

B: Thanks. That would be great!

Listen to the questions and answer them.

1.   Which statement is true about Brian and Tina?

2.   What can we guess about ICD?

3.   What is Tina enthusiastic about?

4.   What is Brian hoping to get?

5.   What does Tina say about job possibilities at her new company?

2. Listen to the conversation and take notes.

A: So, Mr. Kowalski, can you tell me a little about yourself?

B: Well, let's see. I graduated from high school in 1991. I started college but I left after the first year. I was sick of studying and I wanted to work.

A: I see.

B: Well, I couldn't find a job because I didn't have any skills so I went to a technical school and took some courses in electronics.

A: And did you like the technical school better?

B: Absolutely, I really loved electronics. It was hands-on, much better than just studying from books. When I finished that course, I went to work for a small computer hardware company. Innovative Computers Inc. I'd done some computer work in the electronics course and I learned a lot more on the job. When I first got there, the company only had five employees, so there was a lot of opportunity to learn all about the computer business.

A: Sounds like you really liked that job. Why did you leave?

B: Well, I knew that if I really wanted to work in computers I'd need a degree, so I started night school. I did that for two years. And then I decided to get a loan and finish school full time. So I quit my job and went back to college. And now I've just graduated and I'm looking for a job as a systems analyst.

A: Well, we do have an opening for a systems person. Let me tell you about the job...

Listen to the questions and answer them.

1. What is the relationship between the man and the woman?

2. What kind of job is the man looking for?

3. Why did the man leave college the first time?

4. Why did the man like technical school more than college?

5. Where did the man used to work?

6. Which statement is true?

Writing Sample

Choose one of the following topics. Write as much as you can about this topic. You will have 15 minutes to write.

1.   Describe the events that led to your arrival at this school. How did you learn about the school? How and why did you choose it? What preparations did you have to make in order to come here? How and when did you arrive here? What are your perceptions about the school today?

2.   Write a brief (short) autobiography. Tell about your family and your home. Describe at least two or three important events in your life.

3.   Describe a memorable event from your childhood. It could be a good experience or a bad experience. What led to this event? what happened? How did it affect you? Has it continued to affect you today?

4.   Describe a period of social or political or economic change in your country or culture. What led to these changes? What changes occurred? How have the changes affected your country or culture today? Are these changes still going on?

Oral Interview

Time 3–5 minutes (See notes on administration.)

1. What is your name? How old are you? where are you from? What is your native language? How long have you been in (current city)? How long have you studied English?

2. Tell me about your family.

3. Tell me about your arrival at our school. How did you choose it? Why? How did you get here? What did you have to do to prepare?

4. Tell me about your education before now. What have you studied? Where? Compare your previous school and this school. (size, location, etc.)

5. Tell me the story of one important event in your life.

6. Describe yourself. What kind of person are you? Do you have hobbies? How do you spend your time?

7. Tell me about your career plans. What kind of work have you done? What plans do you have the future?

8. If you could change one thing about your life right now, what would it be and why?

9. If you could change one event in the past, what would it be and why?

10. What is the biggest challenge facing your country today?

The Interactions and Mosaic Programs, 2/e

htt://www.mhhe.com

McGraw-Hill

A Division of The **McGraw·Hill** Companies

ISBN 0-07-069604-7

90000

9 780070 696044